# Understanding Language

chap 10

**Also available from Continuum**

*Key Terms in Semiotics* by Bronwen Martin and Felizitas Ringham
*An Introduction to Syntax* by Edith A. Moravcsik
*An Introduction to Syntactic Theory* by Edith A. Moravcsik
*A Critical Introduction to Phonology* by Daniel Silverman
*A Critical Introduction to Phonetics* by Ken Lodge

# Understanding Language

## A BASIC COURSE IN LINGUISTICS

Elizabeth Grace Winkler

continuum

Continuum International Publishing Group
The Tower Building                    80 Maiden Lane
11 York Road                          Suite 704
London SE1 7NX                        New York NY 10038

www.continuumbooks.com

Acknowledgements

The author is grateful to the following publishers for permission to reprint:

Figure 2.1 Round Dance, Figure 2.2 Wagging Dance, and Figure 2.3 Sickle Dance
From 'Dialects in the language of bees' by Karl von Frisch, *Scientific American* August 1962, Vol. 207 #2. p. 80. Reproduced by kind permission of Nelson H Prentiss

Figure 3.1 Left hemisphere of brain Copyright © Laura Maaske

Figure 4.1 Articulators, Figure 4.2 Sagittal Sections: Velum raised and Figure 4.3 Sagittal Sections: Velum lowered
From *An Introduction to Language* 8th edition by Fromkin, Rodman and Hymans, 2007. Reprinted with permission of Heinle, a division of Thomson Learning: www.thomson rights.com. Fax 800 730-2215

Figure 4.4 Drawing of hunters and Figure 4.5 Drawing of hunters
Drawings created by Colleen O'Conner Olson

Copyright © Elizabeth Grace Winkler 2007
First published 2007
Reprinted 2009, 2010, 2011

British Library Cataloguing-in-Publication Data
A catalogue record for this book is available from the British Library.

ISBN: 978-0-8264-8482-6 (hardback)
      978-0-8264-8483-3 (paperback)

Library of Congress Cataloguing-in-Publication Data
A catalog record for this book is available from the Library of Congress

Typeset by Free Range Book Design & Production Limited
Printed and bound in the United States of America

*To my family for all the blessings in my life*

# Contents

Preface                                                                    xi
List of Figures                                                            xiii
Acknowledgements                                                           xv

**1  What every native speaker of a language secretly understands     1**
1.1   The sound system                                                     2
1.2   The lexicon: the human dictionary                                    4
1.3   Morphology                                                           7
1.4   Grammar                                                              8
1.5   How the world's languages differ                                     9
1.6   The boundaries of a language: language versus dialect               12
    1.6.1   How does a standard develop or get chosen?             14
    1.6.2   Standard and written language versus normal
              or non-standard speech                              17
1.7   A linguistic approach to language diversity                         19

**2  Human Language versus Animal Communication Systems              22**
2.1   Naturally occurring animal communication systems                   24
    2.1.1   Black Austrian honeybee communication                24
    2.1.2   Bird calls and songs                                 26
    2.1.3   Dolphins and whales                                  28
    2.1.4   More complex animal communication systems            29
    2.1.5   Primate communication                                29
2.2   Artificially taught animal communication systems                   30
    2.2.1   Chimpanzees and great apes                           30
    2.2.2   African grey parrots                                 32

**3  Language Acquisition                                            36**
3.1   Early theories of first language acquisition                       37
    3.1.1   Challenges to behaviourism and structuralism         38
    3.1.2   The innateness hypothesis                            38
    3.1.3   Support for the innateness hypothesis                39
    3.1.4   Problems with reinforcement and imitation            40
    3.1.5   What children's 'errors' tell us                     41
    3.1.6   Studies supporting the innateness hypothesis         43
    3.1.7   Studies on the living brain                          44
    3.1.8   Critical age hypothesis for first language
              acquisition                                          45
3.2   Stages of language acquisition                                     46
    3.2.1   Learning the sound system                            46
    3.2.2   Sound and meaning                                    48
    3.2.3   From single words to grammar                         48

3.3   Second language acquisition                          49
      3.3.1   SLA and behaviourism                         50
      3.3.2   First language interference in SLA           52
      3.3.3   SLA and feedback or correction               53
      3.3.4   Individual differences                       55
      3.3.5   Critical age hypothesis for second language
              acquisition                                  57
      3.3.6   Recent developments in second language
              acquisition                                  58

4   **Phonetics**                                          62
    4.1   How is speech produced?                          63
    4.2   The consonants                                   64
          4.2.1   Voicing                                  65
          4.2.2   Place of articulation                    65
          4.2.3   Manner of articulation                   66
    4.3   The International Phonetic Alphabet              72
    4.4   The vowels                                       73
          4.4.1   Classification of vowels                 73
          4.4.2   The vowel chart                          73
          4.4.3   Diphthongs                               74
          4.4.4   Vowel length                             75
    4.5   Advantages of a phonetic system                 76
    4.6   Other features of sound: suprasegmentals         78

5   **Morphology: The Makeup of Words in a Language**      82
    5.1   Categorizing the words of a language             84
    5.2   Morphemes                                        85
          5.2.1   Inflectional and derivational morphemes  86
    5.3   Morphology and phonetics                         89
          5.3.1   A final word about morpheme structure    91
    5.4   Our ever-expanding and changing vocabulary       91
          5.4.1   Word formation processes                 92
          5.4.2   Linguistic borrowing                     98
    5.5   The dictionary                                   100
          5.5.1   New dictionary words                     101

6   **Grammar**                                            105
    6.1   Traditional grammar                              108
    6.2   Language word orders                             110
    6.3   Phrase structure grammars                        111
          6.3.1   Advantages of a phrase structure grammar 113
          6.3.2   Determining phrase structure grammar rules 113
          6.3.3   Other aspects of syntax                  128

7   **Semantics: Language and Meaning**                    132
    7.1   How is meaning developed?                        133

| | | | |
|---|---|---|---|
| 7.2 | How is meaning encoded? | | 134 |
| 7.3 | Word meaning: sense and reference | | 135 |
| | 7.3.1 | Proper nouns: the problem of names | 136 |
| 7.4 | What native speakers understand about meaning | | 138 |
| | 7.4.1 | Ambiguity | 138 |
| | 7.4.2 | Synonymy | 139 |
| | 7.4.3 | Antonymy | 140 |
| | 7.4.4 | Levels of specificity | 140 |
| | 7.4.5 | Meaning inclusion | 141 |
| | 7.4.6 | Compositional versus non-compositional utterances | 142 |
| | 7.4.7 | Phrasal verbs | 146 |
| | 7.4.8 | Figures of speech | 147 |
| | 7.4.9 | Irony and sarcasm | 148 |

**8   Pragmatics: Language in Use**   152
| | | | |
|---|---|---|---|
| 8.1 | Speech acts | | 153 |
| | 8.1.1 | Direct versus indirect speech acts | 155 |
| 8.2 | Speaking the unspeakable: indirection as a linguistic strategy | | 156 |
| | 8.2.1 | Euphemisms | 156 |
| | 8.2.2 | Euphemisms for pregnancy | 157 |
| | 8.2.3 | Proverbs as indirect speech | 158 |
| 8.3 | Language and advertising | | 160 |
| | 8.3.1 | Weasel words | 161 |
| | 8.3.2 | Open-ended comparisons | 162 |
| | 8.3.3 | Ambiguous language and modal auxiliaries | 163 |
| | 8.3.4 | Politics as advertising | 164 |
| 8.4 | Meaning and humour | | 167 |
| | 8.4.1 | Humour and the sound system of a language | 167 |
| | 8.4.2 | Humour and morphology | 167 |
| | 8.4.3 | Humour and semantics | 168 |
| | 8.4.4 | Humour and syntax | 169 |

**9   The History of English**   172
| | | | |
|---|---|---|---|
| 9.1 | Periods of English | | 174 |
| | 9.1.1 | Effects of the Norman invasion | 176 |
| | 9.1.2 | The return of English | 177 |
| | 9.1.3 | The influence of Geoffrey Chaucer | 178 |
| | 9.1.4 | The printing press | 179 |
| | 9.1.5 | The influence of James I | 181 |
| 9.2 | Lexical change | | 182 |
| | 9.2.1 | English expands through military and economic expansion | 184 |
| 9.3 | Sound change | | 186 |
| | 9.3.1 | The Great Vowel Shift | 187 |
| | 9.3.2 | Evidence for sound change from Old English | 188 |

| | | | |
|---|---|---|---|
| 9.4 | Changes in grammar | | 189 |
| 9.5 | The spelling 'system' of English | | 190 |
| | 9.5.1 | Fixing the spelling problem | 194 |

**10  Language Variation and Change**    197

| | | | |
|---|---|---|---|
| 10.1 | Why languages change | | 197 |
| | 10.1.1 | Lexical and semantic change | 198 |
| | 10.1.2 | Changes in the sound system | 199 |
| | 10.1.3 | Changes to grammar and morphology | 201 |
| 10.2 | Language variation | | 202 |
| | 10.2.1 | Causes of dialectal diversity | 203 |
| | 10.2.2 | Social attitudes about language varieties | 206 |
| | 10.2.3 | Measuring attitudes about language varieties | 207 |
| 10.3 | Dialects of language contact | | 208 |
| | 10.3.1 | Chicano English and codeswitching | 208 |
| | 10.3.2 | Codeswitching | 211 |
| | 10.3.3 | Pidgins and creoles | 215 |
| 10.4 | Varieties of English | | 225 |
| | 10.4.1 | Appalachian English | 225 |
| | 10.4.2 | African American Vernacular English | 229 |
| | 10.4.3 | Cockney English | 232 |
| 10.5 | Language and gender | | 234 |
| | 10.5.1 | Use of titles | 235 |
| | 10.5.2 | Asymmetries in language | 236 |
| | 10.5.3 | Generic 'he' for unspecified reference | 237 |
| | 10.5.4 | Effects of gender on language | 238 |
| | 10.5.5 | Common beliefs about gendered language | 239 |
| | 10.5.6 | Language and the workplace | 242 |
| | 10.5.7 | Early socialization by gender | 243 |
| 10.6 | The future of English and its dialects | | 244 |

| | | |
|---|---|---|
| **References** | | 249 |
| **Index** | | 253 |

# Preface

Our lives are filled with language. We use it to describe the world around us, to negotiate our way through the complex situations and relationships of our lives, and for the most simple ones as well. In addition, the way we use language defines us to the people around us. Language is not just a tool for communication but an intrinsic aspect of our identity. In fact, Robert LePage and André Tabouret-Keller call every communication event an 'act of identity'. Even though language is so significant in our lives, and we quite easily make use of it hundreds of times every day, most people are not aware of the incredible complexity of all the systems that make up our communication system. The goal of this text is to explore all the fascinating subsystems of language as well as how we make use of them.

Over the past decade, there has been a trend at many universities to offer 'General Education' classes, which are replacing traditional elective classes taken in many departments. These classes are usually multidisciplinary in nature, covering areas of knowledge that universities have identified as critical to the overall education of university students. Because an important function of the university is to prepare students to understand the global society in which we live, many departments of linguistics have been asked to construct courses in the basic understanding of language and its functions across cultures. These classes are often large lecture classes offered to first-year students who are most likely being exposed to the concepts of linguistics for the first time. Students in these classes need materials that provide not only an understanding of the range of linguistic topics, but materials that are preparatory in nature.

Because the needs of students in the general education courses are more interdisciplinary, there is a need for a text that provides a broad-based treatment of both theoretical and applied linguistics. This text, while providing a solid coverage of the theoretical systems of language, provides more coverage than traditional textbooks of language use in our normal lives with many real-life examples to show how theory is played out in real life. Popular culture is also analysed for linguistic content. For example, in any episode of *The Simpsons* television show, there are many examples of language play and manipulation of our language skills which create a great deal of linguistic-based humour. This is not just the simple use of sarcasm or puns to get a laugh, but a profound manipulation of the syntax, morphology and phonetics of the English language.

The text begins with chapters designed to sort out what language is, and just as importantly what it is not, and how it is that all humans acquire their mother tongue so well. Then, I have provided a basic overview of the major structural areas of linguistics including the systems we use to create sound, grammar and meaning. The final third of the book looks at how individuals and groups make use of language in their daily lives. The chapters explore how gender, race and ethnicity, among other characteristics of human communities, affect not just what we say but how we say it. More importantly, the chapters look at how we use language to negotiate our own identities within different communities or contexts.

The text provides a broad coverage of many complex areas of the field of linguistics. Its goal is to provide students with an awareness of human language through brief and clear explanations accompanied by real-life examples and illustrative exercises to help draw attention to the diverse ways in which language impacts our daily lives and the societies in which we live.

Elizabeth Winkler
elizabeth.winkler@wku.edu

# List of Figures

| | | |
|---|---|---|
| 2.1 | Round dance | 24 |
| 2.2 | Wagging dance | 25 |
| 2.3 | Sickle dance | 25 |
| 3.1 | Left hemisphere of the brain | 44 |
| 4.1 | Picture of head with articulators | 66 |
| 4.2 | Sagittal sections: velum raised | 69 |
| 4.3 | Sagittal sections: velum lowered | 69 |
| 4.4 | Drawing of hunters | 78 |
| 4.5 | Drawing of hunters | 78 |

# Acknowledgements

The people I owe thanks to for this book are many. First and foremost are all the professors of linguistics who have taught me over the years at Ohio University and Indiana University, most particularly James Coady and Beverly Flanigan at Ohio, and Albert Valdman, Beverly Hartford and Samuel Obeng at Indiana.

Gratitude goes as well to all the professors at the University of Arizona who helped me survive my first classes of 350-plus freshman non-major students taking the department general education class focusing on the introduction of linguistics. Special thanks go to Andrew Carnie, Simin Karimi, Dick Demers and Michael Hammond who had incredible patience with all my questions, both about how to handle this huge class as well as for their knowledge of their fields. Thanks go as well to the many graduate students who worked for me and contributed many of the creative ideas for how to teach this class to non-majors.

The reviewers for this text provided me with excellent commentaries, suggestions and criticisms, and each reminded me that their fields had much more to offer than I necessarily covered in this brief treatment of their specialties. They provided more guidance than I could have wished for. That being said, any errors in this text are solely mine.

Many thanks go to my special reviewers, first, my parents, who faithfully read every chapter, and as non-linguists, were able to point out to me places where my presentation was not comprehensible to those new to the field. Their unwavering support and confidence in me throughout the writing of this book, as well as my life, made all of this possible. Many thanks go as well to Jennifer Lovel, my editor at Continuum, whose patience, guidance and good cheer never failed throughout this long project. I could not have done this without her help.

Finally I want to thank my husband, Rick Toomey, who, most importantly, didn't leave me over the long time it took to get this project done! I am deeply grateful for his patience with all the missed meals, late nights and missed time together, as well as for all his suggestions and technical help.

# 1 What Every Native Speaker of a Language Secretly Understands

## Chapter Overview

| | | |
|---|---|---:|
| 1.1 | THE SOUND SYSTEM | 2 |
| 1.2 | THE LEXICON: THE HUMAN DICTIONARY | 4 |
| 1.3 | MORPHOLOGY | 7 |
| 1.4 | GRAMMAR | 8 |
| 1.5 | HOW THE WORLD'S LANGUAGES DIFFER | 9 |
| 1.6 | THE BOUNDARIES OF A LANGUAGE: LANGUAGE VERSUS DIALECT | 12 |
| 1.6.1 | HOW DOES A STANDARD DEVELOP OR GET CHOSEN? | 14 |
| 1.6.2 | STANDARD AND WRITTEN LANGUAGE VERSUS NORMAL OR NON-STANDARD SPEECH | 17 |
| 1.7 | A LINGUISTIC APPROACH TO LANGUAGE DIVERSITY | 19 |

If you ask any group of people to define the concept *language*, you are going to get countless definitions ranging from simply a system of communication to 'a system of symbols, generally known as lexemes and the rules by which they are manipulated'.[1] The definition really only becomes relevant for normal people (not linguists!) when we start putting boundaries around a language and try to separate out, for example, what is English and what is not, which we'll discuss in detail in the final chapter on language varieties.

When I rephrase the question and ask, 'what makes up a language?' I usually get a good general list including: sounds, words, grammar, meaning and, more rarely, students tell me about the principles that guide us in combining these features. These are all certainly important features of language, but each aspect represents a complex series of features and rules, and, often, social choices, that are all part of an interconnected system of language. In addition, I get responses about what is *right* and *wrong* about language, for example, that you shouldn't end a sentence in a preposition or use double negatives. Everyone who is a native speaker has a considerable amount of knowledge about the language he or she speaks. Nevertheless, most people have probably lived happily all of their lives without ever thinking about the complexity and elegance of the system because most of this knowledge is unconscious. So, what is it that we all know?

## 1.1 The sound system

All native speakers of a language know what sounds are part, and what sounds are not part, of their language. It is important to note here that I am talking about *sounds* and not *letters*. English, for instance, has 26 letters in its alphabet, but more than 40 distinctive sounds, depending on which variety of English you speak. When we learn a second language, one of the challenges we must meet is learning the sounds, and possible combinations of sounds, that differ in the language we are learning. For example, every English speaker who learns Spanish has to learn the rolled or trilled 'r' sound that appears in words like *carro* (car). Many of us have trouble learning this sound because it is not part of the natural inventory of sounds that English speakers make. On the other hand, Spanish speakers from Latin America learning English frequently have trouble with the 'th' sounds in words like *three* because 'th' is not part of the inventory of sounds of Latin American Spanish, though it is still used in the Spanish of Spain. We are well aware that different languages have these differences because they often appear as stereotypes in television programmes and movies. Many children growing up in the US who have seen the cartoons *Pepe Le Peu* and *Speedy Gonzalez* have heard the stereotypes of second language English from supposedly French and Spanish-speaking cartoon characters. It is clear from the sounds that these characters make that their US creators noted differences in the sounds, stress and accents of certain varieties of these languages and English, and that they expected these would be understood by their audiences.

Native speakers of a language also know where a particular sound can occur in a word. This rule is more unconscious to speakers than knowing which sounds are in their language. Most English speakers are unaware that the last sound in words like *sing,* which linguists represent as [ŋ], can only appear at the end of a syllable or word in the vast majority of English dialects. It is never heard at the beginning of a word or syllable. It does, however, appear at the beginning of many words in sub-Saharan African languages that are not historically related to English. The Liberian language of Kpelle has this sound at the beginning of words: *ŋwana* (wound or hurt, verb).

There are also combinations of sounds in English that can be heard at the beginning of a word or syllable, but may not end them. For example, you can begin a word or syllable with the sound combination [dw] (dwindle, dweeb) but there are no words that end in this combination of sounds. The same is true for the combination [str] as in *street.*

Sometimes there are very subtle differences in sounds depending on where in a word a sound occurs. In most varieties of English, there is a difference in the sound [p] when it is at the front of a syllable from when it is the final sound in a syllable. You can not only hear the difference if you pay close attention, but you can see it as well. If you hold a piece of paper in front of your mouth and say the word *pan,* you will notice that the paper moves a little because you release a small puff of air when you make the [p]. Try the same thing only this time saying the word *taped*. Note how there is much less air escaping after the [p], and the paper hardly moves at all. Most people live their whole lives without overtly noticing this difference, yet they make the correct choice thousands upon thousands of times without thinking when they speak each and every day. There is a sound rule in English, that foreign learners of English must learn, which states that you add a puff of air (aspirate) the [p] sound when it is at the beginning of a syllable but do not when it is syllable-final. Notice the different aspirations of the two [p] sounds in the following sentence:

Put it down and stop it.

It is important to note that there is no physical reason why your mouth is forced to make these sounds differently. There are languages that make both sounds in the same environments. In these languages, it is as if they are different letters. Thai is one of these languages; the difference in initial aspiration of [p] is the difference between the words *aunt* and *cloth*.

pàa = aunt    [p]            phàa = cloth [pʰ]

In addition, only certain sounds can be combined together in any language. Not all combinations of sounds are possible. Above we said that [dw-] was an acceptable combination at the beginning of English words, but how about [wd-]? We also only allow two consonant sounds in a row in the same syllable except for [str-]. Japanese, as well as many other languages, allows no consonant clusters (two or more consonants in a row in the same syllable). Japanese syllables always follow the same two patterns: CV (consonant/vowel) or CVC (consonant/vowel/consonant). You never have a syllable in which there are two consonants in a row in the same syllable. All you have to do is think of all the Japanese company names to test this out:

Ya·ma·ha    Hon·da    Su·zu·ki    To·yo·ta

This pronunciation rule is so strong for Japanese speakers that it even carries over to words that get borrowed into Japanese from other languages. Japanese has borrowed thousands of words from English that people use every day:

lefuto (left field[2])        homuran (homerun)        erebata (elevator)

nekutai (necktie)        sarada (salad)

These words give us a good deal of information about acceptable syllable structure in Japanese as well as information about what other sounds are acceptable in Japanese as well. (For instance, what happens to the [l] sound from the middle of an English word when it gets borrowed into Japanese as in *elevator* and *salad*?) Each language has its own particular set of sounds that are part of the inventory of sounds for that language as well as rules for where those sounds can be found in a word and how they can combine together. There is nothing biological or logical that dictates these rules although they work systematically in every language.

## 1.2 The lexicon: the human dictionary

The most common response I get when I ask students what we know when we know language is that we know the words. Linguists call the words that speakers know their lexicon. Knowing the words of the language is different from knowing the sounds. All speakers of a language know all the sounds of their language. The only exception would be if a speaker has some sort of pathology and physically cannot make a certain sound. The lexicon is different. Each speaker of a language has a different vocabulary depending on the environment in which a person lives and works, his or her level of education and exposure to different social groups, as well as many other variables. There is a subset of words that everyone seems to know. This list would include all the articles like: *a*, *an* and *the*, and the prepositions: *on*, *under* and *by*, etc. Most people also share the most common lexicon as well: words about core family members and activities, food and other things that are common across the English-speaking world. This does not mean that there is no variation for common words. Depending upon which part of the United States you live in, you put your groceries in a *sack*, a *bag* or a *poke*, and you put water in a *pail* or a *bucket*. If you want to go to an all-you-can-eat restaurant you go to either a *smorgasbord* or a *buffet* depending on where you live. In many parts of the USA, a carbonated beverage is referred to as *pop*, in other parts of the country as *soda*, and in the Deep South, it is becoming more and more common to refer to all these beverages as *coke*. When I lived in Georgia, I actually had someone ask me, 'What kind of coke do you want?' When I responded, 'Just regular', the person said, 'No, which kind? Pepsi, Mountain Dew or 7 Up?' This is not just a southern phenomenon; it is spreading slowly to other parts of the States as well. There are thousands of dialectal variations for words and phrases across any country; for example, in Britain, all of the above drink words translate as a *fizzy drink* or a *soft drink*. There are even more lexical distinctions from one English-speaking country to another. I recently heard this joke that gets the point across quite nicely:

> A businessman from the United States was in London for a meeting. After checking in at the hotel, he asked the desk clerk where the elevator was located. The clerk responded that he did not understand the question and asked, 'What is an elevator?' The American responded, 'It's the machine you go upstairs in.' The British clerk looked indignant and in a lofty tone said, 'Oh, you mean the lift.' The businessman got miffed as well and said, 'Look, we invented it; it's called an elevator' to which the British clerk responded, 'Look, we invented the language; it's a lift!'

When we know the words of our language, we also know the slang expressions of our group and idiomatic expressions like *What's up?* Imagine the confusion of many first-time foreigners visiting the United States trying to figure out why in a greeting a person might ask them what's up on the ceiling or in the sky. I ran into the same problem in Mexico when my friends would greet me with *Qué honda?* (basically, 'What's up?') When I looked up the words in the dictionary, they translated as 'how wave?'[3] Native speakers of a language understand when words are to be understood literally and when they are not which means we understand the semantics of our language. We also understand that our utterances are generally not made in a vacuum. If I make the statement 'The lights are on' when we pull up at a friend's house at night uninvited, it is likely that I mean that they are probably still up. If I make the same statement as we are leaving our own house, it is likely that I want to go back inside and turn the lights off. Language is not simply the words, sounds and grammar of a language, but also the understanding of the use of language within a society and its subcultures, which is the study of pragmatics.

As a learner of a second language, it is often a long time before we are able to get jokes because we tend to translate literally, getting word-by-word meaning, and we miss word-play and sarcasm. Much of our humour is based on native-speaker-conscious or unconscious understanding of linguistic processes. You only have to watch an episode of *The Simpsons* to see how language play and manipulation of our language skills in all the subfields of linguistics is the basis for a great deal of humour. This is not just the simple use of sarcasm or puns to get a laugh, but a profound manipulation of the grammar and sound system of the language. There are jokes for every subfield of linguistics, as we'll see throughout this text. Our awareness of language play comes very early in our lives, as we can see from kids' jokes or puns like the following:

Question:    Why can't you play cards on a boat?
Answer:      Because someone is always sitting on the deck.

Question:    What animal could Noah not trust?
Answer:      The cheetah (cheater).

In addition to understanding word meanings and knowing when they are to be taken literally or not, we know how to decide which of a word's possible meanings is needed for a particular context. For instance, we know which meaning of the word *bank* in the sentence 'I'm going to the bank' is necessary depending on the context of the event:

1. You are swimming in the river.
2. You need money.

Many words and phrases are lexically ambiguous (having more than one possible meaning) until they are in a context. Native speakers very naturally access, most of the time, the needed meaning of an ambiguous word or phrase used in a normal conversation without even being aware of the process. This is another source of bad jokes:

> Question:    What did the Zen master say to the server at the hot dog stand?
> Answer:      Make me one with everything.

The humour in this joke is derived from the double meaning of the words *one with everything*. In the context of the hot dog stand, the first reading of *one with everything* would normally mean a hot dog with all the condiments; however, when you throw in the Zen master, it refers to making the speaker one with the universe in this bad joke.

Church signs are often excellent sources for linguistic wordplay. In each of the following signs, a point is being artfully made through the double meaning of the words *jams* and *left*.

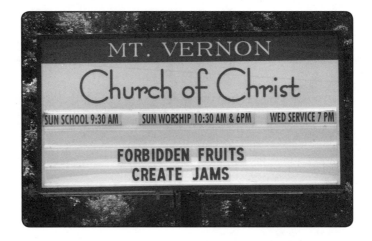

## 1.3 Morphology

Beyond knowing the basic words of a language, all native speakers understand the morphological processes of their language. For example they know where the word boundaries are in a string of sounds like 'doyawannago?' (Do you want to go?). It also means that they understand how some words with the same base forms are related in meaning and how prefixes and suffixes affect both the meaning and grammar of the words. Many of the prefixes and suffixes are quite productive and are attached to many words. Others are left over from earlier varieties of English and are no longer combined with new words. An example of a suffix that has gone out of common use is the use of -en added to a noun to make it plural. The most common remaining words in English that have this ending are *children* and *brethren*. Now when we add a new word to the language, like MP3, we simply add the suffix -s to them (MP3s).

Some prefixes are quite common, for example *un-*. It is attached to many words including: *happy*, *imaginable*, *willing* and *believable*. Each of these words is an adjective, and the addition of the prefix, *un-* simply makes the adjective negative. There are other prefixes that are commonly used in English that mean the same thing: *dis-* (disincentive) and *im-* (impolite) are but two. Knowing which to use is part of the learning process of every child. By listening to their parents speak, children learn these attachments to words and figure out their meanings. They don't always get them right at first: 'I am so dishappy today'. Nevertheless, native speakers learn quickly to say *unhappy* instead of *dishappy* or *imhappy*, though it could be argued that these forms are just as logical as *unhappy*. Non-native speakers learning English also struggle with the many equal forms available to them.

Variation in usage pops up even with native speakers of English. During the 2003 MTV music awards, rapper Fred Durst said 'Everyone is in agreeance'. The word *agreeance* was used by speakers of Middle English, but I doubt Durst is a student of Middle English!

These morphological processes are all about adding new words to the language as well. By adding prefixes and suffixes to new words, we increase the vocabulary of our language. The website *Google* has become so popular that people talk about *googling* to get information that they need. This even happens sometimes when a person just makes up a word by adding a suffix or prefix for a particular situation where none has ever been added before. These may not ever become official words of the language, but people easily understand them nonetheless. In Lewis Carroll's story, 'Alice in Wonderland', the gryphon uses the words *uglify* and *uglification* which are perfectly logical inventions in light of the words *beautify* and *beautification*. The fact that these are not 'real' words in English deters no one from understanding them because we understand the underlying processes.

## 1.4 Grammar

All speakers of a language are also experts in how words or phrases are combined together to make sentences. Nevertheless, many speakers will claim that they know very little about the grammar of their own language, which is for the most part false. What they really mean is that they are unable to tell you all the parts of speech and list the explicit grammar rules that govern their combination. In reality, they know the great majority of these rules implicitly, in other words, they know when something is correct just by instinct. We know this is true because every day they utter thousands of sentences correctly, many of which they have never said before. Their unconscious knowledge of the grammar of their language makes this possible. We will look at how this is possible in more detail in the chapters on language acquisition and syntax.

Even though most speakers claim not to know the rules of grammar of their language, they can actually tell you if a sentence is grammatical or not. This is called our *native speaker intuition*. Linguists have tested this by giving native speakers what are called *grammaticality judgement tasks*. In these tests, speakers are asked to rate the grammaticality of a list of sentences as to whether they are completely OK in any situation, sometimes OK, a little strange but OK, or completely unacceptable. Most speakers find some sentences so weird that they can say with assurance that a sentence is not grammatical in any context in their language; for example: 'Jacques in house the'. No native speakers of English would have to think twice about whether or not this sentence is grammatically correct. They might even be able to give the rule about what is wrong in the above sentence. However, this combination may be perfectly acceptable in another language. In Haitian Creole, the same combination of words results in a perfectly grammatical sentence:

> Jak nan kay-la.
> Jacques is in the house.

In Haitian Creole, the article *the* comes after the noun. In English, we know that articles come before nouns. So native speakers of Haitian Creole would have a very different idea about what constitutes a grammatically correct sentence in their language than English speakers would about theirs.

Sometimes, whether or not a sentence is grammatically correct to a native speaker of a language is much more subtle:

> The blue big round balloon popped.

Although native speakers could say that the sentence sounds funny and declare what sounds better, most could not provide the complete rule for the order of multiple adjectives in a sentence even though they have been applying this rule correctly, though unconsciously, most of their lives.

We may not even think about this rule until we take a foreign language and then have to overtly learn the adjective order rules for that language – which are most likely different from the rules of our own. Here's a brief excerpt of one of the full rules for English:

| (Order from left to right) | | | | | | | | |
|---|---|---|---|---|---|---|---|---|
| article | opinion | size | shape | condition | age | colour | origin | NOUN |
| a | | beautiful | tiny | oval | flawed | ancient | blue | Chinese | *plate* |
| She bought a beautiful tiny | | | oval | flawed | ancient | blue | Chinese plate yesterday. |

Clearly, we rarely produce a sentence like this in a natural conversation, but the rule does explain the problem with *The blue big round balloon popped*. It is weird because *colour* is preceding *size*. There are a number of variations on this rule that provide similar explanations for adjective ordering, but as native speakers of English we don't need to learn this rule overtly because, very fortunately, we intuitively know it.

To native speakers, a sentence like *The blue big round balloon popped* may be acceptable, but they will say it is a little weird. There are other types of sentences though which reflect the division between the way many people normally speak and what our teachers, and maybe parents, tell us is acceptable English. Consider the lyrics from the Rolling Stones' famous song: 'I can't get no satisfaction'.

The violation of the 'no double negatives rule' sends most eighth grade grammar teachers over the edge. In fact, it is one of the most stigmatized features of non-standard varieties of English that you may be judged for using (fairly or unfairly!). Nevertheless, millions of native speakers of English persist in using double negatives in their everyday speech in sentences like 'She can't do nothing right' and 'I ain't got no money'.

As stated above, most of our knowledge of the complex system of English grammar is unconscious – which is very fortunate considering the rate at which we produce and comprehend language in normal conversational settings. Frankly, the quantity of information that we have to know to use a language is astounding, and we generally only become aware of the depth of that knowledge when we have to learn a second language. Then we begin to see that language learning is so much more than just memorizing new words and sounds! All the world's languages have complex rules, though they differ greatly from English. The speakers of these languages are equally unaware of the vast majority of their grammar rules as well.

## 1.5  How the world's languages differ

Every language is highly systematic in its use of features, but the selection of features that appear in each language is arbitrary. For example, the inventory of sounds for a language is limited to a subset of the sounds that the human mouth can make. There are no languages that use every possible distinct sound. Physically, there is no reason that any person without a speech impediment cannot make all the sounds of all the world's languages. Nevertheless, you may be one of the English speakers who has difficulty making the rolled [r] sound of Spanish and Portuguese. As noted earlier in this chapter, some speakers of Japanese have difficulty distinguishing and pronouncing the [r] and [l] sounds in English words. This has to do with familiarity and practice and not with a physical difference of our tongues.

It is also true that there is no inherent relationship between an entity and its name. There is no one logical name for an object or feeling, which is why there are so many different words for things across languages:

| | |
|---|---|
| love | English |
| amor | Spanish |
| pɛ | Akan (from Ghana) |
| влюбленность | Russian |
| 사랑 | Korean |
| sev | Turkish |

Even the onomatopoeic words (like animal sounds) of other languages are not the same or even necessarily understood by speakers of other languages. In English, roosters say *cockadoodledoo*, whereas in Akan (a language of Ghana) they say *kokurokoo*, in Finnish they say *kukko kiekuu*. Dogs in the USA say *bow wow* but in Britain they say *woof woof*, and in Mexican Spanish they say *guau guau*. You will find the same thing if you ask native speakers of different languages about other words like these. Try *ouch, meow* and *ding dong*, for example.

It is not just the words themselves that are arbitrary in their selection. The word combinations that we use to express different concepts vary quite a bit as well. In English, to express discomfort with the temperature, a person might say: *I am hot*. If you translate those words directly from English to Spanish, you end up with *Estoy* (I am) *caliente* (hot). However, in Spanish, this means *I am feeling sexy*. To refer to the temperature, a Spanish speaker says *Tengo calor* (I have heat). You can see that a one-for-one translation here could cause quite a misunderstanding!

Not only is the word choice variable, but the order in which words can appear is as well. The normal word order for sentences differs from language to language, though there are always exceptions. In English, the word order is usually: subject, verb, object (SVO).

> I married Rick.
> S    V    O

However, the word order for most of the world's languages is SOV (subject, object, verb). Some well known SOV languages include Japanese, Turkish and Georgian.

| Japanese: | watashi ga Bob wo naguru |
|           | I          Bob   hit      |

| Turkish: | Ben Bobi severim |
|          | I    Bob   like   |

| Georgian· | me bobi mome'ons. |
|           | I    Bob   like    |

English also has a surprising difference in its grammar from many European languages, of which most native English speakers are not overtly aware – English does not have a future tense ending like Spanish or French (this means English verbs have no special ending like the *-ed* ending for past tense). Romance languages have very elaborate tense marking systems. Anyone who has had to memorize the complicated tense systems of French, Italian, Rumanian, Portuguese or Spanish can certainly attest to this! Let's take a quick look at just the future tense of Spanish:

**Spanish: *dar* (to give) future tense**

| daré | I will give. |
| darás | You will give (informal). |
| dará | You (formal), he, she, it will give. |
| daremos | We will give. |
| darán | They will give. |

In English, we'd simply use the modal *will* and the simple form of the verb *give*. The verb endings do not change for each person like native speakers do with Spanish verbs.

**English: use of *go* for a future reference**

I *will go* tomorrow.
You *will go* tomorrow.
He, she or it *will go* tomorrow.
We *will go* tomorrow.
They *will go* tomorrow.

We can also make a future reference by using the present progressive form of the verb plus an adverb of time in the future like *tomorrow*: 'I am going to go tomorrow'.

Change is another aspect of language that shows us how distinct the world's languages are. It is clear that there is no one true way languages work because we can document that all living languages change, and they change quite differently. Even dialects or varieties of a single language change in different ways from each other – that's how we have ended up with so many varieties of English! Look at how different the varieties of English in the USA, Canada, Nigeria, India and Australia are. These varieties differ in sound system, vocabulary and grammar, as well as in every other linguistic system. If countless differences exist even between the same varieties of a language, imagine the variation across different languages from different language families. All these differences make it seem as if languages are just erratic accidental combinations of features; however, there is quite a lot of the language system that is very systematic which we'll take a look at in following chapters.

## 1.6 The boundaries of a language: language versus dialect

I have been talking very generally about the features and systems of languages in general, but I have left out a very abstract yet important concept that remains difficult for both linguists and non-linguists to define very satisfactorily. Linguists use the word *language* as an umbrella term that encompasses all the possible varieties of a language. *Dialects* or *varieties* of a language may or may not have different names but are related in important ways and similar enough to be grouped together as parts of one language. A simple analogy works well here. We use the term 'tomato' for many different objects because there are hundreds of types which share some qualities of 'tomatoness' but can be wildly different in colour, shape and taste. The same is true for languages. Dialects of a language share many of the same features, but they differ in the grammar, sound, vocabulary and usage. The more different a person sounds, the more features of her or his variety differ from yours. When I first arrived in Samana province, in the Spanish-speaking Dominican Republic, I heard people speaking to each other not in Spanish, but in something I did not really understand that had English words in it. When I asked them what they were speaking, they replied 'English'. This is a variety of an English creole which was transplanted to the island hundreds of years ago but because the Dominican Republic became a Spanish-speaking country, these speakers have had little contact with other varieties of English so their variety of English is quite unique. Furthermore, they are speakers of Spanish as well, which has affected their English too. Obviously, this is an extreme case, but this is the situation for all varieties of English. The more contact between speakers of different varieties, the more likely that their varieties will share features. Speakers of varieties that have little contact will have greater difficulty understanding each other because they will have continued to evolve differently from each other.

Most people have an idea about what they think *proper English* sounds like. They usually point to generalized varieties often spoken by network news announcers. Many will claim not to be good speakers of Standard English, and say they speak in a *sub-standard* dialect or speak *bad English*. Linguists generally prefer to call these varieties *non-standard* dialects because these varieties are just as valuable and systematic as the community standard. To get their point across, there are a couple of sayings that linguists like to teach their classes:

1. The Golden Rule of Dialects: Those with gold get to make their dialect the standard.
2. A language is a dialect with an army and a navy.

These sayings tell us many things about the relationship between a standard language and who holds power. First, if you take a look at the variety of a language that is considered standard in a country, in almost every case, it will be the variety of the people who have some sort of power over the majority. The nature of the power differs depending upon the sociocultural situation of the country. For example, the *Queen's English* in Britain (or *BBC English* as it is sometimes called because it is the variety used by most BBC newsreaders) is the variety considered the standard, yet less than 10 per cent of the populace of Britain speaks an approximation of it. It is the variety of the public school elite. (US English speakers need to translate *public* school to *private* school since the phrases have almost opposite meanings in the two countries.) This is true of other languages as well. For example, in Iraq, previous to the 2002 war, the Sunni variety of Arabic was considered the standard, even though its speakers constituted a numerical minority of the country because they were dominant politically. In the USA, the variety of English most often identified as standard is not the variety of graduates of the northeast private schools (like the voice of John Kerry or TV personality Frasier Crane), but it is more of a Midwestern variety of English, sometimes referred to as *broadcast English* since it is the variety used by many national television news broadcasters. More whimsical names for this variety are *Vanilla English* and *Wonder Bread English* (because they have so little flavour).

If you study any country's situation, you will find that what determines the standard language has everything to do with the social and political situation of the nation and nothing to do with one variety being better than the others in terms of having a systematic rule-based system and extensive vocabulary. Here are several scenarios to consider in terms of their impact on what would have ended up being the standard language in Britain or the United States:

1. What if France had continued to exert intense political, social and linguistic interest in England after the Norman Invasion of 1066 instead of mostly isolating the Norman French?
2. What dialect would be the standard in the United States today if the south had won the Civil War?
3. What if slaves in the USA had revolted and gained political and economic control over the country? What effect might that have had on the variety that became standard American English?

## 1.6.1 How does a standard develop or get chosen?

In actuality, a standard dialect is usually not officially chosen in any way. At no point in our history were our great-grandparents given an opportunity to vote on whether or not they wanted a standard form of English or what features they wanted to be considered standard. No committee of English teachers, great writers or linguists assembled a national convention to make these important decisions. Consider also that the language we speak is not at all the same as the language of the 1800s, so who has been in charge of formalizing or deciding on the constant changes to English that have obviously occurred? Considering how strong many people's feelings are about what is *correct* and *incorrect* in grammar and pronunciation, there does not seem to be an official governing force at work. What's more, it is clear that language has changed greatly over the years and continues to change – even our written forms.

Take a look at English in the USA. The founding fathers discussed the issue of national language as they went about creating the constitution. They even considered languages other than English as possible national languages – including German and Hebrew. In the end, their language policy, or lack thereof, was consistent with their philosophy for other aspects of life in the new country – they opted on the side of personal freedom of choice. Thus, the USA is one of the few major countries of the world that does not have a national language specified in its constitution.

English in America quickly began to diverge from that spoken in England, especially that spoken by the educated classes. The people that emigrated from Britain to the new world were often the economically less successful or less educated. They were, in general, not the elite of England, Ireland and Scotland. The numerous and quite distinct varieties of English they spoke coalesced as they settled in the New World into spoken American English. Written standards came later. The fact that so many people from the USA speak a similar variety of English, at least in grammar, has more to do with the universal public school system than some sort of master plan.

At the same time that Colonial English was developing in America, in England a rising middle class in the mid-1700s allowed for more people to send their children to school. Previous to this, the idea of specifying one 'correct' way to speak and write was not given considerable thought. People spoke the way they did, and great differences were tolerated in grammar, writing and accent. In fact, the political leaders of Britain at this time, and for the next century, had very strong regional accents that did them no disservice in their aspirations. Nevertheless, the parents of the rising middle class had expectations that the children they were sending for schooling would acquire a proper way of speaking that would help them advance in this more open society. Thus, in the 1760s, the Royal

Society was tasked with determining which variety of English would be set down in grammar books for educating children in schools. This committee had a collection of members from various disciplines including Joseph Priestly (better known as the father of chemistry though he also wrote *The Rudiments of English Grammar* in 1761), Jonathan Swift (best known for writing *Gulliver's Travels* and *A Modest Proposal*) and Bishop Robert Lowth (a Hebrew scholar), among others.

They had three basic goals. First, some, especially Swift, were concerned with stopping language change. He feared that one hundred years in the future, no one would be able to read his works – much in the way that school students today have difficulty with and often loathe reading Old English texts like *Beowulf*. Second, they wanted to provide a set of rules that could be consulted by anyone wishing to refine their grammar. Their third goal was to provide a standard form of English that educated people could acquire which would be used for legal works as well as science and literature, that would be consistently understood by people across different dialects.

Because the great majority of English grammar rules were similar across dialects, many of the rules were understood, even if unconsciously, by all the native speakers of English. However, some of the rules that the committee imposed were more in the nature of ornamentation in that they made rules for things that most people did not do naturally when speaking English (like use 'whom' correctly). This may well have happened because these men were focused on writing rather than normal speech. To give them credit, they did not just vote to make everyone learn their dialects. During this era, because there had been no pressure for people to speak the same way, people happily and unselfconsciously spoke the local varieties of where they lived. The committee members themselves did not share a single dialect. Thus, because they were academics, they looked to their professions to find less arbitrary ways to determine the rules they were creating for this new form of Standard English. Interestingly, they resorted to deriving some of their rules from mathematics and Latin.

They chose to derive rules from Latin because they perceived it to be the one perfectly logical language. (Latin is still sometimes perceived this way. Because all the native speakers of Latin have long since died, there are no pesky teenagers to wreak havoc with slang and new forms; thus, it doesn't change like a living language does.) Two rules that they chose from Latin are still quite commonly taught. One is the rule that you cannot end a sentence with a preposition, which is, at least in the USA, regularly ignored in normal speech. Imagine the scene at most workplaces or classrooms if you were to come in on Monday morning and ask your friends 'With whom did you go to the football game on Friday?' Most normal US speakers would simply say 'Who did you go to the football game with?' violating both the preposition rule and the 'correct' usage of *whom*. What makes borrowing this particular rule even weirder, is that English is part of the Germanic family of languages and not the Latin one, and Germanic language speakers regularly, and quite happily, end sentences with prepositions!

They also borrowed another rule from Latin that your eighth-grade grammar teacher taught you, which you more than likely rapidly forgot: 'don't split infinitives'. An infinitive is simply the 'to' form of the verb, for example: *to run*. In Latin, an infinitive is one word, for example, *amare* meaning *to love*. Since *amare* is one word, it is unlikely that a speaker of either a Germanic or an Italic language would split it in the middle of the word. For more than thirty years, grammar teachers all over the English-speaking world have been horror-struck every time either Captain Kirk or Captain Picard have opened a Star Trek episode by saying 'to boldly go where no one has gone before'. The insertion of the adverb *boldly* between the two words of the infinitive phrase, *to go*, is officially a grammar error if one is trying to speak a standard variety of English.

One of the most commonly violated and well-known grammar rules that came out of this committee is the rule concerning double negatives. The members of the committee pointed out that in maths multiplying two negative numbers results in a positive answer; therefore, in language, it is only logical that the same would be true. In most of the world's languages, double negatives are quite common; in fact, they are commonly used in many varieties of spoken English and are replete in the writings of the man many English teachers refer to as 'our greatest writer' – Shakespeare. Here is an example from Henry IV: 'There is *never none* of these demure boys come to any proof.'

The double negative rule does not serve to disambiguate situations in which their use causes problems of understanding. It is pretty clear that when Mick Jagger sings 'I can't get no satisfaction' no one is confused. Nor is anyone confused when one friend says to another, 'He can't do nothing right today.' These rules, and others like them, were artificially created, and despite hundreds of years and millions of grammar classes later, many still commonly ignore them in normal speech. These rules have persisted due to the fact that they were written down and given the status of law. Nevertheless, despite the considerable efforts of grammar teachers and the criticism of grammar mavens in the media to force these rules upon us and to eradicate *bad English*, non-standard English is alive and thriving in every English-speaking country. What we have ended up with are many language systems co-existing side by side, each being used in different contexts depending on the speaker. For linguists, this diversity of form is a marvel. The diversity is extraordinary because despite all the social and educational pressure, people maintain the varieties that have the most meaning for them, and linguists have found that all of these varied forms are systematic in their arrangement of grammar and sound.

## 1.6.2  Standard and written language versus normal or non-standard speech

The reality is that most people do not speak the standard language exclusively in their normal daily life. In fact, most people are not perfect speakers of the standard – including presidents, university professors and broadcast journalists, as we'll see in some examples below. The standard varieties pushed in school are often more reflective of written standards of language rather than spoken ones. They are school varieties rarely used in their complete form except in very formal situations like job interviews and formal business and educational meetings. These varieties are like that suit you put on for your job interview that is never seen again once you get the job! When we are comfortable with people, we speak in the variety that is most comfortable to us, which for only a very few people is perfect standard.

The standard variety spoken in the USA is supposedly modelled by announcers on network news programmes, national public radio and other varieties of educational TV and radio. Yet even in these forums, you can hear normal English that would make your grammar-school teacher cringe. Take a look at the grammar 'problems' in the following examples – all from people your school English teacher would say 'should know better'. First, consider the logo that's been on the Cable News Network (CNN) banner for several years: 'Real News, Real Fast'. Second, notice the same usage on the label of Thai food in the following photograph.

Both of these examples reflect a trend in US English for the *-ly* ending on adverbs to be absent in some contexts. For strict grammarians, *fast* and *easy* are adjectives that *should* be modified by the adverb *really*. I heard the following example on a rainy day weather report from a University of Arizona National Public Radio announcer: 'Do drive as careful as you can'. In this example, the word *careful* is modifying *drive*, and thus, should be *carefully* in Standard English.

The loss of *-ly* on adverbs is not the only variation noted from the standard in some varieties of English. The following example comes from my own speech, taped at an informal event. It reflects various aspects of the Appalachian English dialect that I grew up with: 'I might could do that ifn⁴ you was to give me some time'. The phrase *might could* is called a double modal, and the noun *you* would be paired with subjunctive case *were* in Standard English. And then, of course, there are hundreds of examples floating around on popular websites from United States President George Bush, who is clearly not always a speaker of a standard variety of English: 'Rarely is the question asked, is our children learning?' In this case, there is a singular verb *is* with a plural noun *children*. So if university professors, presidents and network news announcers all violate the rules of Standard English – sometimes even in very formal situations – what does that tell us about the use of pure Standard English?

It may be more useful to think in terms of the standard language as a target that no one hits perfectly all the time but we approximate with different levels of intensity depending on our social needs. I certainly become more conscious of the way I speak when I meet someone for the first time in a professional situation. However, if I used the same overly formal and correct language talking with friends at a casual party, I might well be perceived as being snooty.

Therefore, none of us speak exactly the same way every day, in the same situation, nor do we speak the same as anyone else. For linguists, this is a fascinating phenomenon, but for some teachers and social pundits, this diversity of language use is a cause for alarm. Bad grammar is sometimes looked at as a social ill on the level of political corruption. Some see it as a reflection of the breaking down of our social structure and, for example, equate the use of double negatives as a sign that standards are going down the drain. In reality, no living language is static. They all change despite the ranting of social pundits. Today's 'bad grammar' becomes acceptable to later generations who then have their own ideas about what constitutes an error. Others worry that too much diversity could lead to groups of English speakers being unable to communicate with each other. This certainly has happened in the past. For example, the non-standard dialects of Latin turned into French, Rumanian, Italian, Portuguese and Spanish, among other languages, all of which are now considered languages, and they all have their own dialects.

## 1.7  A linguistic approach to language diversity

To linguists, all the discussions concerning which varieties are good or bad English are irrelevant because all varieties of language, as well as all languages, are created equal. There are no primitive languages, nor primitive dialects of a language. What I mean by that is that there are no languages that cannot express all the possible meanings a group of speakers needs. When speakers need a new concept, they simply create it. The Chinese put together the words *ice* and *box* (just as English speakers did) to create a way to describe a new product. As we have studied the world's languages, we have found that the level of complexity varies between languages and across different systems within a single language as well. The differences don't stop people from saying what they want about anything. We just do it differently. For example, in the West African language called *Kpelle*, spoken in Liberia, there are only four single words for colours. Does this mean that the Kpelle only see four colours? Of course not; their eyes are physically the same as all other humans. English speakers generally distinguish eleven primary colours. Other cultures distinguish thirteen. It's simply a matter of how you divide up the pie. When asked to distinguish between colours like *blue* and *violet*, for instance, the Kpelle will describe the colours as blue as the sky, or blue as a particular flower. They just do not have single words to express these concepts.

Some non-linguists like to claim that some languages are sophisticated and others primitive. This is a personal value judgement, not a scientific analysis. When we analyse the different features of languages, we find that some aspects of a language could be described as simple whereas other aspects may be quite complex. Which aspects are simple and complex varies greatly from language to language. For instance, English is simplistic in many aspects compared to other languages. We have fewer tenses with fewer person forms and fewer classes of nouns (sometimes called genders) than many languages. If you learned French or Spanish as a second language, you had to learn which gender class all the nouns of the language belonged to, and if you are like me, you made many errors in gender agreement while learning the system. When I was learning Spanish, it never made sense to me why the word for *table* (mesa) would be feminine and the word for *floor* (piso) masculine. German has three genders (masculine, feminine, neuter), and many of the Niger-Congo languages of West Africa have more than fifteen. Gender here is really a misleading word; it has nothing to do with masculinity or femininity. It is the linguistic term for classes of nouns. Niger-Congo languages often class words into categories like human, animal, religious items, long things etc. The fact that English does not have a complex noun class system may make it easier to learn, but it does not mean that English is a primitive language.

On the other hand, English is more complex than Spanish in its sound system. English has more vowel sounds (at least twelve depending on the dialect); Spanish has only five or six depending on your point of view. Does that mean that English is a more complex language? No, it just means that it uses more vowels to create the same words that other languages create with fewer vowels.

All languages serve their speakers in significant ways – not just as tools for communication, but also as important markers of culture and identity. For linguists, all dialects of languages warrant the same respect as all languages do, for the exact same reasons. Differing dialects are solely a manifestation of the sum total of our life experiences. Our non-standard voices, which we maintain despite considerable pressure, are a reflection of the social or geographical class with which we identify, as well as our educational experiences. When we choose to approximate the standard, it is usually for some social purpose as well: to impress a new boss or acquaintance or sometimes even to maintain social distance from an unwanted approach. Our language varieties are a useful tool as well as an expression of who we are. In the coming chapters, we'll look at the different systems of language as well as the social contexts in which language is used and shaped.

## Suggested reading

Crystal, D. (2003), *The Cambridge Encyclopedia of the English Language*. NY: Cambridge University Press.
McWhorter, J. (2003), *The Power of Babble*. NY: Perennial.

## Interesting websites

The Linguistic Society of America. Frequently asked questions about linguistics. www.lsadc.org/info/ling-faqs.cfm

The Ethnologue An encyclopedic reference work cataloguing all of the world's 6,912 known living languages. www.ethnologue.com/

## Consider the following questions

1. What attitudes do you, or others, have about non-standard varieties spoken in your country? Which varieties are considered prestigious or undesirable? Why?
2. If you speak a non-standard variety, what attitudes do others have about your own speech? Have you ever been criticized for the way you speak? Explain.

**3.** Do you ever use English that isn't proper? When? Why?

**4.** Which well-known people or celebrities use non-standard varieties of English in either real life or on television? Pick one and explain what it is about his or her dialect that makes it interesting.

## Notes

1   www.wikipedia.org/

2   Left field is a baseball term in the USA. To hit a ball to left field means to hit it to the far left side of the field furthest away from first base. The term has been extended to mean really crazy or way out of line with the norm as in 'She is really out in left field'.

3   This slang expression is generally interpreted as 'Are you tuned in to the same staion as I?' (radio waves. This is similar to the English expression 'Are we on the same page?')

4   'Ifn' is a local variation in pronunciation of 'if'.

# 2 Human Language Versus Animal Communication Systems

## Chapter Overview

2.1 NATURALLY OCCURRING ANIMAL COMMUNICATION SYSTEMS  24
    2.1.1 BLACK AUSTRIAN HONEYBEE COMMUNICATION  24
    2.1.2 BIRD CALLS AND SONGS  26
    2.1.3 DOLPHINS AND WHALES  28
    2.1.4 MORE COMPLEX ANIMAL COMMUNICATION SYSTEMS  29
    2.1.5 PRIMATE COMMUNICATION  29
2.2 ARTIFICIALLY TAUGHT ANIMAL COMMUNICATION SYSTEMS  30
    2.2.1 CHIMPANZEES AND GREAT APES  30
    2.2.2 AFRICAN GREY PARROTS  32

> The trouble is that the differences between language and the most sophisticated systems of animal communication that we are so far aware of are qualitative rather than quantitative. All such systems have a fixed and finite number of topics on which information can be exchanged, whereas in language the list is open-ended, indeed infinite . . . and there are subtler, but equally far reaching differences between language and animal communication that make it impossible to regard one as the antecedent to the other.
>
> (Bickerton 1990, p. 8)

The capacity to communicate is innate in both humans and other species of animals; however, there are significant differences between human language and animal communication systems. The argument is not whether or not animals have communication systems, but whether or not their systems can be defined as language. Human language possesses a number of significant qualities that as yet have not been found, as a group, as part of any other animal communication system. For example, human speech sounds can be arranged in infinite sequences to create new meanings. No animal species has been identified that can combine the sounds or gestures (or whatever) of their system to add new meanings in an ongoing and productive way. Each and every day humans are constantly creating new words and topics of discussion. Language is an open system with almost limitless potential for creativity and innovation as long as the basic system rules are followed. As far as scientists have determined, animal communication systems are generally confined to a very limited set of topics that are significant to the animals' survival: finding food or mates, protecting territory from invaders or keeping the group together when travelling.

In addition, the relationship between the sound of a word and its meaning is almost always arbitrary in human languages, which is why words differ from language to language as we learned in the first chapter. This is evidenced by the fact that all humans are of the same species but that one species' individuals currently speak over 6,000 languages. In animal communication systems, a specific sound corresponds with a specific meaning. Variability is not a feature. For animals, not only is the ability to communicate innate, but also the sounds, postures and gestures are also often biologically fixed according to each species. This is not to say that there is no learned component in any animal communication system; for example, as we'll learn later in this chapter, there are some aspects of bird calls and prairie dog warnings and many aspects of bird songs that are learned, and there is some dialectal variation in some other systems, but by and large, the range of variability is quite small when compared to human language.

Finally, humans do something quite significant with their languages that animals, at least as we currently know, do not; we communicate in the abstract, about events in the future or the past, about things and people not in the immediate environment, and concepts and ideas that have no physical form. Although some animal communication systems may deal, in a very limited way, with items not in the immediate environment, animal communication is limited to reacting to the environment in some way. However, recent research is beginning to focus on whether or not animals possess the ability to think symbolically. As I like to remind my students, our understanding of animal systems reflects our current state of ignorance as well as knowledge. There is much that we do not understand yet about what they do.

So if all of this is true, why do we bother to study animal communication systems at all? Throughout human history, myths, legends and tales from every human culture are full of animals with whom we can communicate and who often instruct us. The Anansi stories of West Africa and the Caribbean, from which Brer Rabbit stories in the USA were derived, are full of wise and foolish animals involved in situations from which we learn important life lessons. The Greek fables of Aesop did the same with a variety of animal protagonists in stories like *The Fox and the Grapes*. More recently, in the movie *Star Trek IV*, the earth is almost destroyed because we hunted to extinction a species of whales with whom we failed to communicate. Beyond stories, in television commercials and magazine advertisements, talking gecko lizards sell insurance and tigers sell breakfast cereal. Many of my own friends are completely sure that their pets completely understand their most abstract communications. There seems to be some sort of universal human compulsion to communicate with animals.

Beyond this urge, a more significant reason to study animal communication systems is that we are not the only animals that communicate in some fashion, and therefore we may be able to understand something about our own system, however different, from studying the systems of others.

## 2.1 Naturally occurring animal communication systems

### 2.1.1 Black Austrian honeybee communication (*appis mellifera carnica*)

One of the most complex and elegant animal communication systems is the gestural one used by bees. A particular type of bee, called the forager bee, has the job of locating food sources for the hive. When a forager bee finds food and returns to the hive, it does a special dance on the wall of the hive to inform the other bees of the location of the food so that they can go and retrieve it. The food can be quite a goodly distance from the hive, so it is important that the distance and direction of the source be very accurate.

Bees do three different dances depending on how far away the source is from the hive. To indicate the location of food that may be found within 5 metres of the hive, the bees do a *round dance*. The *sickle dance*, which imparts more specific information, is performed for food that is more than 5 metres away but less than 20. Food that is located over 20 metres from the hive causes the bees to do the *tail-wagging dance*. Besides providing information about distance from the hive, all the dances tell the observers about the quality of the food source and the direction from the hive where it is located.

In the round dance the returning forager bee dances around in a circle on the wall of the hive, frequently switching direction and stopping occasionally to regurgitate food that he has eaten from the source to let the other bees try it out. The primary function of this dance is to recruit other forager bees to gather the food. In all the dances we'll look at, the number of repetitions of the dance that the bee does, and how intensely he dances, indicate how satisfactory the food source is.

**Figure 2.1** Round dance, performed by moving in alternating circles to the left and to the right, used by honeybees to indicate the presence of a nectar source near the hive

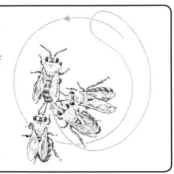

For intermediate distances, the bee dances in a sickle shape with the angle of the open end of the sickle and the vertical angle to the sun reflecting the angle from the hive to the food source. This means that bees use the sun to navigate (solar-oriented flight) and are able to communicate that information to others. For longer distances, the dance must provide very precise information so the bees can locate the food. In the tail wagging dance, the forager bee dances in two semi-circular paths with its tail wagging on the straight line of the path. Depending on the orientation of the dance on the hive wall, the bees know which direction from the sun to fly. The bees know how far to fly because of the duration of the dance. Studies show that they have effectively communicated distances to food positioned up to six miles away.

**Figure 2.2**  Wagging dance indicates distance and direction of a nectar source further away. Bee moves in a straight line, wagging her abdomen, then returns to her starting point

**Figure 2.3**  Sickle dance used by the Italian bee. She moves in a figure-eight-shaped pattern to show intermediate distance

I'm sure you are asking by now, since we cannot talk to bees, how do we know all this? The research to understand animal communication is at least as fascinating as the results. Much of the research was done in the late 1950s and early 1960s by a scientist named Karl Von Frisch. He very methodically created a set of conditions to determine what it is that bees know.

In one experiment, he placed a very fragrant source of food for a forager bee to find, to test whether or not bees are communicating direction. After the bee found the food and flew back to the hive, Von Frisch moved the food to one side a short distance. When the bees from the hive returned to the spot where the food had been, they found nothing and did not find the food nearby, which showed that they were communicating direction and that a heightened sense of smell did not lead them to the food. He did a similar experiment in which he placed the food in a number of locations along a vertical path between the hive and the original source and then on past it. The vast majority of the bees flew right over the food that was closer than the original source and identified it correctly.

In one quite perverse and bizarre experiment, a bee was forced to walk all the way back to the hive after tasting a food source. The dance that the bee did caused the other bees to fly 25 times farther than the food source. Therefore, the bee must have been measuring and communicating flying time.

Finally, in one experiment, the researchers emptied the hive, so that when a forager bee returned with information of a food source, there was no one with whom to communicate. Bees require an audience for their communication efforts, unlike humans! Like humans, however, different types of bees have dialectal differences in their communication system. Studies of other species of honeybees, like the Italian honeybee (*apis mellifera ligustica*), show systematic variations in the dances, and these variations are not trivial. Even though the dancing of two species of bees is similar, they are not mutually intelligible. An experiment was done in which a forager bee of one species was sent into the hive of another species. The bees in the hive got all excited by the dance, but when they flew out to find the food source, they flew right past it.

Unlike human language, which although innate must be acquired through exposure, bee communication systems are completely innate. For example, bees that have been raised in isolation will dance when introduced into a hive. Though there is some evidence that their directional information improves with practice with the sun, all young bees are born fully equipped to dance.

## 2.1.2 Bird calls and songs

I used to visit a cave in Mexico called *El Sotano de Las Golondrinas* (The Pit of the Swallows), which was an upside-down volcano-like opening in the earth that was about 1,200 feet deep. Every morning from the depths of this pit, millions of birds would leave their nests on the lower walls of the cave and fly the full height up and out of the cave in search of food. Every evening, before dark, they would reverse the process and fly back down into the pit to their nests for the night. The total process would take a couple of hours for all the birds to get out. What fascinated me, as I watched them come and go, was that they seemed to do so in waves. They did not all try to fly out at once, which would have been impossible, but seemed to have some sort of plan for an orderly systematic process of who went out in which group and when they would go and in what order. They also seemed remarkably good at avoiding the weird humans ascending and descending the rope in what normally would have been their flight path. The only reasonable explanation for this intricate behaviour is that a communication system must be in place that guides their travel.

Bird communication is bimodal using both vocalizations and visualizations. The focus in this chapter will be on vocalizations, which, according to ornithologists, are of two types: calls and songs. Unlike human language, in which sentences can be broken up into individual words that can be mixed with other words to create other meanings, there is no internal structure to bird calls. The entire utterance is a single message. For some species, bird songs appear to be more complex in their structure. Research shows that bird songs may have an internal structure in that different parts of the song have different functions: one part of the song identifies the species of the bird and the other part provides information about the specific identity of the bird singing and its mated status. Some warblers use different 'accents' in the ending parts of their song to identify whether they have a mate or not. Several species of birds, like marsh wrens, have quite an extensive inventory of songs available to them. They learn over 100 songs for their own repertoire as well as hundreds of songs of their neighbours, and strategically use their neighbours' songs when it suits them.

Bird calls are made up of single notes or short sequences of notes. Calls are used to signal quite a number of activities. For instance, birds employ calls during flight to keep the flock together and to signal takeoff and landing. They also utilize them when they need to sound an alarm or to protect their territory. Birds use different types of calls depending on what type of threat they perceive. If a ground predator is present, a bird will fly over it and sound the alarm, both to scare off the predator and to tell other birds where it is located. If the danger comes from the air, the call is different as well as the reaction of the birds that hear the call. When they hear this call, birds either stop moving or get under cover so they are harder to catch. Alarm calls actually work with many classes of birds, so calls are not completely species-specific.

Bird songs are mostly used by males in courtship rituals and territory protection. Although bird songs sound quite complex, each note does not correspond to a particular meaning, but sections of the song do have a specific function. Early research on bird songs indicated that songs performed very limited functions and that there was little, if any, internal structure. More recent research[1] has shown that songs are more complex than originally understood. For example, the order of the sections of the song is important. As with human language, if you say a sentence backwards, it rarely has any meaning. Some species of birds are not only able to learn the songs of neighbouring birds of the same species, but can learn the songs of other species of birds which they use for defence of their territory. You can imagine how useful it would be to be able to use the 'voice' of a larger, more powerful bird in the protection of your territory.

As with bee communication systems, the acquisition of bird calls is mostly innate, though some species learn parental calls early on, especially in difficult surroundings. For example, Murre chicks learn their parents' calls when they are still working their way out of the egg. When the baby birds are too young to fly, the parents protect them by drawing predators away from the nest so the babies can escape. Later, when the coast is clear, the parents will give their signature call to tell the babies that it is safe to return. The ability to learn a call is useful in other ways. For example, there is a species of finches that learn the calls of the new group if they change flocks.

As with the bees, creative experiments have been conducted to see what it is that birds are doing with their calls. In one experiment, researchers played a particular call over a loudspeaker during the chicks' hatching phase. Later, when the chicks were out of the egg, the call was played over a loudspeaker and a competing call played over another. The chicks ran to the one playing the call that they had heard in the egg and ignored the other loudspeaker playing a different call. This indicates that they learned a particular call during their hatching phase. It's not any bird call that is significant, but the one imprinted at the appropriate time.

## 2.1.3  Dolphins and whales

The communication systems of dolphins and whales are quite similar to those of birds in their functions, and equally complex. For example, the bottle-nosed dolphin creates two kinds of vocalizations: *pure tones*, comprised of whistles and squeaks, and *pulsed sounds*, including clicks, barks, yelps and moans. Dolphins produce clicks to send out sound waves that they bounce off objects to identify them, a process called echo location. Dolphin signature whistles identify the pod and individuals in the pod. Whistles are also used to send out alarms and distress calls. If a dolphin is injured, it can signal other dolphins to come and provide help by raising the injured one out of the water so it can breathe.

Whales are well known for their songs, which can go on for as long as 30 minutes individually or a few hours if there is a group of whales. Scientists have hypothesized that the songs identify individuals and serve to keep migrating herds together in the vast ocean. Whale songs share this function with bird flight calls.

Birds, bees, dolphins and whales all have quite complex systems of communication, but their systems are both qualitatively different from human language, in the limit on their ability to speak abstractly and recombine units of their system to make new messages, and quantitatively different, in the limit on the range of topics they can cover.

## 2.1.4 More complex animal communication systems

Recent studies show that Gunnison's prairie dogs have shown a more complex and detailed system in predator recognition calls than previously studied species of animals with warning calls. Unlike bird alarm calls, which as far as we currently understand are limited to identifying only ground or aerial predators, prairie dog alarms are quite complex, using up to 100 sounds in one alarm to describe a particular predator. More startling, prairie dogs have also created new calls for new predators in their environment, indicating at least some ability to create new messages including specific information about a particular predator. Studies have been done at the University of Northern Arizona in which prairie dogs were confronted with silhouettes of a variety of both predators and non-predators of differing sizes. Their alarm calls were recorded and analysed, and it was found that the alarms provide information about the size and shape of the predator – not just locational information. Nevertheless, these studies still do not offer a serious challenge to most linguists' claims that languages are substantially more complex than animal communication systems.

## 2.1.5 Primate communication

The most studied animals, in terms of communication systems, are the non-human primates, specifically because they are our closest relatives in the animal kingdom. We have not only studied their communication systems, but have made many attempts to teach them forms of human language as well. Part of our desire to teach them language stems from this genetic relationship and the hope that by studying them, we might learn something about the very first languages humans spoke tens of thousands of years ago.

Like other animal systems, non-human primates seem to be limited to reacting to environmental stimuli or to the context in which they are found, and thus are quite limited in the number of topics available to them. Like whales, dolphins, birds and other animals, the topics non-human primates communicate about are feeding, protecting territory and showing dominance, and attracting and keeping mates. They use calls, facial expressions and gestures to communicate with each other.

One of the most studied primates is vervets (*cercopithecus aethiops*), a species commonly found in East Africa. Their vocalizations produce 22 distinct messages using 36 sounds that cannot be combined in other patterns to produce new messages. Most of their calls are dealing with predators, and like the communication system of the prairie dogs, vervets have more varied predators than birds requiring a much more specific set of calls to get across the appropriate warning. In one experiment, researchers played sounds of snakes, leopards and birds of prey to some vervets. In response, the vervets produced three separate alarm calls: 1) for snakes they looked at the ground, 2) for birds of prey, they got out of the trees and under bushes, and 3) for leopards, they returned to the highest parts of the trees.

## 2.2 Artificially taught animal communication systems

At the turn of the twentieth century, a horse named Clever Hans was purported to be able to think and communicate with his human trainer. The trainer would give him simple maths problems, and the horse would use his hoof to tap out the correct answer. This ability was pretty impressive until a sceptical researcher put a blindfold on Clever Hans and found out that he could no longer add. As it turned out, Clever Hans was trained in dressage, which requires that the horse respond to very subtle clues given by the trainer. The trainer was unknowingly moving slightly when the horse reached the correct answer. Thus the horse was skilled at reading the trainer and not at adding numbers and communicating the answer.

Many of the criticisms of the claims that animals are 'using language' stem from the very same type of challenge, though it is quite clear that interpreting the use of complex systems being used by current researchers is hardly the same as evaluating Hans' stamping foot. Nevertheless, because of the intensely close nature of the relationship between the researcher and the animal subject, it is possible that some of the production is a result of cueing. This intense relationship is the cause of another criticism. How much are the researchers reading into the accomplishments of their subjects? How generous are their interpretations? Before strong claims can be made, neutral methods of analysis are required for ensuring that our observations are legitimate. Current researchers are aware of these issues and build into their studies methods for evaluating the data being gathered and for making the most of their observations.

### 2.2.1  Chimpanzees and great apes

A great deal of popular media attention has been given to the teaching of human language to non-human primates. Non-human primates are very much like us in many respects. We have trained them to do so many human activities that we expect that maybe language is within their reach as well. After all, we share over 95 per cent of our DNA with them. The research that has been done is quite interdisciplinary, involving linguists, biologists and psychologists among others. The modes of language that have been employed have also been quite varied: vocalizations, hand-oriented sign language, computer-generated sign language, and different coloured and shaped plastic chips. There have been some interesting claims about how much language these primates can acquire; however, the problems and limitations that surface with each experiment are similar. Because we are biologically similar, some researchers have tried to get apes to form words, even going to the extent of the researcher trying to force the lips of the animal with his hands to help a chimpanzee make human sounds. They had little success because, in part, the physical structure of the musculature in the chimpanzee's vocal tract is quite different from ours and does not allow for the same articulations. More success has been made with communication systems that involve the hands, as chimpanzees and apes have quite good manual dexterity and are very good at imitating movement.

For example, one of the best-known experiments with teaching animals language was Allen and Beatrice Gardner's work in the 1960s and 1970s with Washoe, a chimpanzee. According to the Gardners, Washoe learned to make over 100 signs and could combine two of them together in meaningful ways, for example, 'you drink'. In fact, they claimed that Washoe was actually creating new meanings through the use of compounding. For example, when Washoe saw a swan, she signed 'water bird'. Unfortunately there is nothing to support their contention that this is a compound word for the concept of *swan*. Washoe could just have easily been signing the two consecutive signs for *bird* and *water*, identifying two separate items in her environment. One interesting result of their work was that an infant chimpanzee not being trained by humans managed to pick up several dozen signs from the other chimpanzees in his environment.[2]

In a more recent study in the 2000s, an ape named Kanesa signed the word *badbad* when a researcher picked up a poison mushroom in the ape's habitat. Later, when the researcher faked trying to eat it, the ape dragged him around teaching him which plants were safe to eat and which were not, by signing *badbad* over and over. What does this indicate about the ape's understanding?

Despite the efforts of many well-meaning and skilled scientists, it is quite clear that non-human primate use of human-like language systems is quite 'unhuman'. Although many of the studies seemed quite promising at first, later analysis of the videotapes of the interactions between the researchers and the apes and chimps revealed a number of problems with their claims. First, there seemed to be some completely unintentional cueing by the researchers that calls into doubt whether the animals were responding to the cues or the language, though whether or not all of this challenged behaviour was cueing is still a subject of debate among researchers. Second, there was a considerable amount of misinterpretation or over-generous interpretation of the signs made. This is not particularly surprising. Almost everyone has heard proud parents claim to understand a particular meaning from an unintelligible utterance of their small child, and after working with these animals for some time, it is clear that the researchers were quite involved with them. Beyond these methodological problems, there are more serious challenges to the claims that apes and chimpanzees have acquired human language.

First, unlike human children, who spontaneously pick up many words a day as they are acquiring their first language, the non-human primates have to be taught every single sign or symbol. After 2 years of age, children go beyond two-word combinations and make lengthier and more complex utterances; the other primates do not. If they do use more words, it is likely they will be repetitions. The chimpanzee named Nim Chimpsky once signed 'Me drink Nim', a sentence in which the words *me* and *Nim* both refer to the chimpanzee itself. Some of these criticisms of their ability may be unfair in that the comparison is often made between speaking children and signing non-human primates. Furthermore, the fact that these primates were learning sign from humans who were not native speakers of sign, and may not have always been consistent in their signing, must also be taken into consideration.

Their combinations of signs also vary in word order. They do not develop syntactic patterns like children do even from their earliest utterances. Furthermore, children will chatter to themselves when alone and will talk to everyone around them when given the opportunity. The other primates almost exclusively 'perform' language for the researchers and only very rarely start a conversational exchange, unless they want food, though some of the younger apes in the Gardners' study did sign to themselves on occasion. The chimpanzees and apes imitate researcher behaviours because that's what they do in the wild; they imitate each other. However, we currently lack a sufficient understanding of their ability to imitate either in the lab or in the wild.

The most significant challenge to strong claims about non-human primate communication is that it is still limited to the topics they address with their own communication systems. They react to the environment in which they find themselves.

## 2.2.2 African grey parrots

In college I had a friend who had some sort of parrot that the owner taught to call the dog. The parrot would call 'Here puppy, puppy', and as the dog ran into the room, the bird would go quiet. The dog, totally confused, would exit the room and then the bird would call again and the dog would return. This would go on over and over until the dog would get so frustrated that it would give up. Although this hardly constitutes intentionality (or a sense of humour!) on the part of the bird, it does call into question what it is that animals are doing with the pieces of speech we give to them.

Research in animal communication systems is still ongoing, though fewer researchers are concentrating their efforts on primates. Some interesting research is being conducted on African grey parrots (*psittacus erithacus*). These parrots are being studied, not just to test the extent of their ability to communicate with humans but to understand what complex mental capabilities they may possess. More than just using human speech, can animals think symbolically? Dr Irene Pepperberg, currently at Brandeis University, has been exploring what it is that these parrots can do and understand. Her studies indicate that a parrot called Alex, among others, is able not just to recognize numbers up to six, in both oral and written form, and relate them to objects, but also to understand their relations in terms of size; for example, that five is bigger than three. What makes this even more amazing is that he figured this out on his own and demonstrated it to researchers.

African grey parrots also display an understanding of object permanence. Children under 6 months of age in general follow the rule 'out of sight out of mind'. If an object is removed from their visual field, they do not look for it. When researchers play the shell game with Alex, and hide a nut under one of three cups and switch them around, Alex is able to follow the cups and locate the nut. If they substitute another object for the nut Alex vocally demands the edible nut.

Pepperberg claims that, on certain tasks, African grey parrots have the reasoning ability of a 5-year-old child, which is higher than that of any of the primates that researchers have been studying. The typical bird's brain is quite small in size and quite smooth as well. A primate's brain is covered with fissures and folds that increase its surface area. It is believed that the size of the human brain is what makes the complicated system of language possible. This is one of the reasons that so much focus has been aimed at teaching language to other primates. More recent studies, however, show that a bird's brain may function comparably.[3] Parrots are interesting for another reason: their ability to make the sounds of human language.

Parrots show some of the same abilities that primates do. For example, Alex was once given a piece of cake by some of the students working with him. He had not been taught the word *cake*, but he had been eating banana bread. Since he didn't have cake in his vocabulary, he called it *yummy bread*, which is a quite logical production. Alex expresses his opinion about his workload as well as a research subject. At times, he will turn away from the researchers and say 'I'm gonna go away'.

Much of this research is in its early stages and is yet to be duplicated by other research labs, but it does challenge whether or not there are animal species capable of abstract thought and intentionality and whether or not we will ever be able to figure out what it is that they know.

## Suggested reading

Bickerton, D. (1990), *Language and Species*. Chicago: University of Chicago Press.

von Frisch, K. (1962, August), 'Dialects in the language of bees'. *Scientific American*, 207, 2. 78–89.

McCowan, B. and Reiss, D. (2001, December), 'The fallacy of "signature whistles" in bottle-nosed dolphins: a comparative perspective'. *Behaviour* 62, 6.

Michel, A. (1980), *The Story of Nim: The Chimp who Learned Language*. New York: Knopf, distributed by Random House.

Pepperberg, I. M. (1999), *The Alex Studies: Cognitive and Communicative Abilities of Grey Parrots*. Cambridge, MA: Harvard University Press.

## Interesting websites

The Georgia State University Language Research Center. Research on primate communication. www.gsu.edu/~wwwlrc/

The Alex Foundation. Website dedicated to the research being conducted on African grey parrots. www.alexfoundation.org/

## Consider the following question

Animal 'language' is a popular topic for general and popular news magazines. Because these articles are written by reporters who are not experts in animal communication, they often present new discoveries about the communication of animals as if they have language just like humans. Find two such articles and explain, in light of what you have learned about animal communication systems, how these articles misrepresent the nature of what the animals are doing.

# Notes

1  'Vocal-tract filtering by lingual articulation in a parrot'. By Beckers, Gabriël J. L., Nelson, Brian S., Suthers, Roderick A. *Current Biology*, September 2004, Vol. 14 Issue 17, 1592–7. 'What the white-crowned sparrow's song can teach us about human language'. By Baptista, Luis F. *Chronicle of Higher Education*, 7/7/2000, Vol. 46 Issue 44, p. B8.
2  For more information on the study of non-human primates, see also the work of Roger Fouts, Penny Patterson and Susan Savage-Rumbaugh.
3  'Avian brains and a new understanding of vertebrate brain evolution'. In *Nature Reviews Neuroscience* 6(2), 151–9.

# 3 Language Acquisition

## Chapter Overview

3.1   EARLY THEORIES OF FIRST LANGUAGE ACQUISITION                37
   3.1.1   CHALLENGES TO BEHAVIOURISM AND STRUCTURALISM        38
   3.1.2   THE INNATENESS HYPOTHESIS                           38
   3.1.3   SUPPORT FOR THE INNATENESS HYPOTHESIS               39
   3.1.4   PROBLEMS WITH REINFORCEMENT AND IMITATION           40
   3.1.5   WHAT CHILDREN'S 'ERRORS' TELL US                    41
   3.1.6   STUDIES SUPPORTING THE INNATENESS HYPOTHESIS        43
   3.1.7   STUDIES ON THE LIVING BRAIN                         44
   3.1.8   CRITICAL AGE HYPOTHESIS FOR FIRST LANGUAGE
       ACQUISITION                                       45
3.2   STAGES OF LANGUAGE ACQUISITION                             46
   3.2.1   LEARNING THE SOUND SYSTEM                           46
   3.2.2   SOUND AND MEANING                                   48
   3.2.3   FROM SINGLE WORDS TO GRAMMAR                        48
3.3   SECOND LANGUAGE ACQUISITION                                49
   3.3.1   SLA AND BEHAVIOURISM                                50
   3.3.2   FIRST LANGUAGE INTERFERENCE IN SLA                  52
   3.3.3   SLA AND FEEDBACK OR CORRECTION                      53
   3.3.4   INDIVIDUAL DIFFERENCES                              55
   3.3.5   CRITICAL AGE HYPOTHESIS FOR SECOND LANGUAGE
       ACQUISITION                                       57
   3.3.6   RECENT DEVELOPMENTS IN SECOND LANGUAGE ACQUISITION  58

From the first two chapters, we've learned that acquiring a language is a remarkable achievement requiring an understanding of many linguistic systems each with its own set of complex rules. Nevertheless, practically all children completely acquire their native language with little obvious effort. The vast majority of us take this phenomenon for granted. It is not until we try to learn a second language in school or at university that we confront for the first time the thousands upon thousands of rules and processes that we must understand to be able to communicate effectively in another language. In fact, most native speakers are completely unaware, at a conscious level, of the majority of the rules of their own native language. Despite this, every day we produce and comprehend thousands of sentences, many of which we have never heard or produced before. How is this possible?

# 3.1  Early theories of first language acquisition

In the mid 1950s, behavioural psychologist B. F. Skinner published a study entitled *Verbal Behavior* (1957) in which, after extensive study of groups of pigeons, he put forth a set of theories about how human children acquire their first languages. He posited that the brains of infants were a *tabula rasa* (blank slate) that awaited the input of parents to provide them not only with words to repeat but also overt instruction which would assist children in learning what was and was not acceptable in the language they were learning. He believed that children would hear language, imitate it and then be encouraged (reinforced), either positively or negatively by their parents or other caretakers. Through these mechanisms, imitation and reinforcement, children acquire their native tongue. The logical conclusion of this theory is that environmental and physical factors would affect how each individual child acquires a language. Differences in the quality and quantity of input, each child's level of intelligence and natural talents, and the type of social interaction experienced would have a direct effect on the amount and quality of the language that would be learned. This belief fitted in with psychological theories of the 1950s that viewed normal first language acquisition of language as a behaviour rather than an innate ability.

These psychological theories fitted well with both philosophical as well as linguistic theories of the 1930s to the 1950s, which were rooted in structuralism as promoted by Edward Sapir, Charles Hockett and Leonard Bloomfield among others. Bloomfield's linguistic textbook *Language*, the seminal work of his day, offered a behaviourist view of language acquisition. Proponents of structuralism believed that the basis for understanding language in general, as well as the study of language acquisition, should be limited to observable phenomena and guided by scientific method. Thus, speculation on the internal processes of the mind did not play a role in the development of theories in either psychology or linguistics. Native speaker intuitions about language processes were not explored since they were neither observable nor quantifiable.

This approach not only affected the study of first language acquisition, but the acquisition of additional languages as well. The methodologies for language teaching coming from this period reflect this tradition. Encouraged by Pavlov's famous studies on operant conditioning and stimulus and response on dogs, language methodologists created language methodologies that concentrated on learning through rote memorization with constant practice of structures guided by appropriate reinforcement provided by the teacher. Many of the earliest foreign language classes that I took in school were based on this philosophical approach to language learning. We spent class after class being presented with word lists and grammar rules to memorize. Although I was good at memorizing rules, I was utterly incapable of carrying out even the most basic conversation with a native speaker that did not exactly fit the dialogues that I had memorized. This type of instruction fitted in well with the belief that first language acquisition, and thus second as well, occurred through repetition of forms and reinforcement to encourage correct acquisition.

### 3.1.1 Challenges to behaviourism and structuralism

In the late 1950s, the linguist Noam Chomsky revolutionized the way scientists look at language acquisition as well as the study of language itself. Chomsky's theories went way beyond the structuralists whose goal was to describe the language output of humans. While the structuralists focused their attention on individual languages, Chomsky and the other generative linguists who followed wanted to figure out the principles of human language itself. The structuralists focused solely on the output/performance of speakers, but Chomsky was interested in the speakers' mental competence as well. Language competence and performance do not always match; for example, from many studies we know that both children learning a first language and anyone learning a second one understand more language than he or she can produce. Thus, Chomsky wanted to explain the output by understanding the universal cognitive (mental) processes involved in language and thought. Other theorists of the generative-transformational school of linguistics as well as cognitive psychologists have expanded upon his early theories.

### 3.1.2 The innateness hypothesis

According to proponents of the innateness hypothesis, the brains of all human children are biologically set up to recognize the patterns of whatever human language they are exposed to by their parents and caretakers. This ability to intuitively figure out the rules of the language is guided by the biological resources of the brain. Chomsky called these resources the *Language Acquisition Device* (LAD). There is a good deal of support for this ability which will be discussed below, but one important set of support comes from biology and not linguistics. In the late 1960s, biologist Eric Lenneberg offered a set of criteria to evaluate whether a feature is genetic rather than learned by an animal. If a behaviour is genetic, it will appear before it is necessary for survival, and its acquisition will progress along a path of expected developmental steps until the behaviour is fully functional. The behaviour is also something that cannot be taught before the animal is in the right developmental stage. Lastly, the behaviour must be acquired within a certain developmental stage or it is not likely ever to be acquired correctly. It is easy to see how children's language fits these requirements. Children start to speak very early in life, long before their parents would think of abandoning them, so they don't need it for basic survival. We also know that children's language abilities develop over time in a predictable way (which we'll discuss in more detail below) and no matter how much (or how little) teaching goes on, it still takes children a number of years to fully acquire their language.

The LAD is not like the kidney; we can't just open up the brain, remove and dissect it and explain the functions of the tissues and muscle. Rather, the LAD is an integrated part of the human brain, aspects of which are spread throughout the brain though concentrated in the left hemisphere, as studies have shown. Chomsky declared that the human brain is 'hard-wired' for language acquisition – that language is part of the normal set of abilities that all humans possess just like the ability to walk. Chomsky asserted that language acquisition is not a behaviour that is modified by environmental and social variables that are radically different for each child. He proposed that the LAD takes the highly inconsistent input that each child receives and extrapolates from it the basic rules of the parents' language. Thus, language is a result of the interaction of the LAD and the child's environment.

## 3.1.3 Support for the innateness hypothesis

Skinner and other behaviourists, however, believed that environment is everything, thus exposure, supported by repetition and reinforcement by the child's caretakers, was responsible for a child's acquisition of language. They believed that the environment was everything. Chomsky disagreed, claiming that these processes were insufficient for explaining the complexity of the task that all very young children confront, nor could they explain the uniformity of the behaviour in the process of acquisition by children with varied backgrounds and cognitive abilities. He also pointed out that there is great uniformity in the end product – all children learn to speak their parents' language except for those with very severe developmental issues, regardless of parental teaching style or the type of language that they are learning. Chomsky took issue with a number of the claims made by the behaviourists and pointed out flaws in their argumentation.

First, there is incredible regularity in terms of the patterns of language acquisition and the order of certain grammatical structures across all types of children and languages. Chomsky, and later many other linguists, found that level of education was irrelevant: children of parents who have PhDs in linguistics acquire the basic structures of their native languages no quicker than children of unschooled parents. Differences in culture also seem to play no part in the acquisition process. Children who grow up in cultures in which they are expected to be relatively quiet or are addressed only indirectly learn language as quickly as those in which children are actively 'taught' to speak by their parents. The particular language being learned seems to make no difference either. Children have a marvellous ability to master incredible complexities of their native language no matter what it is. Finally, even differences in IQ have little effect on acquisition: children with IQs as low as 30 fully acquire language. None of these challenges to behaviourist theories of language acquisition can be adequately explained without the existence of a human species endowment for language.

## 3.1.4 Problems with reinforcement and imitaion

Numerous studies have also shown that the role of parents as language teachers is not the critical contributor to language acquisition. Consider the issue of reinforcement: anyone who has been around new parents has probably been amused when the child utters something like 'dimdu' and the proud father exclaims, 'Did you hear that? My baby said Daddy!' Many parents positively reinforce almost anything their children say at first. Later, as their child's production of language becomes less of a novelty, parents' reinforcement of language generally lessens as well. Think about all the challenges new parents have to contend with like the care and feeding of their child and the sleepless nights. It is not surprising that their attention to their child's language diminishes, especially as the child becomes more successful at communication. Thus, it is clear that reinforcement of children's utterances is not particularly consistent. In addition, there are other problems with reinforcement. First, it is not constant enough, nor consistent, enough for children to extrapolate appropriate grammar, sound and usage information. Many children's incorrect utterances go without correction, and many correct utterances go without positive reinforcement. Second, parents are not always concentrating on children's grammar or pronunciation; sometimes their responses to children have more to do with the truth-value of an utterance than a language rule. How is the child to know the difference? Imagine the following scenario: a child visiting a neighbour's house picks up another child's ball and says 'ball mine'. When the mother responds 'no', how does the child know that this is a correction concerning ownership of the ball rather than a lesson in the correct usage of the possessive grammatical structure in English?

Imitation of parents as a primary mode of child language acquisition is also problematic. Chomsky posited the 'poverty of the stimulus' argument that asserts that the input that parents provide is far too limited and too error-filled for children to be able to create the complex rule system that they do so well. You have to ask, are all possible patterns provided by caretakers and in sufficient quantity for children to acquire the grammar of their language? Imagine also understanding the grammatical roles of words, which are rarely limited to only one function. Do parents directly teach children that *running* is a verb, 'She is running fast', as well as a noun, 'Running is fun'? Furthermore, considering all of the speech errors that adults continually make in normal conversation, how is a child to know what is erroneous and what is not? If children are just imitating, then they will imitate our errors as well. Learning solely through imitation creates a situation in which children would learn aspects of their language in an unpatterned way. Because every parent speaks differently, the children would as well. Studies, however, do not bear this out. Hundreds of studies, done on dozens and dozens of languages, show that acquisition patterns are the same for all children.

There is also the phenomenon of *motherese* or *caretaker talk* to take into consideration. Many parents use a different voice and style to talk with children. This speech is characterized by extreme variations in pitch and tone, simplification of grammatical forms and a great deal of repetition. If imitation was crucial, then children would end up speaking this way, which fortunately they do not! Finally, wouldn't you expect that if imitation is the key, then children would learn the most frequently used items in the parent's language? If that were true, then very early on we would expect children to acquire words like *a*, *an* and *the*, which are quite frequent in adult conversation, but appear rather late in a child's vocabulary. Imitation does play a role in language learning; however, numerous studies have shown that it accounts for only between 10 and 20 per cent of children's early utterances and they are mostly formulaic expressions like: 'How are you?'

## 3.1.5  What children's 'errors' tell us

The output of children has also been studied, and it has told us much about their developing systems at different stages. Studies show that children acquire certain structures of language before others and nothing that parents do can force children to produce language beyond what they are developmentally ready for. I tested this out on my own nephew, Alex, who, as a toddler, used the object pronoun *me* in the subject slot: 'Me no go there'. I said to him several times 'Alex, say, 'I no go'. Each time he repeated back to me 'Me no go'. So, I tried another tactic; I had him repeat each word separately. I got him to say 'I' several times. Then he said 'no', and finally 'go'. When I asked him to say, 'I no go' he repeated back slowly 'I no go'. Five minutes later when we tried to get him into the car, he said, 'Me no go'. He just had not reached the developmental stage where he was ready to distinguish subject and object pronouns. Constant imitation and reward were not enough. Eventually, when he was developmentally ready, he used the subject and object pronouns in the correct place in a sentence.

It is clear that when parents try to get children to imitate them, the children are only able to imitate as far as their grammar has developed. If parents use incorrect grammar for play, sometimes children will even tell them they are wrong, but children are only capable of *producing* a form that is within their developing grammar. Furthermore, when they are conversing with others, children are focusing on meaning, not structure. Imagine the confusion of the small child in the following conversation:

> Child: Me went outside.
> Parent: Do you mean, 'I went outside'?
> Child: No me went! You stay here.

Children's errors also give us an idea about the state of their developing grammar systems. In fact, it may be inappropriate even to call them errors since they are often logical forms for the state of development in which the child is currently. The kinds of variations from adult rules that children make are often not ones that parents are likely to have made in any context, so children did not learn these variations through repetition. What parent would say to a child, often enough for the child to have acquired via repetition: 'The baby goed home' or 'The baby wented home', 'My feets hurt' or even 'My foots hurt'? In each of these utterances, it is clear that the child has figured out a commonly used grammar rule, but has not yet learned that there are exceptions to the rule. The speech of children acquiring a language is not erratic combinations of words; the differences show us the underlying systematicity of their developing language.

Mistakes tell us more about what children understand about language than the correct things that they say. Incorrect utterances are evidence that children are not imitating because parents do not overtly teach them incorrect sentences, nor would they positively reinforce them. What is even more interesting is that even in cases where children may have picked up a word via imitation and used it correctly for a while, they may lose that word later and replace it with an incorrect but logical form based on their understanding of grammar. For example, a child may learn the word *went* but upon acquiring the past tense rule – add *-ed* to the ends of verbs – he or she may well lose *went* for a time and start saying *goed* or even *wented*. When children first acquire a rule, they apply it 100 per cent of the time; it takes quite a while before they are able to remember all the exceptions to the rule, which shows that they are constantly forming hypotheses about how language works.

Children's production of these rules has been directly tested many times. One very well-known study was performed by Jean Berko-Gleason in the late 1950s. She showed pictures of an imaginary animal to children, which she called a *wug*. She then showed children a picture with two of them and the children said that there were two wugs, [wʌgz], with the final -s being pronounced like a [z]. She then showed them another imaginary animal called a *bik*. The children correctly identified a picture of two of them as *biks* [bɪks] with the final -s letter making an [s] sound. This shows that children have acquired the very sophisticated understanding that the plural ending in English is not simply pronounced [-s] but varies depending on what word is being made plural. There is a rule guiding when it sounds like [s] and when it sounds like [z]. Most adults cannot tell you what the rule is (even though they apply it correctly dozens of times each day), so it is highly unlikely that they could have directly taught their children this rule. In addition, children do not have a conscious understanding of language processes at all. Just for fun, ask a 3-year-old how the past tense is formed in English.

## 3.1.6  Studies supporting the innateness hypothesis

As discussed before, although scientists have found much evidence to support the idea that language is part of our biological endowment, identifying the specific parts of the brain that guide acquisition is not simple. The brain is a highly complex multifunctional organism that we are really only beginning to understand. Nevertheless, there have been many studies that have provided evidence for a LAD. The most interesting studies have been when we have had the rare opportunity to study a human brain.

Studies in the 1860s and 1870s conducted on cadavers of speech-impaired patients provided two scientists, Paul Broca and Carl Wenicke, with a good deal of information about what areas of the brain controlled language. When these scientists looked at the brains of people who had different types of speech problems, they discovered that they had some sort of injury to the left hemisphere of the brain. As more data accumulated, they noted that it was in two specific areas of the left hemisphere that injury was documented. Depending on whether the front or the back of the brain was damaged, the speech problems differed. These two areas of the brain are now named after these early pioneers in speech pathology. *Broca's area* is located in the front of the left hemisphere in the inferior frontal gyrus; *Wernicke's area* is in the rear of the same hemisphere in the superior temporal gyrus. Damage to these areas often causes a set of different conditions referred to as aphasia.

Injury to Broca's area causes people to have difficulty in expressing themselves verbally. Their speech is often laboured, and words are often partial, mispronounced or incorrect. People with damage to Broca's area sometimes do not produce prepositions or articles or use verbal endings like *-ed* or *-ing*. On the other hand, people with Wernicke's aphasia speak quite fluently and even grammatically, but their utterances make little sense and may not be responsive to the conversational context. Injury to other areas of the brain close to Broca's and Wernicke's areas causes other types of language problems. For example, people may have difficulty with connecting writing with speech when there is injury to the angular gyrus.

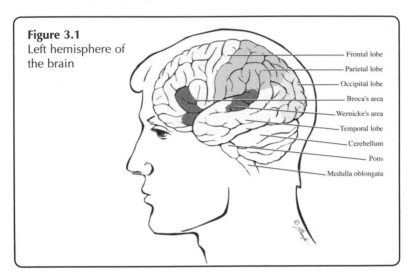

**Figure 3.1**
Left hemisphere of
the brain

Frontal lobe
Parietal lobe
Occipital lobe
Broca's area
Wernicke's area
Temporal lobe
Cerebellum
Pons
Medulla oblongata

### 3.1.7  Studies on the living brain

Further information on language and the brain has been garnered during the observation of people who have undergone hemispherectomies due to acute epilepsy. In a hemispherectomy, the *corpus callosum*, the connecting tissue between the two hemispheres of the brain, is cut to reduce the neural activity between them. Depending on the age of the patient, different effects on speech result. After surgery, linguists conducted tests in which they blindfolded patients and then asked them to identify a common object that they put in their hand, like a key or a pair of glasses. The people were able to verbally identify things put into their right hand, but not their left. This is due to the relationship between the brain and the body being contralateral – meaning the right side of the brain works with the left side of the body and the left brain with the right. Stroke victims, with damage to only one side of the brain, may experience contralateral disabilities. Problems caused by the severing of the *corpus callosum* are more acute in older patients than young children. Children's brains often create new neural pathways to provide some of the functions of the ones that were cut.

Evidence has also come from studying the brains of people who have not had any damage to or surgery on their brains. In the Dichotic Listening Test subjects have sounds played only to one ear at a time, and they are asked to identify the sounds they are hearing, some of which are words and others are sounds like running water. These tests show that when a sound is linguistic, it is heard more quickly and identified more often precisely, when it is heard in the right ear. If the sound is not linguistic in nature, the reverse is true. It is picked up more quickly when it is heard by the left ear. Because the brain is contralateral, the results affirm that language is a left hemisphere process, and also show us that non-linguistic sounds are processed separately in the right side of the brain. Amazingly, the brain is able to sort out sounds that are important for language from those that are not.

## 3.1.8  Critical age hypothesis for first language acquisition

One of the most compelling arguments for the LAD has come from proponents of the *critical age hypothesis*. They have shown that there is a window of time available, developmentally, during which exposure to language must occur or children will not acquire a first language natively or with any degree of systematicity. Proponents of this hypothesis assert that before puberty, children acquire languages effortlessly rather than having to work very hard to learn them as adults do. A child's brain seems to be distinct from an adult's in a number of significant aspects. As each child matures, the neural activity patterns in the left hemisphere of the brain become set and less flexible and the number of pathways being created slows down at some point. In addition, the *corpus callosum*, the set of neural pathways that connect the two hemispheres of the brain, changes, and the transmission of electrical impulses from one hemisphere to another lessens, though certainly to a much lesser degree than for the subjects of hemispherectomies discussed above. Many scientists believe that the ability of the brain to transmit certain information across the two hemispheres is what makes possible the effortless acquisition of language, or languages, in early childhood.

Sadly, some of the most striking evidence to support the existence of a critical period has come from studies of language-deprived children: children that, because of severe abuse or neglect, were not exposed to language during their childhood. One sad example of this was a child named Genie. Her parents abused her by locking her in a room in their house and never speaking to her. Additionally, she was severely punished whenever she made a sound, so she stopped trying to make sounds. When Genie was finally rescued at age 13, social workers put her in the hands of skilled counsellors, teachers and linguists, yet even after more than a decade of intense instruction in English, her linguistic ability was not normal. She managed to acquire some very basic vocabulary but lacked an organizational system for ordering it (a grammar). What very small children so easily do with the language input they receive, Genie was never able to accomplish.

There is even a critical age for acquiring sign language natively. Like hearing children, if deaf children are cut off linguistically from caretakers using sign language, they may have great difficulty developing native-like competence in sign. What happens to profoundly deaf children in environments in which no sign language is available to them? Their parents often create simple signs for common needs and, as they grow, children end up creating as much language as they can. Considering that they have no source to model, these are astounding accomplishments and reflect the human need for communication. I lived in a small village in the Dominican Republic where there were no institutional resources available to the deaf or their families. A deaf neighbour girl used to come over to visit me and after spending some time with her, I began to have a very rudimentary understanding of some of her language system. I found out from her mother that neither she nor her daughter had ever been taught official sign language, but that they had 'worked out' a way to talk with each other over the years. The child seemed to me a happy child, fighting with her brothers and playing with her dolls and other toys. She always had a lot to tell me though she sometimes got frustrated with *my* inability to pick up her language system very efficiently.

## 3.2    Stages of language acquisition

### 3.2.1    Learning the sound system

Although parents' teaching is not critical to language acquisition, their input is. That input becomes significant at some very early point in a child's existence. Scientists have noted that a baby's rate of suckling will remain the same if a particular combination of sounds, for example [ba], is repeated over and over in the same tone. However, if this sound is changed slightly, the rate of suckling will increase. What is even more interesting is that newborns' perception of sounds in some ways actually surpasses that of their parents. The babies can distinguish very slight differences in sound that their parents cannot hear because the alternations don't exist in the parents' language. For example, many native Japanese adults have difficulty differentiating between the sounds [r] and [l] and pronouncing them correctly in English words, but Japanese babies have no difficulty hearing the difference between the two sounds.

Scientists have also discovered that babies begin making many more sounds than are in just their own language. Babbling progresses through stages in which children practise sounds that can be made. At first, their babbling contains sounds not from their native tongue, but as they are exposed to more and more of their parents' speech, they learn that some sounds are significant whereas others are not, which helps to explain why many native English speakers have such difficulty with the rolled [r] sound when they are learning Spanish as adults.

At this point, baby babbling can be identified as being babbling in a particular language. Studies show that parents are able to identify the pre-word babbling of babies from their own language at this stage. Earlier, all baby babbling is quite similar. Thus, English-speaking parents can pick out the baby who is babbling in 'English' from the Arabic, German or Swahili babies babbling.

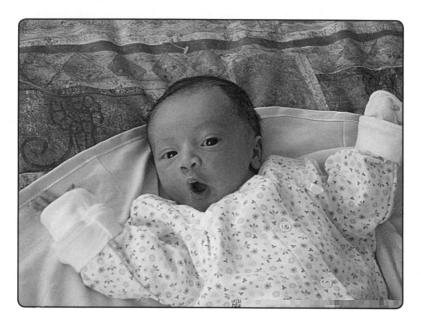

Part of what children do as they are sorting out the important parts of the sound around them is not just to figure out what sounds are possible, but what combinations of sounds are as well. English-speaking babies learn that certain consonant combinations like dr- and bl- regularly occur at the beginning of a syllable and that words never end in these same combinations. This helps them figure out where the word boundaries occur. Japanese babies learn that the normal syllable structure of their language is CV (consonant, vowel – Ya·ma·ha) or CVC (Hon·da). Consonant clusters (CC or CCC, like dw- and str- in English) are not acceptable in Japanese. The babies of every language learn what sounds occur in their language as well as the constraints on how those sounds can combine.

It's not just the choice of sounds that distinguish in which language a baby babbles. Long before words emerge, babies are experimenting with intonational patterns of their language and sorting out what patterns are linguistically significant. They practise with the intonation pattern of a demand or a question long before they can actually make one that an adult can understand.

## 3.2.2 Sound and meaning

Connecting these non-random sounds to meaning is a huge step that all children make. What is also difficult to imagine is that children are eventually able to sort out words from the endless stream of talk with which they are bombarded every day! No normal adult leaves a notable space between each word uttered, so children have to figure out word boundaries and their meanings from streams of speech that may sound like: *Gimmedabanana*. Somewhere around the age of one, babies begin to connect certain combinations of sounds with a particular meaning. For example, a baby in an English-speaking family will learn the family pet is a *cat*, but a baby in a Spanish-speaking family will learn that it is a *gato*. A common language game that parents play with babies is the naming game. Parents ask the name of things (Where's your nose?) and children answer by pointing at them, which they are able to do long before they are able to say the words. An interesting question to think about is how do children actually go about the process of narrowing down all the possible meanings of a word to the one an adult means in a particular context? When they learn *ball*, does that word function as a name for a specific play toy first and then does the meaning become more generalized to mean round object of any shape, including oranges? How does the child learn to broaden and narrow the class of objects that fit with that word? American footballs are not round; eggs look like footballs, but we certainly don't want children throwing them!

## 3.2.3 From single words to grammar

A year later, children are combining the words they have learned to create meaningful sentences. Even their very first sentences follow a pattern. They usually consist of a combination of a verb and a noun or an adjective and a noun, something like: 'Want milk' or 'Pretty Puppy'. The meaning of these sentences is quite clear, especially because children's sentences at this stage tend to be simple requests or responses to things in the immediate environment. What English-speaking children leave out at this stage are the function words like *a*, *an* and *the*, words that are the little extras that add function rather than content to an utterance. Children learning languages other than English leave out the little extras of their languages as well at this stage. Scientists have done a great number of studies on the acquisition of many of the world's languages, and what they have found is startling: the acquisition order for grammatical structures as well as the developmental timetable for the acquisition of these structures is remarkably similar from language to language. There may be a limited number of children who acquire some functions more quickly or more slowly than the great majority of others, but the order of acquisition is the same as well as the end result: the complete acquisition of their native language. By the time they are in elementary school, all children without specific speech impairment will have acquired all the structures of their native language or languages. Don't confuse the acquisition of language with the acquisition of vocabulary: children, like adults, have quite varied vocabularies depending on many variables all related to the vocabularies of the other speakers to whom they are exposed.

There is a great deal of evidence from hundreds of spoken languages to support these claims; however, the first language acquisition of sign language by very young deaf children also provides support for the theory of universal developmental stages of language acquisition. Deaf children go through very similar stages of acquisition to hearing children. Both hearing and deaf children go through a babbling stage before they begin to communicate first through single signs (words) and later by combining two signs. Like hearing children, deaf children pass through predictable developmental stages as they acquire more complex structures and make patterned errors that are predictable because the adult grammars vary from the rule.

As all children age, their sentences increase in length and grammatical complexity along predictable stages of acquisition until they have achieved complete competence in the structures of their language. This does not mean that they never make mistakes, since adults certainly do. What it means is that the basic structures of their language are in place They can embed phrases within sentences: 'My brother, who I hate, broke my doll'. They can use passive voice: 'The ball that I bought is lost'. They even have such a sophisticated understanding of the systems of language that they can create and enjoy all those awful puns that kids love so well, like:

Question:     What flies and wobbles at the same time?
Answer:       A jellycopter!

## 3.3  Second language acquisition

For children, the process of acquiring a language seems so effortless, even when they are acquiring a second language, as many millions of children in the world do. For adults, learning a second language is often, but not always, a difficult and frustrating experience. Nevertheless, many of the same issues that we have discussed concerning first language acquisition are also significant for second language acquisition (SLA). Some linguists do, however, view adult SLA differently from child language acquisition. They refer to getting a first language as *acquisition*, and getting a second one as an adult as language *learning*. The choice of these words reflects the different abilities possessed by each and the differences between child and adult brains.

### 3.3.1  SLA and behaviourism

From the behaviourist position, the acquisition of a second language is just like the acquisition of the first: SLA is simply a process of imitation, practice, reinforcement, feedback and habit formation. For generations, many of the language classes offered across the world have been taught based on methodologies that reflect this approach. The classroom practices associated with this approach concentrate on providing a set of rules to be memorized accompanied by sufficient rote practice to basically 'wear a path' in the learner's mind until the structure is learned. Practice makes perfect.

My first language classes were taken during a time when most classrooms were teacher-centred and behaviouristic in teaching methodology. There was a good deal of memorization of rules and words and lots of overt correction of error during what we used to call 'drill and kill' sessions. Most of the practices provided very rote responses to repetitive exercises with no room for creativity. Because the teachers generally went row by row, I was able to count the number of students and then figure out which question I would have to answer. Thus, instead of listening to all the other students' answers (and maybe learning something), I would spend the whole time working out my own single answer.

Because in a classroom like this most students only get to speak once or twice in the entire class period, I was especially panicked that I would get my answer wrong, and look foolish, so it was more important to me to get that one single answer correct than to learn from the repetitions of the other students. Worse yet, because I was pretty good at memorizing, I was successful at memorizing the book definitions of grammar rules, which I could regurgitate back on tests. However, I could in no way make use of these rules in an actual conversation in French or Spanish. Knowing the rule does not necessarily translate into being able to make use of it in a conversation. Much of the class was conducted in English because the specific course goal was to produce students able to read science and literature in a foreign language not to train students in the normal oral form of the language.

By the time I entered teacher training, the general philosophy had changed. The emphasis had shifted to communicative language teaching with the goal of students being able to communicate with native speakers of the language. The classroom activities changed as well. Teachers constructed activities that would mirror normal life activities that students would engage in when they went to live abroad. Many studies had shown that acquisition of structures was actually better in these classrooms than in those in which students were taught in the traditional behaviourist style. However, when teachers brought these new philosophies into the classroom, there were students who were distressed. How could they really be learning doing all these fun activities rather than memorizing rules and vocabulary? In my own English as a second language (ESL) classrooms, I found that this was not just an individual issue but also a cultural one. Students who came from cultures that placed a high value on rote memorization were often anxious about not being corrected more often and not doing any 'real work'. High verbal and written test scores did little to allay their fears that they were not really progressing. They were accustomed to being tested on their written English and on being judged in speaking exams for using English that more closely reflects writing than normal spoken English. This is not just an issue for students. Over the years I have observed and trained many language teachers and even though the approach to teaching has changed to a more communicative one, many teachers are still focused on fixing their students' errors, based on written standard norms, than on providing students with communicative competence in the language.

## 3.3.2  First language interference in SLA

As we saw with first language acquisition, a behaviourist approach leads to certain assumptions about second language learning. One of the most significant assumptions is that first language habits will interfere with SL learning because they are so familiar and ingrained in the learner's mind. Because a learner has long-standing set patterns, it will be hard to replace these patterns with the new patterns of the second language. For example, if you are a Spanish speaker who is accustomed to putting adjectives *after* the noun, you may have difficulty remembering to put them *before* the noun when you are speaking English because your mind is so accustomed to the Spanish pattern.

> La *vestida azul* es muy bonito.
> The *blue dress* is very pretty.

One methodological practice based on a belief in interference is *contrastive analysis* (CA). Its proponents believed that language learning was largely habit formation; thus, one way of increasing learner success was to look at the native language and the target language to determine where they differed in structure. Once this was determined, lessons could be constructed to specifically address expected problem areas. Although this sounds quite logical and is certainly appealing to teachers looking for lesson plans, studies show that it is not effective as a classroom teaching strategy overall.

The first challenge is that learners do not make all the errors that are predicted by CA. Another problem with CA is that many of the errors adults make are ones that are not simply transferring the rules of the first language to the second one. Sometimes the mistakes students make reflect no pattern from the first language at all, and it is difficult to figure out why they said a particular structure incorrectly. Furthermore, students sometimes even make mistakes when the first and second language structures are the same. Some of the native speakers of Spanish I have had in my language classes struggle with pronouncing the *ch-* combination at the beginning of English words like *chicken*. Some of these speakers pronounce the letters ch- as sh-. Spanish does have the ch- sound in word initial position in many words including *chico* (boy), so this erroneous pronunciation cannot be attributed to transference from the native language.

Unfortunately, placing an emphasis on teaching problem structures does not always lead to acquisition of these structures by students. Just as for babies acquiring language, there is an acquisition order sequence that learners follow pretty closely. They acquire language structures when they are developmentally able to acquire them. Furthermore, when it is a third language that is being learned, that too must be taken into account. I found that while learning Akan, a language of Ghana, some of my errors in grammar and pronunciation could better be accounted for by looking at my second language, Spanish, rather than by comparing Akan to English: the phenomenon of home and other. Perhaps I resorted to Spanish structures because, like Akan, it was not my native (home) tongue.

Although CA is generally out of favour, it can still be useful to teachers in limited ways. It is useful for predicting some of the problems students will confront. For example, I know which students will probably have trouble with the acquisition of articles (a, an, the) and which will have trouble pronouncing -th- sounds. CA, however, is not useful as the basis for curriculum design, especially in classrooms in which students come from many different language groups, for example most ESL classes taught in Britain, the USA and other English-speaking countries.

## 3.3.3  SLA and feedback or correction

Another assumption associated with a behaviourist approach to SLA is that the feedback that second language learners get is appropriate. Just as with parental feedback to small children, teacher feedback is not, nor can it always be, on target or frequent enough to deal with all the aberrations from the norm. Teachers may even have a more difficult time with consistent and sufficient feedback than parents do. Most parents are only dealing with one child at a time, and they have that child for many hours of every day. However, in a language classroom, a teacher may have 20 students to attend to at once and may only meet these students several hours a week. Second, the feedback that provides a positive change for one student may only confuse another student. Worse yet, because interaction in a large language classroom may be quite limited, the teacher will have few opportunities to evaluate and address each student's language ability in sufficient quantity to be useful. If the premise is that use of correct structures will be positively reinforced and incorrect ones negatively reinforced, each learner must get a great deal of the teacher's time to be successful language learners.

Providing feedback to teenagers and adults is not easy even for the best of instructors. First, instructors have to figure out how much correction or feedback is appropriate for each learner. Unlike children, who chatter on despite adult attempts to correct them, adult learners struggle with personal feelings about making mistakes in public. Furthermore, if learners are stopped every time they make mistakes, they will probably get so frustrated that they will stop talking which means that many errors go unaddressed. Unfortunately, some teachers feel that if they let errors pass without correction, then a pattern of error is being established. This assumes that learners are successfully keeping track of everything everyone else says in the classroom and that the error is repeated often enough that it is learned. Other teachers pick and choose which errors they will correct and choose when and how to correct based on their own philosophy of teaching and their knowledge of what individual students are capable of processing and how comfortable they are with being corrected overtly.

Another methodological practice based on behaviourism is error analysis (EA). Instead of studying the languages that students speak and comparing them for differences, in EA teachers study the errors that students make in their classrooms and then create lesson plans to target problem areas. However, there are a number of problems with EA; for example, sometimes a lack of a particular error does not show you what a student does not know because students employ avoidance strategies for problematic structures. When I was living in a Spanish-speaking country, I learned very quickly that I didn't have to learn all the complicated verbal endings for the Spanish future tense because I could simply use the present progressive form and add an adverb of time (*Voy al mercado mañana.* 'I'm going to the market tomorrow'). I also learned synonyms for many words that have the rolled [r] sound which I could not make. Thus, I said *el auto* for *el carro* (the car) and *el tren* for *el ferro carril* (the train). Many learners figure out avoidance strategies that make it difficult for teachers to identify what problems they have with the target grammar.

Another problem with EA is that some structures occur only rarely in conversation, so the opportunity to notice that a student is struggling with a structure may not present itself naturally. The opposite is true as well; some errors are more noticeable because they are structures that occur frequently. However, these errors may be ones that are minor in terms of communicative competence or are structurally quite complicated and are generally acquired at a much later stage of acquisition than the student is in. To complicate issues is the fact that imitation and memorization play a part in SLA, so teachers may get false evidence that a structure is acquired because students have memorized a phrase as a chunk. A good example of this is the passive voice. Most students learning English very early on learn to say 'I was born on June the third'. However, that use of the passive voice is acquired as a memorized chunk. It is not until much later that they are developmentally able to acquire the passive and create sentences like 'The book was written by Cervantes'. Interestingly, when this early usage of passive voice is pointed out to students learning passive voice, they are quite surprised that they have been using this structure already.

What studies have shown us about error correction may also be in contrast to learners' beliefs about how they learn best. For example, although in the 1980s overt error correction became pedagogically unpopular (supported by studies), some of my students continued to request more overt correction than I was providing. In my language classrooms, I tend to model back correct forms when I hear a mistake rather than directly pointing out an error. I believe that reduces embarrassment for the student and provides the correct form for the class as well. Nevertheless, this subtle correction runs the risk of not being noticed by the speaker who, because no overt correction was directed at him or her, continues in the belief that all is well. One of the most important lessons that I have learned as a teacher over the years is that I must constantly adjust my teaching to the individual differences of the students, and provide overt and frequent correction to some and more subtle and less direct modelling to others.

## 3.3.4 Individual differences

Unlike for all babies learning their first language, who acquire it despite differences in personality, exposure and intelligence, individual differences cause variation in how well second language learners acquire a language. Learning a second language as either an adult or teenager can be very stressful – especially since achieving passing grades is often critical. In addition, many students fear making mistakes in front of their peers and thus avoid talking whenever possible. Other learners have a high tolerance for error, and as long as they are communicating successfully, or think they are, they may make little effort to improve their grammar. Students who are more introverted may make considerably more effort to be correct and in the end have a more native-like use of the language but may seem far less fluent than learners who just risk it all and launch right into a conversation without fear of making an error.

When I was living in the Dominican Republic, I had a friend who had been a Spanish major. My grades in Spanish were woeful at best, but because I was sent to a village where no one spoke English, I had to learn to communicate rapidly. When I visited my friend in his village in the mountains, the villagers used to say that I had better Spanish than he did which irritated him to no end because I made many mistakes in grammar and pronunciation. What I did do was talk quickly and without worrying about my grammar or pronunciation, even though if I had spoken more slowly I might have had sufficient processing time to speak more correctly.

My friend's speech was correct, but it was slow and laboured, thus they had difficulty having a conversation with him. They would lose interest in talking with him because it took too long. He was obsessed with not making any errors because he thought that error-free language was necessary to successful communication. Needless to say, it isn't.

One individual difference, your IQ, does not make a significant difference to levels of success in adult language learning. Studies have shown that many types of intelligence and skills are brought to bear in learning a second language. For example, some students can easily memorize new vocabulary and are good at hearing sound distinctions, but may be woeful at remembering rules. Aptitude for language learning is a factor that is separate from IQ and includes such abilities as 1) good memorization skills, 2) being able to figure out rules from utterances, 3) hearing and producing subtle sound distinctions of the new language and 4) understanding the role of a word in a sentence.

Motivation also plays an important role in acquisition. Unfortunately, many students are coerced into language classes in school and college without any real desire to learn a second language or any real appreciation of the wonderful benefits it can bring them. For these learners, grades may be the sole motivation for acquisition. They may even make good grades because they work hard to memorize rules and vocabulary.

However, good grades do not necessarily translate into success in communication with native speakers. Other students may turn out to have better communication skills despite lower grades on standardized tests. Furthermore, in natural language situations, people may acquire local varieties of language that are quite distinct from formal school varieties of language. To the chagrin of my literature professor in graduate school, I came home from the Dominican Republic with a well-developed variety of Afro-Cuban village Spanish, and although I could read the literature from Colombia and Mexico quite well and participate in the lively classroom discussions with the native Spanish speakers, my papers came back with many marks on them. My near-native oral proficiency in Afro-Cuban Spanish was not what my upper-class Mexican professor was looking for in graduate-level research papers!

Motivation is also tied up with attitudes towards the people and culture of the language being learned. It is possible that an entrepreneur who must do business in a foreign country may be highly motivated in terms of work success to learn the second language, but if he or she has negative attitudes about the people or culture, language acquisition may be hindered. This person may concentrate on the mechanical aspects of the language that will serve to advance the business relationship without any attention to the social niceties that make conversation natural. If the pressure to learn the language is external, say from a supervisor, motivation may be low, which could affect success in acquisition.

Success in acquiring a language is also tied up with how people prefer to learn and be taught. When learning in a natural situation, for example, living in a country where the language is commonly spoken, learners may have a good deal of choice in how they go about picking up the language. They can choose social situations in which they can try out different conversational goals. Their feedback will probably be very inconsistent as some native speakers will correct incorrect utterances or problematic pronunciation but others will not. If learners prefer a more structured environment, they can take classes in which grammar rules will be specifically taught, and they can receive very specific feedback either orally or through tests to monitor their progress. However, some people prefer to learn by doing, despite the lack of controlled input and corrective feedback. When you are out in the street trying to buy food or make a transaction at the bank, your progress is measured in the success of the transaction, not in the number of correct sentences that you produce. In these situations, most native speakers will be focusing on the content of your conversation and not on the forms used. Neither of these types of learning is the only right one: each individual learns very differently in distinct circumstances. I'm sure my undergraduate college professors, who despaired of my being able to utter a correct sentence in Spanish, would be astounded that I ended up being bilingual. I am not a classroom learner; I learn best by being in an environment where the use of the language is critical to my social and occupational success. Many people learn best without a teacher or textbook, but the luxury of living in a foreign country is not possible for every language learner.

Success in learning a language cannot be predicted simply by adding up points for motivation, learning skills, personality type or place of learning (classroom or natural learning) among other factors. All of these factors work together to influence the success or failure of students. Teachers who understand these issues, however, can construct classrooms that provide varied types of instruction and evaluation to provide all the students the environment that will give them the most success possible. Students with who understand them can work to make the best of both their own individual differences as well as teaching styles that do not necessarily provide the environment in which they learn best.

## 3.3.5 Critical age hypothesis for second language acquisition

One individual difference that learners have little control over is the age at which they begin to acquire a second language. Most of us who took our first language classes as teenagers or as adults can attest to the fact that it is usually quite difficult to learn a second language. At some point around the time of puberty, the *corpus callosum*, the set of neural pathways between the two hemispheres of the brain, begins to 'harden', meaning that the flow of neural activity between the two hemispheres becomes more limited. This is a highly variable change in state. For some people, it seems that activity between the two is quite reduced, and for others, there is more activity ongoing. Linguists attribute this reduction in activity to most adults' lack of ability to acquire additional languages as easily as they acquired languages before puberty. Babies depend on certain cerebral resources to acquire language from the highly erratic input, resources that are not fully available to adult learners. This is not to say that adults cannot adequately learn a second language. Adult learners do have resources available to them that children do not. For example, adults have access to learning strategies and are capable of reasoning and questioning. Unlike children though, who are not self-conscious about their production nor under direct pressure to acquire a language, adult language acquisition is accompanied by pressure to get good grades or to be successful in a job in which the second language is spoken. Adults also are limited by availability of instruction and time to take classes, and unlike children, they must deal with negative reactions to their language while they are learning.

Studies show that adult learners almost always have a trace of an accent and produce structures that are not quite native-like, long after they are quite fluent in their second language. One only needs to listen to interviews with foreign leaders or diplomats on television to hear that although they are communicating quite well at a very sophisticated level of discourse, differences in accent, word usage and grammar are noticeable. Some researchers assert that the earlier students are placed in second language classrooms, the more likely they are to produce native-like language. However, is full native-like acquisition a necessary or realistic goal? If adult language instruction is sufficient to provide people with sufficient competence in understanding normal written and spoken language, and if people are able to communicate successfully and go about their business of living and being part of their community, does it really matter if they have an accent and have occasional differences in their word or grammar usage?

## 3.3.6  Recent developments in second language acquisition

Chomsky's work since the 1960s has continued to focus on theoretical aspects of how language is constructed in the mind. His focus has not been on aspects of second language acquisition and translating that understanding into methodologies for classroom teachers. That work is the province of researchers in the field of applied linguistics. Some of these researchers have focused solely on understanding the abilities and processes of the human mind in the acquisition of additional language. Others have concentrated their work on applying that knowledge to creating specific methodologies and practices for classroom teachers. There has been an explosion of work in both of these areas.

In terms of more theoretical studies, researchers have continued to analyse how individuals acquire a second language and the challenges to full acquisition. Researchers look at how maturational constraints limit second language acquisition. SLA researchers continue to contribute to studies in cognitive science to expand our understanding of how the brain accesses and archives information including the distinct lexicons of bilingual speakers. Knowledge from SLA research is being applied to our understanding of people with aphasia and language loss due to conditions like Alzheimer's in hopes of helping with language dysfunctions.

SLA research has grown and changed over the years in terms of its direction in classroom research. In the period between the 1950s and the 1970s most of the research focused on figuring out the best methodologies for teaching grammar and correct pronunciation in the classroom. Some of this research was comparative – and quite specific, for instance, what challenges exist for Arabic speakers learning English. Other studies were more broad-based, that is they focused on the acquisition of a particular structure, like relative clauses. This research provided a wealth of materials for classroom teachers meeting the everyday needs of students.

In the 1980s, a shift in classroom teaching philosophy caused a major shift in research as communicative competence, rather than grammatical competence, became the heart of second language teaching. This is not to say that grammar study went out of the window, only that the end product of the language learning experience was the ability to function at some level within a community of first language speakers. The social context of learning became the focus of many studies, and the study of individual differences became significant as well. Researchers compared classroom learning with learning outside the classroom in natural settings to determine how to create classroom experiences that closely mirror learning in 'in the streets', so to speak.

A more communicative classroom means that students are engaged in more task-based activities rather than rote memorization. Task-based instruction implies that learners are engaged in tasks in the classroom that come as close as possible to mirroring tasks that they might do with the second language in a natural language setting. The tasks selected are ones that any native speaker might commonly do, like plan a vacation (which provides a natural opportunity for the use of the future tense). Teachers using these communicative activities may also be helping the learners focus on the particular grammar form being targeted by the activity, perhaps combining the best of grammar-centred classrooms with more communicative ones. Teachers may focus on the form by focusing feedback on it or by talking about the grammar structure or even asking the students questions about the form. ESL teacher and researcher Nina Spada did an experiment in which she varied the learning environment for three classes at the same level. One class was given traditional grammar instruction on a particular structure. A second class was not given any grammar instruction, but practised task-based activities in which the form naturally appeared. A third group was given the same tasks but the teacher also focused on the form with the group, though did not overtly teach it as with the first group. This last group outperformed the other two on tests targeting the structure. The results of this study, and others, show that task-based learning in conjunction with a focus on form leads to higher levels of proficiency.

Research is ongoing to determine the effectiveness of the many strategies and methods that teachers are applying in these more interactive classrooms. One aspect of this is the explosion of research on inter-language pragmatics beginning in the 1990s. Where the focus for so long had been on the form of a grammatical structure, research showed that the function of a construction within a particular discourse community must be learned as well. Speech acts such as apologies, compliments and complaints, among others, are being studied cross-culturally, and we've learned that it is no good to utter grammatically correct sentences if you are in violation of cultural norms as to how to perform common speech acts within a language and culture. Although every culture performs these speech acts, how they are performed and in response to what situation varies widely across cultures. Even speech acts as simple as asking a question may be used for different purposes depending on the culture of the speaker as well as if the speaker is male or female.

We have, however, come a long way from the days of language classrooms being places where students memorize long word lists, decline verbs and repeat sentences uttered by teachers. Several generations of research have taught us much about how the brain learns language in adulthood and has provided a whole new way of looking at classroom learning. Nevertheless, language learning for adults is still difficult. Despite all the television and magazine ads that proclaim that learning a foreign language is easy if you just know the trick (and buy their product!), no magic system has yet been discovered to make adults do what children do so effortlessly.

## Suggested reading

Curtiss, S. (1977), *Genie: A Psychological Study of a Modern-day 'Wild Child'*. NY: Academic Press.

Lightbown, P. and Spada, N. (2006), *How Languages are Learned*. Oxford: Oxford University Press.

Zentella, A. C. (1997), *Growing Up Bilingual*. Oxford: Blackwell.

## Interesting websites

Lectures on SLA by Timothy Mason, Université of Versailles St Quentin: www.timothyjpmason.com/WebPages/LangTeach/Licence/CM/OldLectures/L1_Introduction.htm

Second Language Acquisition and Second Language Learning, by Stephen D. Krashen, University of Southern California. Full textbook. www.sdkrashen.com/SL_Acquisition_and_Learning/index.html

The British Council. Materials for teaching and learning English as a second language. www.britishcouncil.org/learnenglish

## Consider the following questions

1. Reflect on your own second language learning experiences. What kind of classroom experiences did you have in terms of the methods that were used to teach you?

2. What kind of language learner are you? What aspects of the language classroom make you uncomfortable? What aspects do you find helpful in learning a language? What kind of situation is necessary for you to best acquire a language?

# 4 Phonetics

## Chapter Overview

| | | |
|---|---|---|
| 4.1 | HOW IS SPEECH PRODUCED? | 63 |
| 4.2 | THE CONSONANTS | 64 |
| | 4.2.1  VOICING | 65 |
| | 4.2.2  PLACE OF ARTICULATION | 65 |
| | 4.2.3  MANNER OF ARTICULATION | 66 |
| 4.3 | THE INTERNATIONAL PHONETIC ALPHABET | 72 |
| 4.4 | THE VOWELS | 73 |
| | 4.4.1  CLASSIFICATION OF VOWELS | 73 |
| | 4.4.2  THE VOWEL CHART | 73 |
| | 4.4.3  DIPHTHONGS | 74 |
| | 4.4.4  VOWEL LENGTH | 75 |
| 4.5 | ADVANTAGES OF A PHONETIC SYSTEM | 76 |
| 4.6 | OTHER FEATURES OF SOUND: SUPRASEGMENTALS | 78 |

All words are composed of one or more sounds strung together which arbitrarily designate some meaning for the humans who utter them. We know the string of sounds is arbitrary because every language has combined its sounds in a unique way. This explains why the large female bovine animal which English speakers call a *cow* has other names in other languages: *vaca* (Spanish), *корова* (Russian), *saniya* (Chinese, in Pinyin writing style) or *vache* (French). The study of the sound systems of all languages is called *phonetics*. The sound system of each of the world's languages is quite distinct, yet each language shares universal sound features with all the other languages of the world. This chapter will concentrate on articulatory phonetics, which is the study of how the sounds of language are produced by humans.

Speakers of the world's languages do not make use of all of the possible sounds that can be made by the human mouth. Some languages make use of as few as three vowels and a dozen or so consonants. Other languages have much larger systems with dozens of vowel and consonant sounds; nevertheless, languages with fewer sounds can make just as many words as languages with more. Furthermore, they all handle quite well the expressive needs of their speakers to articulate their most complex ideas through the thousands of words they use in their everyday lives.

For words to have meaning, they must be made up of different sounds so that they are distinctive. The English language has about 40 contrastive speech sounds (depending on the variety). Speech sounds are not always well represented by letters. As native and non-native speakers alike understand, the pronunciation of a word and its spelling are often not well matched for English. This is a problem for scientists trying to accurately and specifically describe how the words of a language sound. Thus, to effectively describe a word's sounds, we need a system that provides a direct correspondence between sound and symbol, which means that every symbol would represent one and only one sound, and that a sound could only be represented by one single symbol. Since English has only 26 letters in its alphabet, yet about 40 sounds, clearly the alphabet is not sufficient to provide specific information as to the correct pronunciation of a word. Phoneticians have created a system that does provide a one-to-one relationship between sound and symbol. That system makes use of existing alphabetic characters but also has additional symbols to describe the sounds for which we do not have a separate letter. Using the system that has been created, a person can write down the sounds of any word from any language, and anyone who knows the system will know how that word is pronounced. We will look at the system shortly, but first we need to understand the mechanisms by which sounds are made.

## 4.1 How is speech produced?

The individual sounds of all the world's languages, more than 6,000 of them, are elegantly and simply produced via a very limited number of mechanisms. Most speech sounds are formed when air passes through the larynx past the vocal folds (in common lingo, the vocal cords, though not spelled the same as chords for music!). This sound is modified in the nose, throat and oral cavity to produce the distinctive sounds of all languages.

All of the sounds of English are produced through this process, called the pulmonic egressive airstream mechanism. However, some of the world's languages, like Kpelle, spoken in Liberia, have sounds made through the intake of air which is modified as the air goes into the mouth, a process called the ingressive airstream mechanism. You can make one of these sounds by pressing your lips together as if you were going to make the [b] sound, but instead of sending air out of your mouth, suck in air as you release your lips and make a [b]. You can hear that this is a quite different sound than egressive [b]. It is the first sound in the word ɓanaŋ in Kpelle, meaning *camp kitchen*.

One note here: most native speakers are not accustomed to thinking about the individual sounds of their native languages nor the processes involved in making them. This does take some learning and some practice playing around with individual sounds to get comfortable with them. I tell my first-year students to put on the radio in the living room, then go and lock themselves in the bathroom to practice so their roommates won't see them making funny faces and hear them making weird sounds. An excellent website for learning these sounds and about how speech sounds are produced is the website of the late Peter Ladefoged at the University of California at Los Angeles. Ladefoged was one of the world's foremost phoneticians. At this extensive website, you can hear sound combinations matched with linguistic symbols as well as short video clips of the inside of the mouth in action, among many other phonetic processes: hctv.humnet.ucla.edu/departments/linguistics/VowelsandConsonants/vowels/contents.html

## 4.2 The consonants

Consonants are sounds made by obstructing the airstream in differing ways after it leaves the lungs. They are produced by three mechanisms: 1) *voicing*, the vibration of the vocal folds; 2) *manner of articulation*, the modification of the airstream as it travels though the larynx and mouth; and 3) *place of articulation*, the movement of articulators where the main modification of the airstream takes place.

## 4.2.1  Voicing

When air rushes out of the lungs and pushes past the closed *glottis* (the vocal folds surround the opening called the glottis) the folds open and shut rapidly causing a vibration. You can feel this vibration if you put your fingers on the bump in the front part of your throat and hum. This vibration may not seem all that important at first, but it is the only difference in sound between the words *bus* and *buzz* and many other similar pairs of words. The sound [s] is made exactly the same way as the sound [z] except that for [z], the sound is voiced (the vocal folds vibrate). Put your fingers on the lump in the front of your throat again. Now make the [s] and [z] sounds without any vowel following them. You will feel a vibration when you make the [z]. This distinctive vibration is called *voicing*; it is one of the three features all humans use to distinguish the sounds of their languages.[1]

There are many sets of sounds that only differ by this feature of vibration. In fact, there are many whole words in English for which the entire movement of the airstream and tongue are exactly the same for all the sounds in both words except that one of the sounds in one word is voiced and in the other unvoiced. These sets of words are called *minimal pairs*. The first sound in the following sets of words, *tip* and *dip* ([t], [d]), sip and zip ([s], [z]) and Kong and gong ([k], [g]), only differ by voicing.

## 4.2.2  Place of articulation

A second descriptor of consonants is to note which articulator, in combination with the tongue, is used to modify the airstream to produce a particular consonant. The articulators are the *lips* (labials), the *teeth* (dental or interdental), the *alveolar ridge* (the raised part of the mouth above the teeth), the *palate* (the top of the mouth) and the *velum* (the very back of the roof of the mouth). Using minimal pairs again, you can see how just the movement of the tongue from one of these places of articulation to another generates an entirely different word. For instance, pronounce the words *tight* and *kite* (ignore the spelling). It is clear that the only difference in the pronunciation of these two words is that the front of the tongue is touching the alveolar ridge for the first sound in the word *tight*, and the back of the tongue is raised towards the back of the mouth for the word *kite*. The rest of the movements in the mouth are exactly the same for both words.

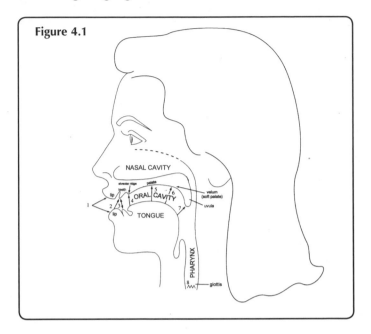

**Figure 4.1**

NASAL CAVITY

alveolar ridge   palate

teeth

lip

ORAL CAVITY

velum
(soft palate)

uvula

lip

TONGUE

PHARYNX

glottis

## 4.2.3  Manner of articulation

The third aspect of making a consonant is how the airstream is blocked and released in the vocal cavity. The airstream may be allowed to flow without obstruction by any articulators as it travels out of the larynx or it may be partially or completely obstructed at different places in the mouth and throat.

*Stops or plosives*

Sometimes, in the production of a consonant, the air cavity is completely blocked for a short time before it is released. These sounds are called *stops* or *plosives* (because a little puff of air 'explodes' from the mouth when the consonant is released). English speakers use three sets of consonants made in three places in the mouth. The sounds [p] and [b] are made with the lips closing completely to block the air which is then released. The only difference between the two sounds is voicing. A second pair of stops is [t] and [d] which are produced when the tongue blocks the air from escaping at the alveolar ridge. The last set in English is [k] and [g] which are produced when the back of the tongue rises to close off the air at the back of the mouth, at the velum. There are lots of minimal pairs that show that pairs of sounds are distinct. Pronounce the words *bet* and *get, time* and *kind*, and note how either the front or the back of the tongue or your lips are used to completely block off the air for a brief moment.

There is one additional stop that is not in a paired set and only occurs in some varieties of English: the glottal stop. The glottal stop does not occur in American English except in the non-word expressions uh-oh [ʔʌʔo][2] (meaning 'whoops!'), and uh-uh [ʌʔʌ] (meaning 'no'). Some students have a difficult time feeling the difference between the glottal stop and the [h] sound. There are a couple of pairs of expressions in American English that make the difference more obvious. Compare the middle consonant sounds in the expressions *uh-uh* (no) and *uh-huh* (yes). The second one has a very obvious [h] sound in the middle. You can also say these same two expressions with your lips held shut [mʔm], 'no' and [mhm], 'yes' and feel the difference in the production of the consonants as well. Nevertheless, the glottal stop is not all that common in varieties of American English.

The glottal stop occurs commonly in Cockney varieties of English, where it systematically replaced the [t] sound in words like *bottle* [bɔʔl]. According to a number of linguists, the use of glottal stops has recently been spreading to other British varieties of English spoken throughout the United Kingdom.[3]

*Variation in stop sounds*

There is some variation in the production of stops depending on where in a word the sound appears. If you hold a piece of paper closely in front of your mouth and make the [p] sound alone, you will see that the air escapes from the mouth with sufficient force that the paper moves. This is called aspiration. In English, significant aspiration only occurs whenever [p] or another voiceless stop are the first sound in a word or syllable, like in the word *pepper*. When these sounds occur at the end of a syllable or word, like in the word *step*, they are unaspirated: meaning the puff of air is greatly reduced.

You can test this out by switching between the normal pronunciation of the words *pat* and *stop*. This is a phonetic rule in English that all native speakers acquire without conscious knowledge. It is possible to aspirate the final [p] in stop, but it is not normal English pronunciation. The over-aspiration of [p] is noticeable to native speakers of English. As a child, when I heard other children aspirate their word initial [p] sounds, other children would tease them and say 'Say it, don't spray it' because of the unfortunate tendency for spittle to accompany the puff of air.

There are languages, like Thai, for which [p] and [pʰ] (aspirated [p]) are important distinctions in terms of meaning. In Thai, the word [pàa], with an unaspirated [p], means *aunt*, but when the sound [p] is aspirated, then the word means *cloth* [pʰàa]. This difference may be difficult for a non-native speaker of Thai to hear. You can, however, hear a demonstration of these sounds on Ladafoged's website mentioned above.

Slight changes in tongue position can also make a noticeable difference in the pronunciation of stops. Speakers of Latin American varieties of Spanish make some sounds differently from speakers of English. For example, for

Latin American Spanish speakers, the [t] and [d] sounds are dental; the blockage of the airstream is made at the teeth and not the alveolar ridge. This difference in tongue position makes a slight variation in pronunciation and is one of the thousands of tiny differences that can give native speakers of either Spanish or English an accent when speaking the other language.

### Stops and the past tense in English

One property of the stop is a significant feature in the systematic production of past tense endings in English. Most native speakers of English do not really think about it, but there are three pronunciations of the -ed past tense ending: [ɪd], [t] and [d]. Consider how you pronounce the following words:

| | | |
|---|---|---|
| elect/elected | drag/dragged | roam/roamed |
| judge/judged | record/recorded | believe/believed |
| push/pushed | load/loaded | look/looked |
| sob/sobbed | watch/watched | count/counted |

Take a minute to see if you can figure out what rule determines which of the three endings that each of the above words gets. (Answer in the next paragraph). To begin, see if you can identify a pattern in the root words.

The answer has to do with the final sound in each of the root words. If the root ends in a voiced sound (the vocal folds vibrate), then the suffix that gets added is also voiced, that is, the [d] ending. For instance, the word *roam* gets the voiced [d] suffix. For a root word that ends with an unvoiced sound, the [t] suffix is added. Therefore, the word *walk*, which ends in an unvoiced sound, gets the voiceless [t] suffix. This works for all of the words except the root words that end in [t] or [d]. It would be very strange to add a [t] sound to the end of a word already ending in [t], so we insert a vowel [ɪd] to make it easier to say (elected). We do the same for root words ending in [d] (recorded).

The rule is so firmly embedded in our brains that when we create new verbs or change existing nouns or adjectives into verbs, we automatically add the appropriate phonetic string of sounds to create the past tense. One example is quite frequently heard in American offices and universities in sentences like 'She xeroxed the paper yesterday' [zirokst]. In businesses, you hear the same process in sentences where the company name of Fed-Ex is being used as a verb, as in 'He Fed-Exed the contract to her yesterday'.

Native speakers implement this rule unconsciously dozens of times each day, even though most have never heard of the rule. Interestingly, non-native learners of English do not make mistakes with matching the voiced and unvoiced sounds. The mistake they most commonly make is to pronounce the full -ed on the end of all the past tense verbs. Thus, they pronounce every single letter in the word *walked*.

*Oral and nasal stops*

The three features detailed above are sufficient to illustrate all the basic consonants of the world's languages created in the oral cavity of the mouth. They are called *oral sounds*. However, there is another small, but very significant, class of stops that need an additional descriptor. At the very back of the roof of the mouth is the velum, which is moveable.[4] When the velum is lowered, the air coming up from the lungs escapes through the nasal cavity instead of through the mouth. The sounds created when the air passes over the velum and out through the nose are called *nasal sounds*.

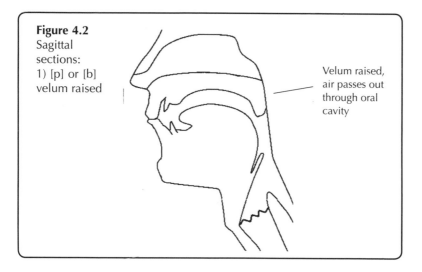

**Figure 4.2**
Sagittal sections:
1) [p] or [b] velum raised

Velum raised, air passes out through oral cavity

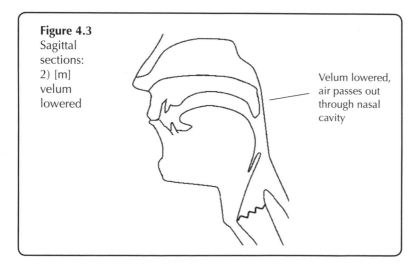

**Figure 4.3**
Sagittal sections:
2) [m] velum lowered

Velum lowered, air passes out through nasal cavity

English has three nasal stops. One is the [m] sound, which can be described as a voiced bilabial stop. Try making an [m], and then pinch off both sides of your nose so that no air escapes. The sound will disappear because being a bilabial stop means that no air is escaping from between the lips. A second nasal sound is the [n], which is a voiced alveolar stop. Both of these sounds and symbols are quite obvious to English speakers. There is a third nasal sound, however, which is not so obvious. It is the last sound heard in words like *sing* and *ring*. Although English speakers write these words with four letters, there are really only three sounds pronounced. To test this, say one of these words and note what your tongue is doing when you hold the last sound for a few seconds. You are not pronouncing the word *sin* plus a hard [g] sound. The back of the tongue raises to cut off the air at the back of the mouth, so it must escape through the nasal cavity. Again, if you pronounce this sound and pinch off your nose, the sound will disappear. Unlike all the other stops, which can occur at the beginning, middle or end of a word, the sound [ŋ] never occurs in word-initial position.

ENGLISH STOPS

| Place of articulation: | bilabial | alveolar | velar | glottal |
|---|---|---|---|---|
| | [p] [b] | [t] [d] | [k] [g] | [ʔ] |
| Nasals: | [m] | [n] | [ŋ] | |

## Fricatives

Fricatives are another manner of articulation. Fricative consonants are formed by bringing two articulators close together and forcing the air through the remaining space, with the movement of air generally causing a hissing or rushing sound. English has pairs of voiced and unvoiced fricatives at several places of articulation.

The *labiodental* fricative sounds, [f] and [v], are made with the teeth resting on the bottom lip (as in the first sounds in *fat* and *vat*). These sounds differ only in voicing. These are the only two labial-dental sounds found in the inventory of English.

There is also a pair of *interdental* sounds made with the tongue extended slightly out from between the teeth. English speakers all know the letter combination -th- (thought); however, most are unaware that this two-letter combination is really only one sound. They also don't realize that there are two forms of -th-, a voiced and an unvoiced pronunciation. Consider the initial sound in the words *though* and *thought*. As you pronounce each one, you can feel the vibration of the tongue and the vocal folds quite distinctly in the word *though* but not in the word *thought*. Both sounds have the same manner of articulation (fricative) and are made in the same place of articulation (interdental); they differ only in voicing. Phoneticians have chosen letters of the Greek and Latin alphabets, the *theta* [θ], to represent the unvoiced interdental fricative, and the eth [ð] was adopted from the Latin alphabet for the ~~un~~voiced interdental fricative. There is a pair of words for which there is only a difference in voicing in the initial letter, otherwise the rest of the word is the same. Linguists call sets of words like this minimal pairs. The first consonant sound in the word *ether*[5] is [θ] (same pronunciation as Ethernet) and the first consonant in *either* is [ð]. The only difference between these two words is the change in voicing in the initial consonant.

Fricatives are also made at a third point of articulation: the *alveolar ridge*. The ~~voiced~~ (voiceless) alveolar fricative is the [s] as the initial sound in the word *sip*. The ~~un~~voiced alveolar fricative is the symbol [z] in *zip*. These sounds, like most of the others above, can occur in the middle or ends of words as well: *trucks, zoo, mistake* and *buzzard*.

Two sounds are produced with the tongue raised towards the centre of the palate which differ only by voicing: [ʃ], the first sound in the word *ship*, and [ʒ], the first consonant in the second syllable in the word *pleasure*. Like the sound [ŋ], the distribution of [ʒ] is limited. There are no native English words that begin or end with this sound, but it is the initial sound in the literary term *genre* (borrowed from French) and the name *Jacques*, well known by English speakers because of the exploits of French oceanographer Jacques Cousteau. Other English words with [ʒ] include: *measure* and *leisure*.

The final point of articulation used by English speakers to create fricative sounds is the glottis. The fricative, [h], as in *hot*, is unvoiced. It is made with the air passing without obstruction or modification through the glottis and out of the mouth.

ENGLISH FRICATIVES

| Place of articulation: | labiodental | interdental | alveolar | palatal | glottal |
|---|---|---|---|---|---|
| | [f] [v] | [θ] [ð] | [s] [z] | [ʃ] [ʒ] | [h] |

## Affricates

A third manner of articulation is created when the airstream is stopped for a very brief instant at the palate and then forced through a narrow space, making these sounds a combination of a stop and a fricative. English speakers only have one pair of these sounds. The first [tʃ] is usually represented in spelling as -ch- as in the first and last sounds in the word *church*. The second, the voiced sound [dʒ], is heard twice in the word *judge*. The word *judge* is also a good example of why a phonetic alphabet is necessary. The sound [dʒ] is spelled with a j- at the beginning of the word but with a -dg at the end. Spelling provides little help in understanding how to pronounce this word.

ENGLISH AFFRICATES

Place of articulation:      palatal
                            [tʃ] [dʒ]

## Liquids and Glides

The final two categories for English manner of articulation are the liquids and glides. These sounds are produced with little or no obstruction of the airstream. The glides, bilabial[6] [w] and palatal [j], as in the initial sounds in the words *wet* and *yellow* respectively, are both voiced. The glides are produced with almost no restriction of the airflow at all.

The liquids are both alveolar, and unlike the rest of the symbols which have been in voiced and voiceless pairs, both of these are voiced. They are characterized by more restriction of the airstream than glides, but much less restriction than typical consonants. They are [l], as in *let*, and [r] as in *red*. This is another set for which the spelling alphabet and the phonetic alphabet are equal. These sounds, however, are problematic for speakers of some languages, commonly Asian languages that do not have these distinctions. If you switch back and forth between these two sounds, it is clear that they are both alveolar, but it is how the tongue moves which distinguishes them.

ENGLISH LIQUIDS AND GLIDES

| Place:   | bilabial | alveolar | palatal |
|----------|----------|----------|---------|
| Glides:  | [w]      |          | [j]     |
| Liquids: |          | [l], [r] |         |

# 4.3 The International Phonetic Alphabet

The International Phonetic Alphabet (IPA)[7] represents all the sounds of the world's languages and is quite complex. There are no languages that make use of all of the consonants that can be made in the mouth. It is not obligatory to do so to create all the words necessary for speakers to express themselves about any topic in the world. The inventory of sounds of any language is an arbitrary collection of sounds that may reflect some of the history of contact between speakers of different languages. However, as we will see in the chapter on the history of English, we have often borrowed words from other languages without borrowing their native pronunciations, for example, *ballet* [bæle] (from French) for which we pronounce the final syllable according to French pronunciation rules rather than English ones and *khaki* [ka:ki] (from Urdu) for which we ignore the highly aspirated [h] which is the normal Urdu pronunciation.

Below I have provided a summary of the full IPA chart reflectin
the consonants of standard varieties of worldwide English. A v
reference to the full chart may be found at the end of this chapter.

| | Bilabial | Labiodental | Interdental | Alveolar | Palatal | Velar | Glottal |
|---|---|---|---|---|---|---|---|
| Stops | p b | | | t d | | k g | ʔ |
| Nasals | m | | | n | | ŋ | |
| Fricatives | | f v | θ ð | s z | ʃ ʒ | | h |
| Affricates | | | | | tʃ dʒ | | |
| Liquids | *ignore* | | | l r | | | |
| Glides | w | | | | j | | |

# 4.4 The vowels

Written English has only six vowel letters, but it actually has 11 (or more)
vowel sounds that are commonly pronounced by speakers of varieties
of English across the world. Just like for the consonants, there are more
sounds than letters, so more phonetic symbols were created to provide a
one-to-one correspondence between sound and symbol.

Vowels differ from consonants in that the airstream is never blocked
or even seriously constricted by any of the articulators. In addition, unlike
most consonants, they can stand alone. They can be sung – you can't sing
a high C note solely on a [k] sound! The few consonants that you can sing,
like the nasals and the liquids, are sometimes referred to as semi-vowels
because of this quality among others. A more linguistic description of this
quality is to say that they may serve as the nucleus of a syllable like vowels
do. Consider the second syllable in the words *able* [ebl] or *vixen* [vɪksn].

## 4.4.1 Classification of vowels

Like consonants, there is a systematic way to classify vowels by four basic
features: tongue height (high, mid or low in the mouth), the part of the
tongue being raised (the tip, middle or back) and the shape of the lips
(spread, neutral or round). There are also a couple of minor descriptors.
Vowels can be described as tense or lax depending on the muscular tension
used to produce them, and for languages like English (but not Spanish),
some vowels have a longer duration than others.

## 4.4.2 The vowel chart

The vowel chart is made to represent, very loosely, the shape of the
tongue with the tip of the tongue at the left side of the chart. It is

divided into three rows to represent tongue height and three columns that represent which part of the tongue is involved in the production of a particular vowel. As with the consonants, many of the sections contain two phonetic characters representing distinct vowel sounds. Unlike the consonants, the difference between each vowel in a set is not voicing, but tongue position among other characteristics that we'll talk about below.

| TONGUE HEIGHT | FRONT | CENTRAL | BACK |
| --- | --- | --- | --- |
| HIGH | i | | u |
| | ɪ | | ʊ |
| MID | e | ə | o |
| | ɛ | ʌ | ɔ |
| LOW | æ | | a |

Here are some common words that should help you identify each of the sounds represented by the phonetic characters. Dialectal diversity does play a part in each individual speaker's pronunciation of the words of their language. For example, in both my varieties of English, standard and non-standard, the words *caught* and *cot* are pronounced exactly the same way, as are the names *Don* and *Dawn*. The two low back vowels have merged. A sizable proportion of speakers in the United States no longer distinguish between these two sounds. Another pair of vowels which are pretty close are the two mid-central vowels. An example word that is useful that has both sounds is *above* [əbʌv].

Vowel symbol examples
(US English)

| | | |
| --- | --- | --- |
| [i] meat | | [u] dude |
| [ɪ] quit | [ə] sofa | [ʊ] foot |
| [e] mate | [ʌ] cut | [o] coat |
| [ɛ] bed | | [ɔ] caught |
| [æ] cat | | [a] cot |

## 4.4.3 Diphthongs

Three very common vowel sounds in English that have not been dealt with yet are the diphthongs. These sounds are not listed on the chart because they are a combination of two sounds (a vowel plus a glide) resulting in a single unit. When you pronounce these sounds, you can hear how the timbre, or vowel quality, changes, whereas for the other vowels, the quality remains the same throughout the articulation of the vowel.

Diphthongs

| | | | |
| --- | --- | --- | --- |
| [aw] | flout | cow | cloud |
| [aj] | I | fly | wide |
| [ɔj] | toy | toil | moist |

## 4.4.4 Vowel length

Native speakers of English rarely notice that some vowels are longer in duration than others. In English, vowel length is not a contrastive feature, meaning that there are not pairs of words where the double pronunciation of a vowel signifies a completely different word. There are many languages worldwide for which vowel length is significant. One is Finnish, for which the single iteration of a vowel is in contrast with the double pronunciation of it because that difference in sound results in a different meaning.

| | |
|---|---|
| Tapaan sinut puistossa. | I'll meet you in the park.[8] |
| Tapan sinut puistossa. | I'll kill you in the park. |

In English, two levels of vowel length are present. The lax vowels, [ɪ], [ɛ], [ʌ], [ʊ] and [a] are all short vowels. The remaining vowels, [i], [e], [ə], [u], [o] and [ɔ] are slightly longer in duration. They are not double vowels like the Finnish vowels, but there is a perceivable difference in their duration. To test this, pronounce the following three sets of words in which the vowel in the first set is short and in the second long:

| | |
|---|---|
| bit [bɪt] | beet [bit] |
| bet [bɛt] | bait [bet] |
| foot [fʊt] | food [fud] |

For speakers of languages like Spanish, which has only five vowels [a], [e], [i], [o] and [u], this distinction is particularly hard to hear. It is not uncommon for Spanish speakers learning English to use the same vowel length for all of the vowels in English, which causes them to pronounce the word *sister* with the long sound [i]. The difference in the production of [i] and [ɪ] is only a slight movement of the tongue and a small lengthening of the sound, so it is easy to understand why this is a difficult sound for some learners of English as a second language to produce.

## 4.5  Advantages of a phonetic system

Not only is a phonetic system better than an alphabet for specifying exactly which sounds to pronounce, it also takes care of other problems related to the English spelling system. For example, there are many words in English that have sounds in them that are not represented by letters. Consider the following two words: *coot* and *cute*. They are quite similar in pronunciation; however, there is nothing in the spelling of the word *cute* to tell you that the second sound in the word is a glide; the transcriptions provide that information: *coot* [kut] and *cute* [kjut].

You can see a couple of other things from these transcriptions. The letter -c-, like many other letters, has more than one pronunciation. It can be pronounced as either [s] or [k], as in the US pronunciation of the  word *circumstance* [sɪrkʌmstæns], in which we get both pronunciations of -c-. Another example of a letter with more than one pronunciation is the letter -x-, which can be pronounced as a [g] in words like exit [egsɪt] (or [eksɪt] and [ɛksɪt] in other dialects), or as a [z] in words like xylophone [zajləfon].

In addition, silent letters are quite common in English. Consider the word *thought*; it has a total of seven letters, but there are really only three sounds in the pronunciation of the word: [θɔt]. You can only begin to imagine the frustration of second language learners of English trying to figure out how to pronounce words in English from their spelling!

The phonetic system also allows us to capture dialectal variations. In the USA, the word *coupon* has two common pronunciations: [kupan] and [kjupan]. There is also a pronunciation feature called r-insertion, in which the [r] sound is added to the end of words where it does not appear in standard varieties (nor is indicated by spelling). These dialects are found in the northeast of the United States as well as parts of the southern USA, and are also found in southwestern England.

If you have heard speeches from US president John F. Kennedy, during the Cuban Missile Crisis, you may have noticed his non-standard pronunciation of the country name Cuba [kubaɹ]. Furthermore, although the Spanish pronunciation of the word is [kuba], native speakers of English pronounce it quite commonly as [kjuba]. If you 'google' 'Kennedy' plus 'Cuban Missile Crisis' plus 'audio', you will come up with dozens of websites where you can hear examples of Kennedy's speech in which this pronunciation is frequent.

When I taught in southwestern Georgia, my linguistics students put together a set of features of the local dialect. One of the features was vowel insertion. Here is the list of word variants they came up with:

|  | Standard English | English in Columbus, GA |
| --- | --- | --- |
| tomato | [təmeto] | [təmeder] |
| potato | [pəteto] | [pətedər] |
| delta | [dɛltə] | [dɛltər] |
| Jonah | [əonə] | [əonər] |
| spa | [spa] | [spar] |

In contrast, sometimes these speakers actually lost the [r] sound in words which are followed by a schwa sound: Standard English *darling* became [dɔlin] and *never* became [nɛvə].d3

Another advantage to a phonetic system is that it allows us to capture the words of languages for which there are no writing systems. Many years ago I compiled the first dictionary of a language called Kpelle, a Mande language spoken in Liberia. There is no writing system for Kpelle. Its speakers are mostly bilinguals, and when they have a need to write, they use Liberian English which is the lingua franca for the country (with more than a dozen languages commonly spoken, English serves as a neutral means of communication across ethnic groups). Because my goal was to represent how Kpelle sounds to other linguists, I used phonetic characters to describe each word rather than create an alphabet for the language and all the rules to explain how all the letters related to individual sounds.

Finally, phonetic transcriptions tell us how to pronounce new words in our own language or a language we may be studying. Most hard-copy monolingual English dictionaries use some kind of archaic system they have created to represent pronunciations of words, often using a couple of letters to represent a single sound. However, online versions have been increasingly switching to phonetic systems. The Merriam-Webster Online Dictionary[9] uses a phonetic system that transcribes the word *cute* as [kyüt]. The online version of the Oxford English Dictionary transcribes it as [kju:t][10]. Many of the international students in my linguistics classes have very sophisticated hand-held dictionaries that also use a phonetic alphabet. Many of the ones created in Asia reflect British pronunciations whereas the ones from Latin America reflect US pronunciations.

## 4.6  Others features of sound: suprasegmentals

The vowels and the consonants are only a part of the sound system of a language. Speakers of languages also make use of rhythm and the stress patterns in the creation of meaning. Consider the following phonetic sentence: [lɛts] [hʌnt] [sæm]. There are two possible interpretations of this:

Drawings created by Colleen O'Conner-Olson

When the utterance is written, we have the comma in place to disambiguate which meaning the sentence has. There are no commas in speaking, but the pronunciation of these sentences varies slightly in some subtle but very significant ways. First is the difference in intonation. The intonational contour of the first sentence is quite flat, possibly falling slightly at the end of the sentence, whereas the intonation rises slightly at the end of the second sentence. There is also a difference in sentence stress. In the first sentence, the major sentence stress is on the verb *hunt*. In the second sentence, the stress is on the object of the hunt: *Sam*. Thus, although the phonetic string of sounds is the same for both sentences, different meanings are created via variations in sentence stress and intonation.

There are pairs of words in English that reflect how stress patterns affect meaning, like *White House* and *white house*. In spelling, the use of capital letters would indicate that the first expression refers to the residence of the president of the United States. Speaking, however, has to provide us with a different set of clues.

[aj] [wɛrk] [ɪn] [ðʌ] [wajt] [haws]

If you are referring to the presidential mansion in Washington DC, you will put the sentence stress on the word *white*. If you are pointing at one house in a row of houses all painted different colours, in Los Angeles, you would put the stress on *house*. The same is true for distinguishing the red-winged blackbird from any old black bird (species unknown). The proper noun receives the main sentence stress on the adjective, *black*, and the generic use of the word gets the stress on the noun *bird*.

Stress patterns of language, which are quite easily acquired as children, are quite difficult for adult language learners, and are the major features contributing to the foreign accent that many adult have when learning any language. When learning a foreign language, it is not all that difficult to memorize a lot of words and even the basic sentence patterns of a language, but the subtle differences in tongue position, aspiration, word and sentence stress and intonation are what can mark us as non-native speakers. Most of these differences are quite small when taken individually, but the compounding of them has the effect of creating a foreign accent. These slight differences are also what create the differing accents of the native English speakers of New Delhi, London, Cape Town, Sydney, Vancouver, Accra or Boston.

## Suggested reading

Fromkin, V., Rodman, R. and Hyams, N. (2006), *An Introduction to Language*. 8th Edition. Boston: Thompson/Heinle.

Tserdanelis, G. and Wong, W. Y. P. (eds) (2004), *The Language Files*. The Ohio State University Linguistics Dept. 9th Edition. Columbus: Ohio State University Press.

## Interesting websites

International Phonetic Alphabet: www.arts.gla.ac.uk/IPA/index.html

Phonetics website of Peter Ladafoged, University of Southern California: hctv.humnet.ucla.edu/departments/linguistics/VowelsandConsonants/vowels/contents.html

## Practice exercises

A. Identify the following sounds by their phonetic character and provide a word that begins with this sound (one not found in the chapter examples).

1. voiceless glottal fricative
2. voiced interdental fricative
3. voiced bilabial glide
4. mid back lax vowel
5. high front tense vowel

6. voiced bilabial stop
7. alveolar nasal
8. voiceless palatal affricate
9. low front vowel
10. high back tense vowel

B. Transcribe the following words:

| | | | |
|---|---|---|---|
| 1. fang | 5. chunk | 9. renown | 13. capture |
| 2. treasure | 6. cucumber | 10. with | 14. flight |
| 3. circus | 7. bath | 11. bathe | 15. yes |
| 4. wedge | 8. exits | 12. queen | 16. recourse |

C. Transcribe the following. Put each word in a separate set of brackets.

1. Your full name
2. Your mother or father's name
3. The city of your birth
4. Your major area of study
5. The name of your street or residence hall

# Notes

1   Although, as we will see in this chapter, this is a distinguishing feature of many pairs of consonants, it is easiest to feel with pairs of fricative sounds because they have more duration than other consonants.

2   The ʔ is the linguistic symbol for the glottal stop which we'll see in the consonant chart in a couple of pages.

3   'Phonological resistance and innovation in the North-West of England' by Kevin Watson, 2006. *English Today* 86, Vol. 22, No. 2.

4   There is an excellent interactive website from the University of Toronto that shows the position of the velum and the other articulators for all the consonants. www.chass.utoronto.ca/~danhall/phonetics/sammy.html

5   Ether is a colourless liquid that used to be used as an anaesthetic.

6   There is some argument for a velar classification for [w]; however, since this is an introductory text, we'll limit the description to the bilabial.

7   Grateful acknowledgement is given to the International Phonetic Association (Department of Theoretical and Applied Linguistics, School of English, Aristotle University of Thessaloniki, Thessaloniki 54124, Greece) for the use of this chart.

8   Examples from, *The Wonders of the Finnish Language* website at: www.ecml.at/html/finnish/html/Finnish_Finnish.htm

9   www.m-w.com/netdict.htm

10   The colon in this transcription represents vowel lengthening.

# 5 Morphology: the makeup of words in a language

## Chapter Overview

| | | |
|---|---|---|
| 5.1 | CATEGORIZING THE WORDS OF A LANGUAGE | 84 |
| 5.2 | MORPHEMES | 85 |
| | 5.2.1  INFLECTIONAL AND DERIVATIONAL MORPHEMES | 86 |
| 5.3 | MORPHOLOGY AND PHONETICS | 89 |
| | 5.3.1  A FINAL WORD ABOUT MORPHEME STRUCTURE | 91 |
| 5.4 | OUR EVER-EXPANDING AND CHANGING VOCABULARY | 91 |
| | 5.4.1  WORD FORMATION PROCESSES | 92 |
| | 5.4.2  LINGUISTIC BORROWING | 98 |
| 5.5 | THE DICTIONARY | 100 |
| | 5.5.1  NEW DICTIONARY WORDS | 101 |

Words, words, words. Everyday we use thousands of them not only to conduct our daily interactions with other people, but also for our own internal dialogues. At the most basic level, they give form to our experiences and thoughts; if we are good with them, they can express the subtle nuances of our lives as well.

Because of its unique history, English is a particularly rich language in terms of the scope of its vocabulary. There are more than 450,000 words in the English language, which is double the number of words in any Romance language, like French or Spanish, or any other Germanic language, like German or Dutch.[1] This wealth of words is not due to any special quality of the English language; it is due to the fact that English speakers have borrowed many words from every language with which its speakers have been in contact. Even when English speakers already had a perfectly good Anglo-Saxon word for something, they added words from other languages and thus greatly enriched the vocabulary of English. We'll look at the process of borrowing in detail in the history chapter later in the book.

Most people who have taken a foreign language in high school or college have spent a good deal of time memorizing long lists of words, often divided into grammatical categories like nouns and verbs. You may have memorized thousands of words as well as grammatical rules for how to put them together and all the possible prefixes and suffixes that can be attached to them. If you were lucky, you might have travelled to a country where that language is used and had the opportunity to converse with native speakers. All of a sudden, you may have found yourself completely confused by the people's language, confronted with long strings of sounds which seem to all be connected together instead of neatly spaced individual words like you learned in school. Writing on the page has words separated in a way that normal human conversation rarely does. I spent a good deal of time completely confused by a Spanish expression I kept hearing in the Dominican Republic: *pana*. I asked many people what it meant and everyone kept telling me it was not a word. I finally heard someone say it again and immediately asked what they had said and found out that it was a clipped form of two words: *para nada*, 'for nothing'. Two complete syllables had just gone missing, and most native speakers were not even aware that they were doing it!

Of course, we do the same thing when we have normal conversations in English. Imagine being a foreign student in the southern part of the USA and overhearing the following conversation between two friends just before noon:

| John: | Waassup? |
|-------|----------|
| Bill: | Nutin. |
| John: | Jeetyet? |
| Bill: | No, djew? |
| John: | No, yauntu?[2] |

Like the speakers above, we do not consciously pay attention to word boundaries, and we create many contractions, both official (like *isn't*) and unofficial (like *hafta*). Contraction is a normal process for anyone who is a native speaker of a language. Language teachers do recognize that these strings of sounds may be problematic for learners of English and often modify their speech when speaking to their students to help them understand more easily in beginner language classes. A wonderful example of this type of speech modification can be heard on the United States government international radio station called *Voice of America* which is broadcast all over the world. They have been broadcasting a programme for at least 30 years called *Voice of America in Special English*. 'Special English' means that there is a slight (and unnatural to native speakers) pause between every single word uttered. Many of the international students I have taught over the last few decades have reported listening to this programme in their home countries to help them acquire English.

Even having a clear understanding of single words is not enough to understand them in a particular context. You have to know what the possible prefixes and suffixes of a word can be and what they can mean. Additionally, speakers must understand variation in meaning in different contexts as well as know both regular and idiomatic meanings. Native speakers of any language have this knowledge and much more.

Most people live happy lives never learning the grammatical terms that English teachers and linguists apply to the words of a language or the explicit rules about how they can be combined into sentences. This knowledge is unnecessary to being a competent, or even eloquent, speaker or writer of a language. Nevertheless, all native speakers of a language have a wealth of information about the words that they access continually, and unconsciously, as they are having a conversation, writing or thinking to themselves. For example, although many speakers of English cannot identify what an *adjective* is, they certainly know how to use one, where it can appear in a sentence, and, possibly, if it has more than one meaning. If you asked a native speaker to construct a few sentences with the word *cool* in different places in the sentences or with different meanings, the speaker would have no trouble producing the following sentences:

> The water is too cool to swim in.
> Please get me a cool cloth for my head.
> That rock band is so cool.
> Cool music from the 1980s is very rare.

Linguists, however, have noted that all the words of a language pattern into describable categories that have certain characteristics and differing functions that native speakers understand intuitively.

## 5.1  Categorizing the words of a language

All the words in a language can be divided up into two simple categories: *content words* and *function words*. Content words are the largest category including the following parts of speech: nouns, verbs, adjectives, adverbs and interjections. This class of words is also called the *open class* of words because we are always adding new words to it. If you take a quick minute to list a few of the new slang words that have been added to your language in the past few years, you can see what part of speech they are. Some recent (past ten years) examples from the United States include: *blog* (noun), *phat* (adjective), *Iraqnophobia* (noun) and *bling-bling* (noun). *Blog* and *bling-bling* have spread to other parts of the English-speaking world as well. Blog has even expanded to other parts of speech: *blogger* and *blogging*.

The remaining parts of speech make up what linguists call the *function words*. These are the *prepositions* (e.g. *of*, *in*, *on*) *articles* (e.g. *a*, *an*, *the*) and *conjunctions* (e.g. *although*, *but*, *and*, *nor*). They are termed function words because their most significant role is connecting the content words in a sentence together – showing how the nouns and verbs of the sentence relate to each other. This group is also called the *closed class* of words because it is a limited set that is not being added to as our cultures change or our technology grows.

## 5.2 Morphemes

Another, more complete way to describe words and their parts is to look at their *morphology*. Morphology is the field of linguistics that studies the structure of words and their components. All words are made up of one or more parts that have meaning. For example, the word *unhappy* has two meaningful parts: *happy*, describing an emotional condition and a prefix *un-* meaning *not*. The combination of these two parts gives us the complete meaning of the word *unhappy*. Each of these distinct parts is called a morpheme. Any further divisions of the word *unhappy* would leave a string of letters that have no meaning. Un- is not the only prefix that performs the same function. Think of all the other prefixes that we use to mean *not*: *dis-* (disappear)[3] *il-* (illogical), *im-* (impossible) and *in-* (incorrect). For some reason, English speakers have chosen only prefixes to make words negative. The choice of *un-* to precede happy was arbitrary; *unhappy* could just as logically be *dishappy* or *inhappy*.

The two morphemes in the word *unhappy* are quite different. The morpheme *happy* can appear by itself in many different sentences; the morpheme *un-* cannot. It must always be attached to another morpheme. If it is attached to an adjective, it means *not*; however, when it is attached to a verb, it means to reverse a process (undo). We speak of words like *happy* as being *free morphemes* because they are free to appear alone, and prefixes like *un-* as *bound morphemes* because they are always attached to (bound to) a free morpheme. Bound morphemes like *un-* are also called *affixes*, which is a class of words that includes suffixes, prefixes and infixes. Grammatical suffixes and prefixes abound in English, but infixes do not. An infix is a bound morpheme that appears in the middle of a word. There are languages like Turkish and Tagalog that regularly use them as part of their grammar to get across variations on the meaning of the same basic root word. In Tagalog, spoken in the Philippines, infixes are used to change present tense verbs into past tense ones. The rule (which seems quite complicated to those of us whose languages don't do this) is to infix a syllable composed of the phoneme [n] plus the initial vowel of the root word (the present tense is the base form of the verb in this language). This pattern can be determined from the following examples:[4]

bili 'buy'       binili 'bought'
basa 'read'      binasa 'read' (past)
sulat 'write'    'sinulat' (wrote)

English does not make use of infixing as a productive grammatical process, though infixes do appear in a few somewhat negative or slightly obscene slang expressions: *AlaDAMbama*, *AbsoBLOODYlutely* and *FarFREEKINGout*. In fact Michael Adams says that 'because it is a species of swearing; even if an insert isn't profane, or a euphemism for something profane, it amplifies only negative emotions (anger, frustration, dismissiveness, disbelief) those that swearing usually conveys'.[5] A counter example to this may be the use of infixing by the character Ned Flanders of *The Simpsons*. With expressions like *okelly dokelly* (okey dokey) and scrumdiddlyumptious (very scrumptious), he expresses his unflagging, and often completely irritating, cheerful nature. A more detailed analysis of infixing can be read about in the Adams article listed at the end of this chapter.

Another productive bound morpheme in English is *re-*, meaning 'to do again' (relive, rework, rewind). Do be careful not to jump to any conclusions though. What about the word *repeat*? Is the *re-* in this word a bound morpheme? Does this word mean 'to peat again?' Consider the word *revive*. Sometimes the answer is that the root word (the free morpheme) that the prefix is attached to is no longer a productive word but was at some point in Middle or Old English. This is the case with *revive*. According to the Oxford English dictionary the verb *vive* means 'to endue with life'. It is listed both as a transitive and intransitive verb as well as an adjective. Thus it is possible that *vive* and *revive* were both in use at some point in English. For other words, like *repeat*, the letters re- at the beginning of the word are just a random combination of letters which have no separate meaning as *do again*, any more than the combination of letters -hi- found in the word *which* means the slang version of *hello* (hi).

## 5.2.1  Inflectional and derivational morphemes

Not all bound morphemes function in the same manner. In English there are two classes of morphemes based on their functions: *inflectional morphemes* and *derivational morphemes*. Inflectional morphemes may be identified by the presence of several features. First, when they are added to a word, the grammatical class of the word does not change. If the root word is a noun (dog) it will stay a noun after an inflectional morpheme is added (dogs). Second, in every case but one, only one can be attached to a word. The exception to this is plural possessive (*dogs'*, for which the -s' represents both the plural and the possessive case). Finally, they are all suffixes, though in other languages they can be prefixes as well. In English, the inflectional morphemes are a very limited group of suffixes that can be easily remembered.

*Inflectional Morphemes of English*

| | | |
|---|---|---|
| -s | (plural morpheme) | dogs |
| -s | (3rd per. sing. present) | lives |
| -ing | (progressive) | living |
| -ed | (past tense) | lived |
| -ed | (past participle) | had lived |
| -er | (comparative) | taller |
| -est | (superlative) | tallest |
| -'s, -s' | (possessive) | Adrian's, The Jones' |

Of course, like everything else in English, there are exceptions to the rule. There are some words that have irregular plural forms like: child → children, foot → feet, hypothesis → hypotheses, goose → geese, as well as many others. There are even some words for which the singular and plural forms are the same: one deer → two deer, one sheep → two sheep and one fish → two fish. In addition to irregular plural forms, there are also irregular comparative and superlative forms: good → better → best or bad → worse → worst, though you may occasionally hear a speaker of a non-standard variety of English say something like 'He's the baddest dude in town'. These exceptions to the general pattern are the headache of every second language learner of English. Nevertheless, the vast majority of English words do follow the patterns in the inflectional morpheme list.

The other type of bound morphemes is *derivational morphemes,* which can be both prefixes and suffixes in English (*dis*regard and happi*ness*). Unlike the inflectional suffixes, derivational suffixes usually change the grammatical category of the words to which they are attached (*govern*, verb → *government*, noun or *happy*, adjective → *happiness*, noun). However, the derivational prefixes generally do not change the grammatical category of the word. These prefixes usually make a word negative (*un*happy or *dis*appear) or have some numbering or ordering function (*bi-* or *tri*cycle or *pre*nuptial) that does not change the category of the word but changes the meaning in some way.

There are dozens of derivational morphemes including but not limited to: *-ment, -ize, -able, -bi, -tion, -sion, -cion, ate, -ness, -ity, -er, -ent, -ive, -tial, -ed, -ic, -ly, dis-, un-, il-, in-, pre-, bi-* and *post-.* Many of these perform exactly the same function, like turning a verb into a noun: *-ment* (establishment), *-sion* (comprehension), *-er* and *-or* (teacher, actor) among others. There is no rhyme or reason why a particular affix was chosen as the only one to attach to a word. Again, imagine what fun it must be to learn English as a second language and try to decide from which of these many endings to choose. These morpheme choices factor into current language change as well. In the last decade, I have noticed in some varieties of African American English, the word *conversate* is being used in place of *converse,* and this usage is spreading to speakers of other varieties of English as well (e.g. 'We was conversating about it'.) Whether it continues to spread or not, we'll only know at some future point in time. Morpheme alternations of this sort are also found in historical records and literature. You do not have to read very many stanzas of Shakespeare's sonnets before you run into a word with a different derivational morpheme than we use currently.

> As an *un*perfect actor on the stage. (Sonnet, 23.1)
> By willful taste of what thyself refus*est*. (40.8)
> When I was certain o'er *in*certainty . . . (115.11)
> The painful warrior famous*ed* for fight, (25.9)

There are many semantic gaps in English, meaning there are words for which the root of a word is no longer (or never was) productive, but the derived form is. Thus, we say an employee is *disgruntled*, but never *gruntled*. We can be *overwhelmed*, but not simply *whelmed*. Your mother can describe your appearance as *unkempt* when you are a mess, but she will never compliment you for being *kempt*!

Derivational morphemes are also different from inflectional morphemes in that you can add as many of them as you like to a root word as long as the word remains sufficiently comprehensible to the listener. Consider the word *nationalist*. The root word is a noun, *nation*. The suffix *-al* changes the noun to an adjective, *national*, and the suffix *-ist* changes it back into a noun, but a noun describing a person, *nationalist*. You can even add the inflectional morpheme *-s* to it making it plural, *nationalists*. For practice, let's take the word *disappearances* and analyse its bound morphemes.

Root word: *appear*

| bound morpheme | type | function |
| --- | --- | --- |
| dis- | derivational | change meaning *not* |
| -ance | derivational | change verb to noun |
| -s | inflectional | change singular noun to plural noun |

Just for fun, take this long word and do the same thing: *antidisestablishmentarianism*. You can cover up the rest of the page while you figure it out yourself.

Root word: establish (yes, I have had students argue for *stable*)

| bound morpheme | type | function |
| --- | --- | --- |
| anti- | derivational | change meaning *against* |
| dis- | derivational | change meaning *not* |
| -ment | derivational | change to noun (thing) |
| -arian | derivational | change to noun (person) |
| -ism | derivational | change to noun (philosophy) |

**DEFINITIONS**

*content words*: the open class of words like nouns, verb, adjectives and adverbs. Speakers of languages are always adding new words to these grammatical categories.

*function words*: the closed class of words including prepositions, articles and conjunctions. Native speakers do not create new words for these categories because they are functional words rather than meaning words.

*free morphemes*: words that can stand alone in a sentence and have meaning (e.g. happy).

bound morphemes: attachments to words that extend the meaning of a word. They cannot stand alone in a sentence (e.g. -ed, past tense)

*prefixes*: bound morphemes that are put on the front of free morphemes (e.g. il-illogical)

*suffixes*: bound morphemes that are put on the ends of free morphemes (e.g. -ed walked)

*infixes*: bound or free morphemes that are inserted in the middle of a free morpheme.

*inflectional morphemes*: in English, a small set of bound morphemes, all suffixes, that do not change the grammatical class of a word but do alter it in some way. (e.g. -est, big→biggest)

*derivational morphemes*: a large set of bound morphemes, including prefixes (which do not change the grammatical category of the root, e.g. *multi*cultural) and suffixes (which usually do change the grammatical category, e.g. move*ment*).

## 5.3  Morphology and phonetics

No linguistic system exists in a vacuum untouched by other systems, even though sometimes we teach them as if they were. An example of how different language systems affect each other can be seen when we look at how some morphemes are specifically crafted because of sound characteristics of the free morpheme. There may be several spelling forms or several pronunciations that mean the same thing but fit a particular pronunciation pattern. An interesting example is the past tense morpheme. Although it has just one spelling, -ed, it is actually pronounced in three slightly different ways. Most native speakers are not even aware of the difference, until you point it out to them, yet they make the correct pronunciation choice dozens of times a day.

Say the following words, and see if you can note how the endings are pronounced differently. Keep in mind the three basic features of consonants learned in the chapter on phonetics. Then figure out the pattern. The answer is below, so you may want to cover up the rest of the page after the example words.

| | | | |
|---|---|---|---|
| believed | pushed | judged | booted |
| dripped | roamed | wetted | sobbed |
| elected | watched | talked | dotted |

The answer:

1) Final -*ed* is pronounced [t] after final *voiceless* sounds in the free morpheme. In other words, if the last sound in the root word is voiceless, then voiceless [t] is added. Thus, the word *drip* ends in [t], which is a voiceless alveolar stop: [drɪp]. The plural form is [drɪpt].

Words: pushed, looked, watched, talked.

2) Final -*ed* is pronounced [d] after final *voiced* sounds in the free morpheme. For example, the word *sob* ends in [b] which is a voiced

bilabial stop, so the voiced [d] is added to make it past tense: [sobd].
Words: believed, judged, roamed, sobbed.

3) Root words that end in [t] or [d] are left. It's hard to repeat the same consonant twice in succession, so we don't simply add a [t] or [d] as with the other two patterns; we pronounce the vowel as well.
Words: booted, wetted, elected, dotted. Others: loaded, defended, added.

We add voiceless [t] to root words ending in voiceless sounds and voiced [d] for words ending in voiced sounds. Thus, we match voiceless sounds together, and we pair voiced sounds together; when we cannot, the -ed is pronounced [Id] after [d] and [t] ending root words: an elegant combination of morphology with phonetics.

There is a similar pattern with the addition of the plural morpheme -s to root words as well. Three patterns are used, but they vary from the past tense morpheme addition above. When we think of spelling, we tend to think of the plural morpheme as -s, an inflectional bound morpheme. However, both the pronunciation and the spelling vary. A phonetic rationale is the answer for why the sound varies. Again, think about the last sound you hear in the root word. In each of the following, the phonetic transcription is given within the bracket; focus on that.

|  |  |
|---|---|
| boot [but] | bead [bid] |
| date [det] | road [rod] |

Now make each one plural:

|  |  |
|---|---|
| boots [buts] | beads [bidz] |
| dates [dets] | roads [rodz] |

Just as with the past tense variations, the plural variants match the voicing of the root word with the appropriately voiced plural ending, so for the word *boots* which the root ends in the voiceless [t], the plural ending added will be the voiceless [s]. Voiced [d] gets added to the word *bead* because the final sound in this root word is voiced. Again, one group does not follow the pattern: the sibilants, sounds that manifest turbulence in their production (they make hissing or rushing sounds). The following sounds are sibilants: [s], [z], [ʃ], [ʒ], [tʃ] and [dʒ]. The plural ending for words that end in these sounds is a vowel plus a consonant [ɪz]. Sample words include: *watches, judges, dashes, messes* and *churches*.

## 5.3.1  A final word about morpheme structure

Some warnings are necessary about identifying morphemes. First, do not confuse the number of morphemes with number of syllables. We are looking at smallest meaning units, not sound units. Second, make sure that something that looks like a bound morpheme really is one. Consider the word *remember*. Does this word really mean 'to member again'? There is a derivational morpheme *re-*, meaning to do again, as in *relive*, but the letter combination *re-* is not always a bound morpheme. Make sure you focus on function, not spelling.

## 5.4  Our ever-expanding and changing vocabulary

The vocabulary of a language is in constant flux. Words enter and leave our language all the time, and although people may comment on the entrance of new words, especially if they are the slang words of particular groups, their demise is less often noticed. Some people think a person's vocabulary varies from others mostly because of level of education. However, vocabularies are quite varied for many more interesting reasons. If you watch international television shows and read books written by people from outside your country, it is obvious that people from other places where English is spoken use different words. The British use the word *boot* to describe the storage compartment of a car, and they *queue up* at the market cash register. People in the United States put their bags in the *trunk* of the car and stand *in line* at the grocery store (or stand *on line* in the East Coast region of the USA). These local words and expressions gain wider currency through books, television and movies. For example, the movie *Crocodile Dundee* brought Australian English words to both the United States and Britain. Some of the better-known Australian words are *barbie* (barbecue), *cobber* (mate), *dunny* (toilet) and *daks* (trousers). Thousands of words differ from country to country, where people are supposedly all speaking the same language.

Television provides more evidence for words and expressions coming in and out of the language. If you watch programmes more than a generation old, you will hear all kinds of words no longer in use like *groovy*, *far out* and *telegraph* (quickly disappearing everywhere!). If you go even further back in time to black and white movies and programmes, you are likely to hear other words and expressions that are no longer in vogue. When these words disappeared, the concepts they defined usually did not disappear like the telegraph did, they were simply replaced by other words. Groovy was replaced by many other words throughout the years including *tubular*, *rad*, *fly* and *fresh*. Words will continue to come and go as new generations of people create novel and expressive terms to define their experiences. So, how do all these new words come into our varieties of English?

## 5.4.1 Word formation processes

*Derivation*

One process, which was discussed in detail earlier in this chapter, is *derivation*: the adding of bound or free morphemes to root words to extend the meaning of an existing word as well as just extending a word to another grammatical category. There was never a point in language development when someone sat down and made a list of all the nouns and said, 'Let's verb these nouns by adding new endings'. Sometimes a word began life as a noun and was affixed to make it an adjective. For other words, the base form was the verb and endings were added later to make adjectives, adverbs and nouns. For instance, the word *snack* was first used as a noun; then later, the same word began to be used as a verb as well. The inflectional morpheme *-ing* is now commonly added to the verb *snack* to form the present progressive tense, *snacking*. Derivation is a very easy way to extend words, and people do it all the time to words they commonly know when they have a need. Sometimes the word catches on like the verb *snack* did, and at other times it may not. A few years ago, one of my neighbours in Georgia, who had his Weedeater (a lawn trimming device) in his hand, told me: 'We need to *weedeat* the yard'. He needed a verb, so he just created one on the spot. In September of 2003, the host of the television show *Animal Planet* was reading letters from viewers. After reading a particularly tender one he said, 'At the risk of getting all *Hallmarky* about it . . .' (a reference to sentimental greeting cards from the Hallmark Company). Although it is unlikely that *weedeat* and *Hallmarky* will catch on, hundreds of other words that underwent similar processes have caught on over the years. We know what these utterances mean because we understand the process of derivation and how affixes change root words. Notice how the sign below effectively uses derivation to turn the noun *office* into a verb.

One of the funniest new words created through derivation in the last few years is for a new product. The creator of this product combined the processes of derivation and clipping (shortening) to create a name for the new product, *Neuticles*, which are fake testicles for neutered pets. *Neuter* was clipped to *neuti-* and the now-unproductive Latin bound morpheme *-icle* (as in Latin *cuticula* 'cuticle' for which the root word is *cutis*, 'skin') is added to the base *neuter*. According to their website, 'Neuticles allows your pet to retain his natural look, self-esteem and aids in the trauma associated with neutering'.[6] You have to ask yourself if the dog is really traumatized or if the human owner is projecting his or her own feelings on the dog!

### Compounding

Another very productive process by which words are added to language is *compounding*, the process of merging two pre-existing words into a new concept. There are thousands of examples of these, for example, the breakfast cereal *cornflakes* and many new computer terms like *download*, *upload* and *hard drive* as well as other words like *editor-in-chief, home-schooling* and *drive-thru*. We sometimes even borrow compound words as in *après-ski* and *schadenfreude*.[7] Customs concerning hyphenation also contribute to confusion over word boundaries. The presence or absence of a hyphen has more to do with how integrated a word is into a language than whether or not something is a compound word.

### Clipping and blending

A very productive word formation process in American English is *clipping*, in which you simply cut off part of a word: laboratory → lab, dormitory → dorm, and influenza → flu. The Australians do this frequently as well, including: *servo*, (service station), *barbie* (barbecue) and *roo* (kangaroo). The process of clipping is quite frequent for commonly used longer words. Note the shortened form of the word *tomato* in the following sign from rural Kentucky: *mater* is used in speech as well as in writing in this area of the USA.

Sometimes new words are formed by the use of more than one process. The words *sitcom* involves clipping the phrase *situation comedy* and then blending *sit* and *com* into one word. The same goes for *simulcast* (simultaneous broadcast), *blog* (web log), and two of the most well known examples: *motel* (motor hotel) and *brunch* (breakfast lunch).

Compounding, clipping and derivation are put to use often for a humorous effect to create words that reflect a political or social issue. Members of the *American Dialect Society* collect new words each year to discuss at their annual meeting. One of my personal favourites from a few years back was *Iraqnophobia*, defined as an unreasonable fear of Iraq. More fun are all the words created by the media in 2004 after the sex scandal involving governor Arnold Schwarzenegger: the *governator*, the *gropenfurer* and the *gropenator*. *The New York Times* also sponsors a competition each year among its readers to create words that should exist but do not. Recent entries include: *reintarnation* (coming back to life as a hillbilly) and *glibido* (all talk, no action).

### Coinage

Sometimes when we create new inventions, discover new things or come up with new concepts, we create totally new words for them, a process called *coinage* (these words may be called *neologisms* as well), for example, the words *gizmo*, *teflon*, *nerd* and *quark* (a subatomic particle) are all fairly recent inventions. No one person, however, has contributed to the English language as many words as Shakespeare. There are more than 1,000 of his creations in current use including: *buzzer, cater, dawn, frugal, hint, hurry, hobnob, obscene, rant, torture* and *zany*.

At other times, meanings of old words are extended to cover new territory. In both Mandarin Chinese and English the words *ice + box* were put together to name the first refrigerators. The term *hacker* to describe a person who illegally breaks into a computer program can easily be derived from the original verb 'to hack' meaning to cut up. According to Fred Shapiro, a contributor to the *American Dialect Society* list, 'The computer term is probably from the metaphor of continually hacking or chopping away at something until it finally gives way.' The word 'spam' has also taken on a new meaning. The website of the *Association of Online Professionals* comments that the origins of the term *spam*, to refer to unsolicited mass electronic mail postings, is unknown. They provide two plausible possibilities:

> Some accounts attribute the term to a sketch on the Monty Python television series in which Vikings who loved the Hormel meat product named Spam[8] sang the word over and over, rising in volume until the other characters found it impossible to hold a conversation. The term may also have been an acronym related to 'Simultaneous Posting of a Message'.[9]

## Reduplication

Another type of word creation is *reduplication* in which part or all of a word is repeated for the effect of intensification. Older examples include: *hanky panky*, *boogie woogie*, *hoity-toity*, *helter skelter* and *super-duper*. A more recent one is *bling-bling*, popularized by Rap artist Snoop Dogg. Snoop Dogg has made this word formation process a part of his style, examples of which can be found on various websites that map his language usage.

## Generification

Words also enter the language through a process called *generification*, by which a proper name for a product becomes so popular that the name becomes the word for the product no matter who sells it. Most users of the *Frisbee* are unaware of its origins at *Frisbee's Bakery* where pie pans were thrown around for fun. The most classic examples though are the use of the company name *Kleenex* to refer to facial tissues and *Band-Aid* for small adhesive bandages. Most of my undergraduate students can't readily come up with facial tissue or a generic word for Band-Aids when queried. Other examples of this process are the terms *ohms* (a unit of electrical resistance) and *watts* (an international measure of power), the last names of two scientists who made significant contributions to the study of electromagnetism.[10] These terms are no longer capitalized because they were co-opted so long ago. A very recent example is the name of the search engine *Google* being used as a verb. I hear students in the library talk about *googling* information for their papers. On a prime-time episode of the television show *E.R.* in the USA, a nurse told one of the doctors: 'We're googling your blind date,' meaning they were checking him out on the Internet.

## Onomatopoeia

New words may also enter a language through *onomatopoeia*, a process by which a sound is turned into a word that is supposed to be pronounced like the sound itself. This would include words like *whoosh*, *bang*, *hiss* and *click*. However, if you look at other languages' words for these same sounds, as we did in Chapter 1, you'll note that there are a wide variety of words that people have created to supposedly represent these same sounds, so there still is a cultural and arbitrary aspect to them.

*Acronomy*

An alphabetic abbreviation, in which each letter of a word represents a whole word, is another word formation process called acronomy. You can tell how old one of these words is or how integrated it is into a language by whether or not it is still represented by all capital letters or now looks like a regular word. Good examples of words that are now clearly completely integrated are: *scuba*, *radar* and *snafu*. Most people cannot easily come up with the words that each letter represents anymore (*scuba* = self contained underwater breathing apparatus; *radar* = radio detection and ranging; *snafu* = situation normal all fouled[11] up). The history of *snafu* is particularly interesting. It came into English during World War II as an informal military term. This is not particularly unusual – many official, and unofficial, military terms are cut down to their initial letters: MP (military police), IED (Improvised Explosive Device). Lots of these words end up in non-military English through news reports and movies as well as through friends and family of military personnel. Military slang often becomes quite popular with civilians. The world of computers and technology is another rich source for these kinds of words as well. Consider *jpeg*, which Microsoft Word did not require me to capitalize!

*Morphological misanalysis*

One prolific and interesting process by which we get new vocabulary is called *morphological misanalysis*. In this process, there has been some play in dividing up a word into the root and the bound morphemes in a way that is not traditionally done. One of the best known of these is *chocoholic*, a person addicted to chocolate. Consider the original word from which this word was derived: *alcoholic*. The root word (free morpheme) is *alcohol*, which is attached to a bound morpheme *-ic* (meaning one who does this a lot). If we put the same logical process to work on *chocolate*, the addicted person should be called a *chocolatic*. For some reason, this possible word does not sound as good as *chocoholic*. For many years the word *chocoholic* stood alone, but in the last decade, the *-aholic* bound morpheme has really taken off. We now hear: *drugaholic*, *shopaholic* and *workaholic* among others. In another misanalysis, the painter of this sign has combined the words 'garden' and 'antiques' to create a new word that is easily understood by readers.

Another example of morphological misanalysis is the use of *-gate* to signify a political scandal. In the 1970s, the *Committee to Re-elect the President* (Richard Nixon) funded a break-in at the Watergate Hotel in Washington DC to bug the headquarters of the Democratic Party; thus the *Watergate* scandal was born. Since then we have had *Irancontragate* (Ronald Reagan) and, more recently, *Monicagate* (Bill Clinton). The word *gate*, previous to the Watergate scandal, was not a productive bound morpheme, nor did it carry any meaning associated with scandal. During the 2006 baseball World Series, I heard several sports announcers use the expression *Dirtgate* to refer to the accusation that Detroit pitcher Kenny Rogers had an illegal substance on his hands that enhanced his grip for pitching.

The drive for gender-neutral or reverse gender-biased words has also stimulated some new creations based on the misanalysis of the morphemes in a word. I have heard a number of people over the years use the creation *herstory* in place of *history*. The word *history* comes into English via Greek and is not the result of combining the words *his* plus *story*. I have also heard *sheroes* used in a number of contexts, including a programme on National Public Radio. Since the word *hero* is Latin in origin, the *he* in it is an accidental match with the Anglo-Saxon pronoun *he*. Most people who have uttered the word *hero* have probably not made the assumption that *he* is a significant subunit of *hero*, and that its utterance could have larger political and social ramifications for some people.

More entertaining is the case of a man in a small town in Texas who actually petitioned the city council to change the town's greeting to *heaveno*, in place of *hello* because the word *hello* contains *hell* and the devil should not be encoded in the most common of everyday greetings! It is doubtful that people saying this greeting intend this bizarre man's meaning.

Morphological misanalysis is actively used on many television shows for humorous effect. There is a hysterical episode of *The Simpsons* television series in which Homer Simpson is having a really bad day, and he is angry with and yelling at everyone. In a reflective moment, he says to himself: 'I'm a rageaholic. I'm going to have to give up rageahol.' In an episode of *That 70s Show*, the character named Hyde says to his friends, 'I have two jobs. It's like I'm a workaholic. That's not the kind of holic I thought I'd be'. Because this type of word formation process is so common in language, no one has difficulty following the characters' meaning when they invent these words. If people think they are useful terms, their usage may spread, and they may even become officially part of the language at some point in the future if their use becomes commonplace.

Definitions:
*derivation*: create new words by adding derivational morphemes to root words (snacking)
*compounding*: the joining of two free morphemes to make a new word (download)
*clipping*: cutting off part of a long word to make it shorter (laboratory → lab)
*blending*: blending parts of two words to make one (brunch)
*coinage* or *neologism*: the complete creation of a word, never before used (quark)
*reduplication*: repetition of all or part of a word, usually for intensification (super-duper)
*generification*: a company name is used for the name for the product (Kleenex, Xerox)
*onomatopoeia*: a word is created from a sound (whoosh)
*acronomy*: a word is created from the initial letters of the words in a phrase (scuba)
*morphological misanalysis*: the morphemes of a word are misanalysed and a new morpheme is attached to other roots (chocoholic, shopaholic)
*borrowing*: when a word is taken from another language (ballet)

## 5.4.2 Linguistic borrowing

English owes the wealth of its vocabulary to borrowings from other languages. Estimates of borrowed words in the lexicon of English are higher than 80 per cent, referring to words in current use that do not have an Anglo-Saxon origin. One of the reasons that this figure is so high, and maybe even higher, is that English language speakers have borrowed words from almost every group of people with whom we have been in contact. Early borrowings into Old English are discussed in detail in the chapter on the history of English. In this chapter, we'll look at more recent acquisitions.

Borrowings differ in each English variety: Australians have borrowed words from Aboriginal peoples in their country, as have Canadians, New Zealanders and Americans. Examples of these words in US English include: *caucus*, borrowed from Algonquian, *moccasin* (from Natick) and *squash* (from Massachuset). The Australians borrowed the words *billabong* (a small branch of a river), *kookaburra* (a small kingfisher bird) and *corroboree* (a party) among many other words, from the aboriginal groups they encountered when settling in the Australian *outback* (a word now commonly understood by Americans as well). English spoken in India has been enriched by borrowings from Hindi, Urdu and Marathi, as well as India's other languages, for example the noun *tamasha* which means 'a fuss', and *darshan*, a verb meaning 'to worship'. Specifically borrowed from Hindi or Urdu are the words *hawala*, which is the Indian version of a *moneygram* (a telegram that wires money to another location) and *lathicharge*, a street demonstration. These words appear frequently in online newspapers of Indian origin although they will be unfamiliar to speakers of other varieties of English.

Some English speakers in colonial territories where other European colonial groups were settling augmented their English vocabulary with borrowings from the languages of other settlers. For instance, English-speaking Canadians have borrowed Quebecois words and phrases into their variety of English, like the Quebecois term for 'happy hour'. English-speaking Canadians will say to co-workers at the end of the workday, 'Let's go for a cinq a sept' (a 5:00 to 7:00).[12] American English has borrowed hundreds of common words from early Dutch settlers (*boss*), as well as the Spanish (*rodeo*), French (*levee*) and German (*sauerkraut*) settlers in the colonies.

Some language speakers (more often governments), most notably the French and the Quebecois, are increasingly concerned with preserving the 'purity' of their languages and have created laws and academies to protect them. In both French-speaking Quebec and France itself, the governments have passed laws legislating against the use of anglicisms, in the case of France, or the use of English signage in the public domain, in Quebec. Each government has created committees whose sole task is to create French-derived words for new inventions and concepts. In Quebec, they even have a language police who go around measuring English commercial signs to make sure they are smaller than the French ones. Needless to say, you can control the public domain in areas like television broadcasting and advertising, but you can't stop normal French or Quebecois-speaking people from commonly using anglicisms like 'le weekend' and 'le sandwich' any more than you can stop the typical American from using a double negative (I ain't got no money) or saying *who* instead of *whom*. There are language critics, generally not linguists, who write books and articles about the corruption of the pure English language and how the youth of today have debased the spoken form of English so much that it is of little value. They complain about many things like the 'overuse' of *like* by young people, borrowing of 'foreign' expressions, and the use of slang. They equate language change, which is inevitable, with the moral corruption of the society. The truth is, there never was one true form of pure English. As linguist James Nicholl (1990) put it so well: 'the problem with defending the purity of the English language is that English is about as pure as a cribhouse whore. We don't just borrow words; on occasion, English has pursued other languages down alleyways to beat them unconscious and rifle their pockets for new vocabulary.' This is part of the vitality of English: our fascination and acceptance of new ideas and words that we make part of our language and culture.

## 5.5 The dictionary

*Dictionary, n. A malevolent literary device for cramping the growth of a language and making it hard and inelastic.* Ambrose Bierce, *The Devil's Dictionary*, 1911.

The words of a language are made available to individuals through their experiences, but the meanings and connotations of these words are codified through the publication and use of dictionaries. Many people view dictionaries as the one true source of knowledge on a word's meaning and use. However, most people are unaware of how dictionaries are created and how their makers decide what a word means or even if something may be classified as a word. Currently, dictionaries are the work of committees who periodically meet to update long-existing previous versions. If we go back in time though, we find that the first dictionaries were monumental works created by people labouring under quite difficult circumstances with little in the way of technology to speed up their efforts.

The first full dictionary of English, as spoken in England, was completed in 1746. Samuel Johnson, a well-known writer and grammarian, was selected by the Royal Society (a group which will be discussed in detail in the chapter on the history of English) to create a dictionary to provide a norm for spelling and usage. Johnson hired half a dozen assistants to help him compile all the words of English and to write meanings for them. Of these men, most were actually speakers of Scots English and one was a convicted felon (hence the jokes about how punishing the work of writing a dictionary could be). The work took almost a decade to complete and two of the assistants did not live to see its publication. A decade sounds like a long time, but the French Academy, with many more lexicographers dedicated to the task, took over 40 years to produce the first complete dictionary of the French language.

Johnson and his assistants filled over 80 large notebooks with what they learned about the vocabulary of English. Their final work contains over 40,000 words and definitions. Unlike modern dictionaries, Johnson's did not include a pronunciation guide. He recognized that there was wide variation in pronunciation across Britain and was not interested in normalizing pronunciation in the same way that he would end up normalizing spelling. Many of the definitions he wrote reflected Johnson's sense of humour:

> Oats: A grain which is fed to horses in England and to people in Scotland.
> Lexicographer: a writer of dictionaries, a harmless drudge.

Two things make Johnson and his dictionary very interesting. One is his attitude to language use, and the second is concerned with who is the appropriate source of knowledge concerning a word's meaning and usage. He was not interested in being a prescriptivist, someone who decides for the masses how they should speak and write. Johnson was more interested in describing the English language as spoken by all of its users – not just the educated elite. Unlike some of his contemporaries, Johnson did not believe that the creation of the dictionary would halt language change. That was not his goal. He was interested in spreading knowledge about English and helping to normalize spelling and usage. Sometimes his diverse spelling selections for related words seem a little arbitrary; however, his philosophy on spelling was to choose the form that seemed most popular to him. He did not see it as his job to create a systematic set of rules and change popular spellings to fit a pattern, thus he too contributed to the erratic nature of English spelling. Current English spelling is even more mismatched with its pronunciation than in Johnson's day because his dictionary served to more or less freeze the spelling of English when the pronunciation of the language was still in great flux. Thus, spellings that would have made more sense during his time do not necessarily do so today.

## 5.5.1 New dictionary words

Current dictionaries are revisions of previous ones. No one starts out with a blank computer screen and starts collecting words and meanings. Words are added to or removed from new dictionaries; definitions are modified; and both the connotations of words and their official status changes. Words are classified in the dictionary by how the editors interpret their usage. A word may be labelled *archaic*, but remain in the dictionary because the editors are well aware that the word commonly appears in the writings of commonly read authors of earlier varieties of English. Dictionaries also include words that are particular to a certain region of the country. For instance, one *regionalism* found in the online version of the American

Heritage Dictionary is *gum band*, a word used in and around Pennsylvania to refer to what is more commonly known in the rest of the US as a *rubber band*.

When new words enter the dictionary, they may be labelled as regionalisms, slang, or listed as new technical or scientific terms. In 2004, both the *Oxford English Dictionary* and *Merriam-Webster's Collegiate Dictionary* added new words to their pages as they do with every new edition. The editors of a dictionary come from many backgrounds. They are not required to be teachers, nor linguists, nor English scholars, nor great writers (nor do they necessarily need to be!) but these unelected wordsmiths make decisions about how people should use the words they find in the dictionary. I thought it would be fun to present some of these new words to my undergraduate students to see how many of these words had gained currency. Some seemed to be excellent additions for a US dictionary, like *road rage*, *tree-hugger* and *chick-flick*, though it is interesting that only the last two are hyphenated. Others, like *bling-bling*, seem too new to guarantee that they'd survive their current popular usage, and my students commented that *bling-bling* has already been reduced to *bling*, which I have noted on some television shows as well. Other words added to the dictionary were completely unknown to everyone I spoke to: *anoraky*, defined as 'socially inept and studious or obsessive, with unfashionable and largely solitary interests'. The choices made by these committees are in a certain sense arbitrary in that a large group of people does not vote on them, nor are they required to show that the word has appeared a certain number of times to qualify as a new word. Is this a problem? Not really. The written language is often out of sync with the spoken one and a new word may survive or die despite its status in any dictionary. As I said earlier in this chapter, it is pretty much a mystery why millions of people still say *cool* when they like something but *groovy*, despite the Austin Powers movies, has passed on in the US and remains mostly in the memories of those who were young in the 1960s.

All languages change over time, but it is in their vocabulary where these changes are the most obvious. The native speakers of any language, especially the young speakers, constantly play with their language, inventing new combinations of free and bound morphemes, creating new words and changing the meanings of words already in use. Because all native speakers understand morphological processes, when someone creates a new word on the spot, like *workaholic*, everyone understands it. Just like for every past generation, the words being created by the youth today will either become part and parcel of English or will disappear as the next generation takes over the language.

# Suggested reading

Adams, M. (2001), 'Infixing and interposing in English: a new direction'. *American Speech*, 76.3, 327–31.

Harley, H. (2006), *English Words: A Linguistic Introduction*. Oxford: Blackwell.

Lakoff, G. (1990), *Women, Fire and Dangerous Things: What Categories Reveal about the Mind*. Chicago: University of Chicago Press.

# Interesting websites

American Dialect Society: Words of the Year: www.americandialect.org/index.php/amerdial/categories/C178/

English slang and colloquialisms used in the United Kingdom: www.peevish.co.uk/slang/

# Consider the following questions

1. For the following words, identify the number of morphemes in each, and if there is an affix or more than one, tell if it is derivational or inflectional and define what function that affix performs.

unhappily   inevitable   Susan's   governmental   news
repeatedly   photography   remembers   recommendations   phonological

2. Two words in the group have a different morphological structure than the others. One has a different type of bound morpheme, and one has no bound morpheme at all.

teacher   taller   sliver   actor

3. Derivational Prefix = NOT
There are many ways to add the idea of NOT at the beginning of adjectives in English:

unhappy   disincentive   illogical   inoffensive

Some of these are pronounced in ways that reflect a phonological pattern. Figure out the pattern from the following words and write a rule/rules to explain the pattern.

impermeable   incorrect   illogical   impossible   illegal
indivisible   immovable   incalculable   innumerable   incorrigible

# Notes

1   *The Story of English* (2002) by Robert McCrum, William Cran and Robert MacNeil. Penguin Books, New York.

2   John: What is up? Bill: Nothing. John: Did you eat yet? Bill: No, did you? John: No, do you want to?

3   dis- can also have the meaning of 'to undo', as in to disassemble or to dismember something.

4   From *Contemporary Linguistics* (2001) by William O'Grady, John Archibald, Mark Arnoff, Janie Rees-Miller. Bedford St Martins.

5   Adams, Michael. 'Infixing and Interposing in English: A New Direction' (2001). *American Speech*, 327–31.

6   www.neuticles.com/index1.html

7   schadenfreude – a spiteful pleasure gained from other people's troubles.

8   SPAM is short for 'spiced ham'.

9   www.usiia.org/pubs/spam.htm

10  Georg Simon Ohm and James Watts.

11  Or a more obscene word as reported by some.

12  For more on Canadian language, the website www.cbc.ca/cestlavie/ has a 'word of the week' and looks at Canadian language.

# 6 Grammar

## Chapter Overview

| | | |
|---|---|---|
| 6.1 | TRADITIONAL GRAMMAR | 108 |
| 6.2 | LANGUAGE WORD ORDERS | 110 |
| 6.3 | PHRASE STRUCTURE GRAMMARS | 111 |
| | 6.3.1 ADVANTAGES OF A PHRASE STRUCTURE GRAMMAR | 113 |
| | 6.3.2 DETERMINING PHRASE STRUCTURE GRAMMAR RULES | 113 |
| | 6.3.3 OTHER ASPECTS OF GRAMMAR | 128 |

Most students dread the thought of studying grammar in either their native or foreign language. This is frequently the case because traditional grammar classes often consist of endless memorization of unfamiliar vocabulary to refer to things we use every day and for which we have never felt a need to have a label. Grammar is such a staple of the US school system that older Americans even refer to elementary school as grammar school! In addition, many teachers still resort to the dry exercise of diagramming sentences to get students to overtly understand the complex rules of the language that, as native speakers, they already know intuitively. It all seems kind of pointless to most students. The other goal of traditional grammar classes, especially in the teenage years, is to weed out all the 'deviations' in each student's speech so that everyone will know the 'proper' way to speak and write. Unfortunately, this has the negative result of making most students hate what can be an insight into something they do every day, and second, it misses giving them an appreciation of how varieties of the same language differ systematically.

For linguists, grammar includes all the systematic structures of language. The grammar that we hear about in school is concerned with making sure students learn the correct way to combine the parts of speech of our language. Linguists call this *prescriptive grammar*, because as a doctor prescribes medicine to cure your ills, the teacher, or grammar book, prescribes rules that tell you what you should do to 'fix' your natural way of speaking and writing to fit the official rules of the language (like not to end a sentence with a preposition). Linguists are interested in understanding how the natural grammars of languages are structured, including how the sound system of a language works and how people combine sounds and words into phrases that are meaningful for them. *Syntax* is the branch of linguistics that is concerned with the principles by which the phrases and words of a language are combined to make sentences. By studying the sentences of a language, syntacticians are able to create a finite set of rules for illustrating the patterns of a language.

Although most people claim that they do not know very much about syntax, the reverse is quite true. The very fact that people successfully communicate with others quite naturally all day long is proof that they do know a great deal about the structures of the languages that they speak. That is not to say that they can name all the parts of speech using proper terms, nor list all the rules of English, but all humans know the syntax of their language just the same. We know that speakers intuitively know the syntax of their language because every day they create long and complex sentences that they have never heard or produced before, and they understand the same types of sentences spoken by others without difficulty.

Native speakers of any language are capable of making grammatical judgements about their language even if they have never had a linguistics class. If someone asks an English speaker if the following sentence is grammatical: 'car the parked is the in front of school', no native speaker would say 'yes'. They would say that the words are in a funny order. However, if the same person said: 'The blonde tall girl is happy', the native speaker would probably be a bit less sure of the answer because although the sentence does not sound quite right, the problem is much more subtle. Hardly anybody, including English teachers, can list the complex rules for the ordering of adjectives in English (or Mongolian, if you are learning it); nevertheless, speakers do it correctly every time they produce a noun phrase that has more than one adjective. These rules are ingrained in our mental grammar even though we are unaware of them.

When you know a language, your *native speaker intuition* tells you whether a sentence is grammatical or ungrammatical. This intuition is based on the set of syntactic rules for your language that specify which arrangements of words and phrases can be combined into sentences and which cannot. As a native speaker of a language, you have this knowledge mostly without being aware of it. You may have been taught artificial rules like when to use *whom*, and not to end a sentence with a preposition (though I bet you do it anyway!), but no one taught you the adjective order rule or the multitude of other grammar rules that you use correctly every single day. Does that mean everything we say is grammatical?

Even with native speaker intuition, every utterance from your mouth is not necessarily perfect. Even though you have the rules embedded in your brain, your output can be affected by stress, fatigue, alcohol or excitement. Our performance does not always measure up to our ability. Furthermore, any normal conversation between two or more people is not a string of uninterrupted grammatically correct sentences. At your next family gathering or any gathering of close friends, listen carefully to the conversations around you, and you will note that a great number of the sentences are not fully formed, or the speaker changes direction in the middle of a thought, or entire chunks of a sentence may be missing because good friends and family often talk in sentence fragments and code and rarely pay attention to the niceties of formal written language. Nor should we. This does not mean that we lack a systematic language structure. Sometimes the 'errors' are just dialectal differences that reflect different linguistic customs, as in the following sign in which standard English 'hidden' is replaced by the locally accepted 'hid', that is, local to Tennessee hill country. Dialectal variation is also alive and well despite globalization, universal education and the relative sameness of television news announcers.

Our normal speech is also affected by many other factors including our age, social class, geographic location, race or ethnicity, as well as the particular social circumstance of each conversation. Most of us speak quite differently at a backyard barbecue with close friends than at a formal business meeting or job interview. Nevertheless, the vast majority of the syntactic structures of English are remarkably similar across dialects. In this chapter, we'll be looking at the major features of English syntax; in later chapters, we'll address dialectal variation.

The focus will also be on normal spoken English. In formal writing, each sentence, at least according to our English teachers, must be able to stand on its own grammatically. Spoken language, however, is more like a call and response system. Because you are involved in a dialogue, the other participants may be filling in some of the missing bits. If someone asks you, 'Where did you go with Christopher last night?' a likely, yet officially ungrammatical response is 'to the Kung Fu festival'. You are less likely to answer, 'Last night Christopher and I went to the Kung Fu festival'.

Grammaticality also depends on other factors. Consider whether or not the following sentence is grammatical:

Bush thinks bananas.

At first glance, most would reply that this is not grammatical. Some might say that it is not because it is missing the word 'about'; others may give a more complex answer and say that it is not because the verb 'think' must be followed with an adverb like 'often' or a prepositional phrase like 'about bananas'. However, would this be a grammatical response to the question 'What fruit does Laura like?' Clearly, the grammaticality of an utterance must be judged within the context in which it is stated.

## 6.1 Traditional grammar

Most people remember, maybe with dread, learning at school the traditional definitions for the parts of speech. A *noun* is a person, place or thing. A *verb* is the action of the sentence. An *adjective* modifies a noun. An *adverb* modifies an adjective or a verb. Other parts of speech are a little more complicated because they are often more about function rather than meaning. Try describing to an international learner of English the purpose of articles (a, an, the) and demonstratives (this, that, these, those). Or worse yet, explain why you get married 'to' someone rather than 'with' someone. What do prepositions really do?

The disadvantage to the traditional system is that it is purely descriptive. You can take the words of a sentence that has been written or said and tell what part of speech each word represents. If I ask what part of speech the word *running* is, most will reply, 'a verb'. However, think about the following sentences:

1) Peg is *running* away from home.
2) *Running* is fun.
3) Bob loves *running*.
4) *Running* water stays cool.

Only in the first sentence is *running* a verb. In 2), *running* is the subject of the sentence; thus, it is a noun (a gerund). *Running* answers the question: What is fun? In 3) *running* is the object of the sentence, again a noun (gerund). And in the final example, it is an adjective describing what kind of water it is. There are thousands of words like this in every language that change part of speech depending on how they are used in a sentence. So, simply saying that *running* can be a noun, verb or an adjective is overly general information. Take a look at the use of the word 'safe', most frequently used as an adjective, on the instructions on the side of this military aeroplane:

Another way to describe the parts of speech is to describe what prefixes or suffixes categories of words can take. For example, nouns combine with a variety of -s endings to make words plural or possessive:

> computers (plural)
> computer's (possessive)
> computers' (plural possessive)

English adjectives can combine with only two endings that are used in making comparisons:

> shorter (comparative)        shortest (superlative)

Verbs combine with a variety of suffixes in English. Other languages, like the Romance languages (Spanish and Rumanian, for example), have dozens of verb endings. In the Niger-Congo languages of West Africa, verbs combine with many prefixes. English, however, only has three possibilities, all of which are suffixes:

> talks (3rd person singular, -s)
> talked (past tense, -ed)
> talking (progressive/present participle, -ing)

There certainly are many exceptions to these combinations (we'll learn why English is like this in the chapter on its history). These exceptions really frustrate international learners of English. They have to learn that the plural of *man* is not *mans* (even though the plural of *human* is *humans*). They learn that the comparative form of *good* is not *gooder*, nor is the superlative form *goodest*. There are thousands of words in English that do not take the regular endings of their particular class. One of my ESL students pointed out that there really were not that many past tense verbs that end in *-ed*, so maybe we should call *-ed* verbs, like *walked*, the irregular ones!

Describing a system based on accepted endings certainly provides us with more description than simply saying a noun is a person, place or thing, but it does nothing to enhance the definitions of other parts of speech like conjunctions, prepositions and articles that take no endings. The most important limitation of this system, however, is that it does nothing to specify in what combinations these words can be arranged to form phrases or sentences. The syntax of a language does just that.

## 6.2 Language word orders

Modern English is an SVO language (meaning in most sentences, the *subject* comes first, then the *verb*, and the *object* is somewhere near the end of the sentence). Some sentences deviate from this, but they are marked in special ways by changes in the grammar. This is not the only possible word order, nor is it the most common. More of the world's languages are SOV languages, though the total number of their speakers is less than that for SVO languages. In fact, Old English was an SOV language (see Chapter 9 for more discussion). Currently, all of the Romance languages like Spanish and Italian and most of the Germanic languages like Dutch and Frisian are SVO languages. People use SVO languages throughout Africa including the Bantu languages like Kiswahili, which is widely spoken all over East Africa with more than 800,000 speakers. Vietnamese is SVO as well as the South American Amerindian language Guarani. SVO languages exist on every continent where there are people.

SOV languages are also quite common and are spread through the world. They include Farsi (Persian, from Iran), Turkish, Hungarian, Korean, Japanese and Hindi. VSO languages are also not uncommon. Celtic languages like Welsh and Irish are VSO as well as Hawaiian and Nahuatl (Aztec). Nahuatl is still spoken as a minority language in Mexico and Central America.

The remaining word orders for languages, VOS, OSV and OVS, are much less common, though there are millions of speakers who daily use these orders. The distribution of speakers is quite broad though some of the languages only have a few hundred speakers left and are at risk of becoming extinct. There are others, however, that are quite stable.

| Word Order | Language Name | Country(ies) | Number of Speakers |
|---|---|---|---|
| VOS | Tumbalá | Mexico, Guatemala | 30,000 |
| VOS | Kiribati | Fiji | 58,000 |
| VOS | Malagasy | Madagascar | 2,606,000 |
| VOS | Bushi | Madagascar | 767,000 |
| OSV | Apuriña | Brazil | 2,000 |
| OSV | Kemak | Timor Islands | 50,000 |
| OSV | Xavánte | Brazil | 10,000 |
| OVS | Macushi | Brazil | 15,000 |
| OVS | Huarijio | Mexico | 5,000 |
| OVS | Guapuyngu | Australia | 450 |

These word orders are all the combinations possible. There are, however, some highly inflected languages that have a free or fairly free word order, like Latin and Dyirbal. In Latin, this is possible because all the nouns in Latin sentences are grammatically marked to indicate whether they are the subject of the sentence or some class of object, so it does not matter in what order the words appear. Both of the following sentences translate as 'The dog bit the boy', The word for *boy* in Latin is marked for accusative case (the direct object) by the suffix *-um*, so it does not matter where in the sentence the word appears; we know it is the *boy* that got bit and not the *dog*.

Canis mordit puerum.
Puerum mordit canis.

## 6.3 Phrase structure grammars

All of these types of languages have been systematically represented by a set of algorithms called a phrase structure grammar or a generative grammar. From a finite set of rules, based on phrases, all the grammatical sentences of a language can be generated.

Syntactic structure is both linear and hierarchical, as we'll see from the tree diagrams below. Linear means that the placement of words in a certain order is significant for a sentence to be grammatical and to convey the meaning the speaker intends. In the sentence, 'John ate the tacos', the word order is significant. You cannot say, 'the ate John tacos' because this is not an acceptable word order for English. You can rearrange the words to, 'The tacos ate John', but this is a problem for meaning in that it expresses a completely different meaning from the original sentence. When I say the structure of a sentence is hierarchical, it means that certain groups of words in the sentence are meant to be viewed as a coherent unit, both in structure and meaning. Consider the sentence, 'The very naughty children were sent to bed without their dinner'. There are a number of units that logically go together: 'the very naughty children, were sent to bed, without their dinner'. These are phrases of the sentence. Thus a phrase, also called a constituent, is a word or a set of words that behave as a grammatical unit. Take the following sentence:

The dog bit the man on the leg after the fight.

There are lots of ways to divide this up. First, you could divide a sentence up like you did in high school English classes into *subject* and *predicate*:

| The dog | bit the man on the leg after the fight. |
|---------|------------------------------------------|
| subject | predicate                                |

This is a pretty natural division. I doubt anyone would divide it in the following way:

> The dog bit the          man on the          leg after the fight.

This is native speaker intuition at work again. The two main phrases of the sentence, the subject and the predicate, linguists call a noun phrase (NP) and a verb phrase (VP).

The VP can be divided up into smaller phrases. First, you can see a number of other NPs in the sentence: *the man, the leg* and *the fight*. Then, we have the words *on* and *after* to describe. Traditional grammar tells us that these are prepositions. In this sentence, they tell us *when* something happened and *where*. Prepositions are at the head of prepositional phrases (PP). Thus, just from this simple sentence, we've figured out some of the pieces of the English grammar puzzle: A sentence has a subject noun phrase and a verb phrase, and a VP can have prepositional phrases, and PPs all have NPs. This is how syntacticians go about determining the phrasal patterns of their languages: they simply look at many different types of sentences and describe the patterns they see.

Other than our sense that these words go together naturally (our native speaker intuition), there is other evidence or tests that show that phrases are real. One such test is the substitution test. A single word, like a pronoun, can substitute for a phrase. Let's go back to our sample sentence: The dog bit the man on the leg after the fight.

*The dog*, an NP, can be replaced by *it*.

> *It* bit the man on the leg after the fight.

The NP, *the man*, can be replaced by *him*.

> The dog bit *him* on the leg after the fight

The PP, *on the leg*, can be replaced by *there*.

> The dog bit him *there* after the fight.

Furthermore, phrases can sometimes be moved, as a unit, to a different part of the sentence. This is called the movement test.

> After the fight, the dog bit the man on the leg.

Phrases can also be answers to questions asked (aptly named the stand-alone test):

> Who bit the man?          the dog.
> Where was the man bitten?          on the leg.
> When was the man bitten?          after the fight.
> Who did the dog bite?          the man.

Finally, some phrases can be joined by conjunctions like *and*, *or*, *but*, *nor* and others:

The dog bit the man *on the leg* and *on the arm* after the fight.

## 6.3.1 Advantages of a phrase structure grammar

The ability to describe how phrases combine to make sentences in a language has many advantages over traditional descriptions of grammar because a set of algorithms (a phrase structure grammar) could be used to generate all the grammatical sentences of a language, not just describe them after they are uttered. This is significant for artificial intelligence and machine translation because computers operate on algorithms. It is also significant for explaining the ease with which human toddlers acquire such a complex grammatical system. Chomsky proposed the language acquisition device that was guided by universal grammar (UG) as the means by which all children acquire their first language. If this is accurate, there must be a set of mathematical-like algorithms that the brain uses that could generate all the possible sentences of a language. This is easy to test. If you take any page of a book and write down all the sentences on it and study their structure, you will be able to note many of the most common patterns of the language. Phrase structure rules capture generalities about how phrases combine. This is much more efficient and easier to learn than a system that would call for a rule for how every individual word combines with every other word, requiring an infinite number of rules making a language quite difficult to learn!

## 6.3.2 Determining phrase structure grammar rules

We learned previously in the chapter, and already knew from our native-speaker intuition, that every sentence in English must have a subject NP and a VP. To set up our algorithm to generate sentences, we need to start with a master rule that specifies the mandatory features of a sentence. Our first phrase structure rule needs to specify that a sentence is minimally composed of a noun phrase and a verb phrase (the subject and the predicate). Here is the notation to represent the rule:

S → NP VP

Only one type of sentence seems to violate this rule and that is imperatives (commands), for example, *Shut this book right now!* In this sentence, there does not appear to be a subject; however, all native speakers understand that the subject is *you*; it just happens to be null in command sentences.

The above sentence rule only gives us the most general specifications for a spoken sentence. We still need to figure out all the possible phrases and create rules that cover all of the details. This sounds more complicated than it really is. All we need to do is figure out all the possible phrase and sentence patterns.

### Phrases and heads

There is a pattern to how heads combine with other words in the phrase. Each head may be modified by a specifier, as a noun can be modified by a word like 'the', which in English always comes before the noun and never after it. The same is true for the other phrases and heads:

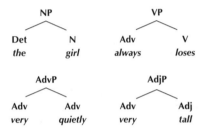

Each head, in English, may also be followed by one or more complements depending on what is possible for each particular head. The complement is another phrase that may be embedded within the first phrase. In the tree below, you can see that the prepositional phrase, 'on subjects', is modifying the NP 'tests'.

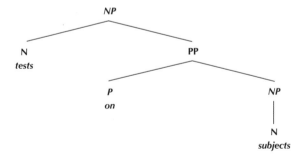

The phrase structure rules specify which phrases take complements and which do not.

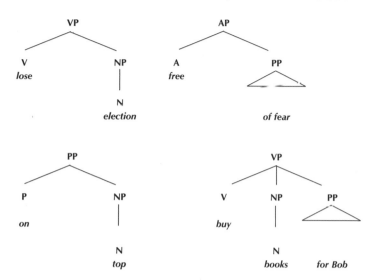

## The noun phrase

The phrase structure rules of a language are the rules that these trees are generated from. They are, however, just a representation for what it is that every human speaker knows about the combination of phrases into sentences in his or her language. The rules give us a written representation that expresses what order the words in a phrase have and the order of phrases in a sentence as well. They also specify which categories are mandatory in creating a sentence or a phrase and which are not. For example, a noun phrase may be preceded by a determiner[1] and may also be accompanied by a PP and an AdjP, though neither is mandatory. How can we figure this out? First, make a list of the possible combinations that you can think of:

> Jessica (N)
> I (PN)
> the girl (Det, N)
> the clever girl (Det, Adj, N)
> the very clever girl (Det, Adv, Adj, N)
> the very clever girl in California (Det, Adv, Adj, N, PP)

From this list of phrases, all of which are headed by a noun, we can see that a noun may stand alone (Jessica), may be accompanied by a determiner (the girl), or a determiner and an adjective (the clever girl) or it may have a determiner, an adverb and an adjective precede it (the very clever girl). A noun phrase may also be headed by a pronoun (I), but that is just a different type of noun. In the final example above, the NP even includes a prepositional phrase. We can write a rule to specify what constitutes an NP based on this limited information:

$$NP \rightarrow (Det)\ (AdjP) \left\{ \begin{array}{c} N \\ PN \end{array} \right\} (PP)$$

A brief explanation of the notation is needed here. The brackets around the N (noun) and PN (pronoun) indicate that at least one of these must occur in every NP. The parentheses in the above rule indicate that these phrases and parts of speech *can* occur in a NP but are not obligatory. In an NP, the only obligatory element is the noun or pronoun (the head) as illustrated by the NPs in the following sentence:

*I* ate *tacos.*

Native speakers also know that more than one of these elements can be repeated in a single phrase but not all of them. Any native speaker can tell you that it is possible to say: *The very very hot tacos* (two adverbs) or *The large hot tacos* (two adjectives), but not *The the very hot tacos* (two determiners). In English, it is ungrammatical to have two consecutive determiners in a single noun phrase. For our phrase structure rules to work, we must be able to indicate this. A simple superscripted notation asterisk is used (*) to indicate that an element may be repeated:

$$NP \rightarrow (Det)\ (AdjP^*) \left\{ \begin{array}{c} N \\ PN \end{array} \right\} (PP^*)$$

This rule now allows us to generate phrases like *the very very big grey elephant in a bikini on the desk in my office.* The rule allows that each noun may be accompanied by multiple adjectives, adverbs and prepositional phrases. Frankly, there is no longest noun phrase or sentence in terms of grammar – though there certainly is in terms of our ability to produce a very long one or our patience to listen to one. Little children love to make sentences like:

There is a big big big big big big big big big big big big monster under my bed!

Nevertheless, most noun phrases generated in normal conversations do not have this quantity of repetition. Many are quite simple like the ones in the following tree diagrams:

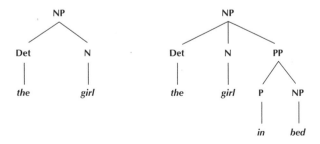

*The prepositional phrase*

In our NP rule, we specified a PP, but we have not as yet described what can occur in a prepositional phrase. In the sentence right above, *in bed* is a PP. A PP must have a preposition like *at, in* or *on*. If you can't remember what a preposition is one of the students in my English syntax class told me a pretty good trick that gets most of them: a preposition is anything you can do with an aeroplane. This definition actually works pretty well. An aeroplane can land *on* the tarmac. Planes can fly *by* or *over* a building or sadly go *under* the sea. They can be parked *in* the hangar, *behind* it or *beside* it. All of these prepositions are locative propositions because they indicate the location of a noun. Prepositions also serve to introduce NPs in other ways. We get married *to* someone. We bet money *on* the team *of* our choice. We buy gifts *for* our mothers *on* their birthdays *with* our credit cards. The grammatical function of prepositions is much harder to explain. Note that in each one of the phrases above, the preposition is followed by a mandatory noun phrase. So the basic PP rule is really quite simple: PP → P NP.

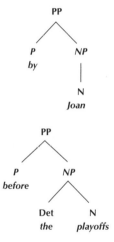

A prepositional phrase may be part of a VP, NP or AdjP. In English, all prepositional phrases must have a NP as a complement. We know that NPs also have an optional PP specified in their rule. This is a property we call recursion. Recursion is an important aspect of our set of rules because for a finite set of rules to be able to produce an infinite number of sentences there must be mechanisms that provide for the embedding of one phrase structure within another. Because an NP and a PP can each generate the other, we can create phrases like: 'the girl with the kitten in a cage':

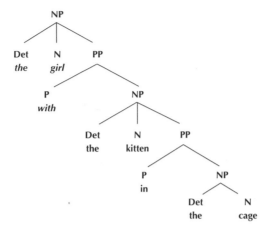

Infinity can also be achieved by using 'that clauses' or conjunctions (*and*, *or*, *but*), which also can be used to embed phrases and clauses within a sentence.

> I bought a car that needed new tyres that had too many miles on it, that cost too much and that was not worth the money I paid for it.

A wonderful example of the use of conjunctions to increase the length of an utterance are old folk songs in which each verse is longer than the first by the addition of another line following a conjunction. Here is the final verse of a song called 'When I first came to this land':

> When I first came to this land, I was not a wealthy man,
> so I got myself a son, and I did what I could. And I called my son, my work's done,
> and I called my wife, run for your life, and I called my horse, lame of course.
> and I called my farm, muscle in my arm, and I called my duck, out of luck.
> and I called my cow, no milk now, and I called my shack, break my back.
> But the land was sweet and good, and I did what I could.

Another grammatical category that many people confuse with prepositions is particles. English, like other Germanic languages, has a large number of two-word verbs (called phrasal verbs) that look like a verb and a preposition, but in reality are a verb and a particle. In the case of phrasal verbs, the particle is grammatically and semantically connected to the VP whereas the preposition is directly tied to the NP that follows it. Here is an example that will clarify the difference:

> The boy *called up* his mother.
> The boy called *up the stairs*.

In the first example, the phrase *called up* is a synonym for *telephoned*. In the second, the word *up* describes the direction of the shouting: from downstairs to upstairs. There are hundreds of verbs like this in English including:

**Verb + out:**   go out, break out, punch out, figure out, run out, turn out, strike out, pass out, flow out, tire out, knock out, work out, stand out, act out, black out, put out, come out, hand out, wear out, take out, burn out, look out, go out

**Verb + down:**   put down, keep down, go down, turn down, break down, cut down on, run down, back down, get down, burn down, strike down, play down, stand down, knock down

**Verb + up:**   give up, put up, take up, string up, buy up, play up, throw up, keep up, back up, cut up, turn up, burn up, look up, make up, break up, get up, knock up, work up, act up, punch up

You can come up with hundreds more examples with *over, on, by,* etc. These have to be dealt with differently from prepositions because they clearly are part of the VP and not the PP.

## The adjective phrase

In English, adjective phrases may be modified by a degree specifier like an adverb, and they may also be followed by a PP as a complement.

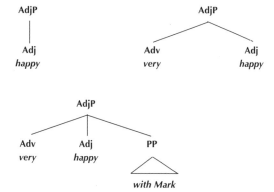

## The verb phrase

With our simplified phrase structure grammar, we are only going to deal with simple one-word verbs as the heads of phrases. The verb phrase (the predicate) is the most complicated set of phrase structure rules to write. Consider the following sentence:

Bob built the deck with scrap lumber this afternoon for his daughter.

The subject NP is simply *Bob*; the rest of the sentence is the VP. There are a number of phrases within the VP that we can identify including four NPs: *the deck, his daughter, this afternoon* and *scrap lumber*. There are also two prepositional phrases: *for his daughter* and *with scrap lumber*. So far the VP rule we need to describe all these phrases is:

VP → V (NP) (PP*)

Since we have already described all the elements of the NP in the NP rule, we don't need to specify them again in the VP. It is sufficient just to list NP as one of the constituents of the VP. However, we can add other words to a verb phrase that will require that we add more elements to the VP rule:

She worked *very quickly*.

*Quickly* is an adverb describing how she ran, and *very* is another adverb intensifying the adverb *quickly*, thus, with our addition, our rule changes to:

VP → V (NP) (PP*) (Adv*)

A sentence can have more than one consecutive NP, so the rule needs to expand again, which will generate sentences like *Bill bought his friend dinner.*

VP → V (NP*) (PP*) (Adv*)

There is one last frequent element that can appear in a VP: an adjective. They commonly follow linking verbs like *feel*, *touch* and *seem* as well as transitional verbs like *become*.

The students seem *frustrated* with the PSG rules.
The workers became *tired* after so much lifting.

These additions result in a final modification of our VP rule:

VP → V (NP*) (AdjP*) (PP*) (AdvP*)

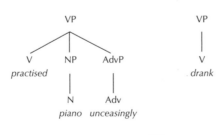

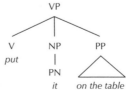

*The adverb phrase*

An adverb phrase may contain solely an adverb or the head may be modified by another adverb that will precede it.

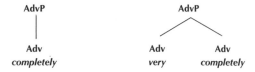

Sometimes an adverb phrase or a prepositional phrase will modify a verb.

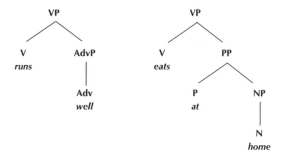

*Tense and aspect*

*Tense* tells when the action of the sentence takes place. Tense in English is pretty simplistic compared to many of the world's languages in that we have only three tenses and only one of them is represented through grammatical inflection. The present tense in English is unmarked in terms of tense (walk), though we mark third person singular with -s (walks). The past is marked with -ed suffix (walked) for regular verbs. We'll get to the future below.

The concept of tense is all a bit fuzzy when you consider what types of sentences the present tense is used to cover. The present tense can be used to describe a habitual action as in:

I always walk to school.

It is also used when stating many simple facts and general truths about the world.

Brittany is not really a blonde.
The world is round.

It can even be used to indicate a future event when we combine it with the right adverb or prepositional phrase functioning as an adverbial.

> Rick leaves the airport in an hour.                Rick leaves the airport soon.

The future in English is never marked grammatically, but always lexically as in the example on the right above. There are two other ways to make a future sentence: 1) use a present progressive sentence and add an adverb of time (I *am going* to Sydney *tomorrow*) or 2) use the modal auxiliary *will* plus the simple form of a verb[2] (I *will go* to Sydney tomorrow). Modal auxiliaries like *will* operate differently from verbs. Take a look at what happens when we change the subject of the previous two examples to 'he':

> He is going to Sydney tomorrow.
> He will go to Sydney tomorrow.

Note that following a modal like *will*, the third person form of the verb does not get an -s ending as it would if it were a verb. Neither of the following sentences is correct:

> *He wills go to Sydney tomorrow.
> *He will goes to Sydney tomorrow.

The tense system is really very easy for international learners of English to master. Other languages have much more complex systems. Some, like Spanish and French, have dozens of endings that you have to learn for all the tenses that reflect first, second and third persons both singular and plural. If you have taken these languages (and other similar ones), you probably spent a good deal of time memorizing all the possible endings. Other languages also have different ways of dividing up the timeline. They may have one tense and a set of endings that refer to the recent past and a full other set of endings for the *remote past* like Italian, or the Bantu language ChiBemba (which also has a *remote future* tense for things that will happen in the distant future rather than the near future).

Along with tense, sentences in English may have aspect as well. The aspect of a sentence describes how the activity of a verb unfolded, for example, has the action been completed or is it ongoing (in progress). In English, the perfect aspect is formed through the use of *have*, used as an auxiliary verb combined with the main verb in the past participle form:

> The pianist *has performed* the concerto.

From this utterance, we know that the action was completed in the past at some unspecified point up until this moment in time. This tense is actually called the *present perfect* because the present form of the verb *have* indicates present tense. The *past perfect* uses the past tense of *have* (had):

The pianist *had performed* the concerto before last week's performance.

In this case, the activity of performing was completed before some other activity that happened in the past. The other aspect very commonly used in English is the *progressive* aspect (sometimes called *continuous* aspect in ESL textbooks). This grammatical formula is used to stress the duration of an activity or to show that it is ongoing. It is formed through the use of the 'be' verb, as an auxiliary, with the present participle (the *-ing* form of the verb):

Jenny *is studying* electrical engineering at the university.

This verbal structure tells us that she is not done yet with the act of studying. We know that this is the *present progressive* because the helping verb 'be' is in the present tense. Past progressive is also possible in English:

Jenny *was studying* electrical engineering before she shifted to nuclear physics.

It is also possible to combine aspects in the present, past and future to create differences in meaning:

I am studying pharmacology.
(action taking place now)
I will have studied by the time you get home tonight.
(action completed before some time in the future)
I will have been studying for almost three hours by the time you arrive.
(action will have been under way for some time before another happens)
I was studying last night.
(ongoing action)
I have been studying pharmacology for almost three years.
(ongoing action for a period of time up until now)
I had been studying for almost an hour when you arrived.
(duration stressed of action that happened before another in time)

Tense and aspect are sentence-level phenomena in that these auxiliaries set the time and the unfolding of the activity of the entire sentence. Therefore, we must add a couple of features to our PSG rules to account for them. First, we need to include both tense and aspect in the sentence rule:

S → NP AUX VP

Then we need to specify what elements are part of the auxiliary (AUX). We need to be able to specify the features of tense (present, past, future) and the perfective aspect (represented by *-ed*) and the progressive aspect (represented by *-ing*).

AUX → T (perf) (prog)

ny readers have already figured out that there are still a number of ence patterns that we have not described above. The goal of this chapter is not to give you a full course in English syntax but to give you a brief insight into how a generative grammar of English works. Thus, we are not going to create a complete PSG system in this chapter. Here is the sum of the rules:

> S → NP AUX VP
> AUX → T (perf) (prog)    *aux → T (m) (perf) (prog)*
>
> NP → (Det) (AdjP)* { N / PN } (PP)
>
>                     *perf → have + en*
> VP → V (NP*) (AdjP*) (PP*) (AdvP*)    *prog → be + ing*
> PP → P NP                              *T → { pres / past }*
> AdjP → (Adv) Adj
>
>         *m = modal*
>         *\* = can be repeated*

### Tree diagrams

The PSG rules provide us with a way of creating a visual representation of the sentences of a language. With them we can create tree diagrams, which are simply a technique for showing what the brain knows, not an actual representation of the brain's processes. Tree diagrams actually look like upside-down trees. They begin with the largest unit, the sentence, and work their way down through the major phrases until we can specify the grammatical category of each individual word. Let's start with a very basic sentence: *The boy bought a boat.* We begin with the first rule from above describing the three main features of a sentence and then describe the remaining phrases of the sentence and each word in the phrase. The tree that results looks like this:

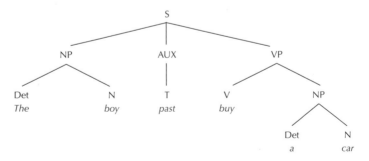

This simple diagram provides all the necessary information about the sentence. It reflects that sentences are minimally made of a subject (NP) and a predicate (VP). The tree diagram shows the relationships between the individual words in the sentence. It also tells us when the activity occurred. Let's complicate each of the phrases. We know from our rule above that an NP can contain many elements. The NP node of the tree can have many forms depending on which elements are present.

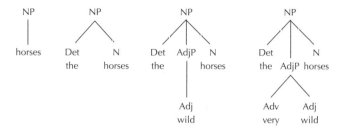

These NPs could be further complicated by the addition of other adverbs and adjectives. We can do the same thing with verb phrases. We know that verbs can stand alone, or that they can be accompanied by NPs and PPs or even adjectives and adverbs. All we have to do is follow the rules above to successfully represent each part of the phrase.

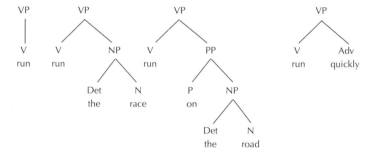

To draw a tree diagram of a full sentence, all we need to do is to combine the individual phrases and to add information about the tense and aspect of the sentence. Here's how the sentence *The very wild horses were running in the woods* will look:

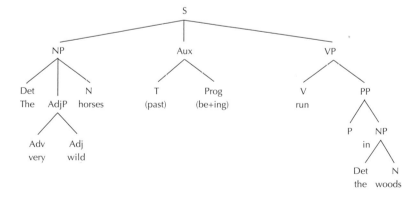

The diagram describes a sentence in the past progressive. The main verb is *run*, found under the V node of the VP. Its tense and aspect are described under the Aux node. If we changed the sentence to the present tense, the only thing that would change is the labelling under tense. This would give us the sentence: *The very wild horses are running in the woods.*

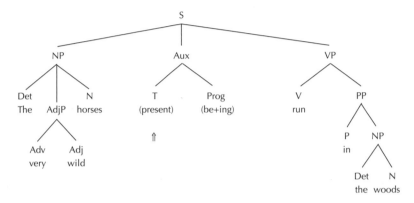

You can even complicate the aspect. Take the sentence: *The horses had been running in the woods.*

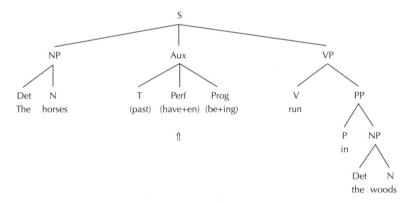

At the end of this chapter you can find exercises to help you get more comfortable with creating tree diagrams.

*Limitations to phrase structure grammars*

Even a full set of PSG rules, like those used to program computers for machine translation or artificial intelligence, are not perfect. Mostly this is due to the fact that although we teach grammar/syntax as if it is a completely separate entity, it is not. Humans use grammar in differing social contexts to create meaning. Grammar, meaning and context are all part of a whole. A number of limitations result from the fact that the PSG rules focus only on the ordering of words and phrases into sentences. For example, they create not only all the meaningful grammatical sentences of a language, but also the meaningless grammatical ones like Noam Chomsky's famous example:

> Colourless green ideas sleep furiously.

This is problematic if you are trying to create an algorithm for generating computer language because you want a set of rules that will only create sentences that make sense. Going back to Chomsky's sentence, if you replace each of these words by another from the same grammatical category, you can get a meaningful sentence:

> Long thin spaghetti cooks quickly.

Linguists are not the only ones who recognize that grammatical sentences are not always meaningful. Most of you will remember Lewis Carroll's poem *Jabberwocky* in which he strung together sentences that seem grammatical, because there are enough real English prepositions and determiners mixed with made-up nouns and verbs with appropriate prefixes and suffixes to sound English even though each sentence has no meaning.

> 'Twas brillig, and the slithy toves
> Did gyre and gimble in the wabe;
> All mimsy were the borogoves,
> And the mome raths outgrabe.

Or the poetry of e.e. cummings, where all the words are common English words in their appropriate grammatical spots, but the resulting sentences do not fit traditional concepts of meaning.

> Love is more thicker than forgot, more thinner than recall.
> More seldom than a wave is wet; more frequent than to fail.

In addition, the PSG rules alone do not limit which specific words can and cannot be combined together. The PSG rules do not specify which verbs are transitive and which are not. *Transitive verbs* are those that require a direct object to follow them to be grammatical. *Intransitive verbs* may not be immediately followed by a direct object. Take a look at the following sentences and determine why they are not grammatical:

> I threw.
> The mother broke.
> The sun rose the morning.
> John fell the stairs.
> The mayor spoke the speech.
> He sneezed the cold.
> The magician disappeared the rabbit.

Verbs like *broke* and *threw* require direct objects that tell *what* was broken or thrown. However, verbs like *rose*, *slept*, *disappeared* and *sneezed* may not be followed by a direct object, though they may be followed by adverbs or other grammatical constructions:

| | |
|---|---|
| The sun rose quickly. | She slept soundly. |
| John fell down the stairs. | He sneezed forcefully. |

Some verbs, like *put* and *set*, even require both a NP and a PP, but our PSG rules only say what is possible, not what is required.

| | |
|---|---|
| *She put. | *She put the book. |
| *She on the table. | She put the book on the table. |

For some speakers, certain sets of transitive/intransitive pairs cause difficulties, for example: *raise/rise* and *sit/set*. This example comes from a Laundromat in South Dakota:

Phrase structure rules also do not limit the placement of pronouns in NPs. For example, it is grammatical to say *The green chair is on the veranda*, but it is not grammatical simply to replace *chair* with the pronoun *it*, as in *The green it is on the veranda*. You can substitute the entire NP *the green chair* with *it*, but you lose the determiner and adjective specifiers.

### 6.3.3   Other aspects of grammar

The set of phrase structure rules we have been working with in this chapter is only a very limited fragment of the whole. For the introductory student, they provide an idea of how a very complex system works. Other introductory books, as well as websites you may find, do this as well, but may focus on a different set of objectives. Your particular teacher may present this in a different way as well. As you look at different presentations of this material, look at the common denominators that are present and appreciate the systematicity involved in any presentation of the syntax of the language.

Phrase structure rules were the result of early work in syntax, and as complete and as elegant as they may be, they are not sufficient to handle by themselves the full complexity of the structure of a language. They do, however, give us an appreciation for the universality of the structures of language as provided by the human mind and universal grammar, the collection of principles that are part of the biological endowment of every human brain.

This simple type of generative grammar was just the beginning of a great deal of research concerning syntax and what it tells us about the human brain. Chomsky has continued his research and this research has been extended by many other syntacticians and cognitive scientists as well. One of the early additions was the work on transformational grammar (TG). Proponents of TG said that many types of related sentences were all generated from a base sentence (called the deep structure). These variations of the deep structure sentence, the actual sentence uttered, thought or written were the surface structure realization of the original deep structure sentence. The deep structure sentence is an assertion or declarative sentence, and everything else generated from that sentence, like questions, passives, negative sentences, etc. were the surface structures. To get from the deep structure to the surface structure, the mind performs transformations, the movement of certain sentence structures to other parts of the sentence.

For example, to shift a declarative sentence to a yes-no question, the transformational rule 'Move-Aux' (move the auxiliary of the verb) must be applied so that the auxiliary element of a sentence moves to a position in front of the subject. Thus:

> The car is moving. (deep structure, declarative)
> Is the car moving? (surface structure, interrogative)

There are many other transformations that happen. For a full understanding of transformations, I suggest the texts in the list at the end of this chapter.

Chomsky began working with English, but his work quickly extended to other languages as well. If syntax gives us an understanding of the human brain, then there must be universal structures that are present in all human languages because our brains are biologically identical even though we speak different languages. The concepts of universal grammar we looked at in the chapter on language acquisition are guided and framed by specific *principles* and *parameters*. A principle is a rule that describes a structure present in all languages. A parameter specifies that certain structures may only behave in a limited number of ways. For example, specifiers, like determiners, can only come before or after their head, in the case of determiners the noun. With exposure to English, children learning their first language learn that the word 'the' precedes words like 'church', not follows them. Children exposed to Haitian Creole learn the opposite: determiners follow the noun as in *legliz la* (church the). Another parameter is the option of dropping the subject pronoun of a sentence. If you took Spanish or Portuguese, you learned that in many sentences an overt subject is optional; it can be dropped because endings of the verb indicate what the subject is anyway. So in Spanish it is possible to say: 'Voy al cine' rather than adding the subject pronoun to the sentence: 'Yo voy al cine'. You can't do this in English where the verbs lack distinct marking to indicate the subject to which they refer. Thus, we call languages that can do this *pro-drop languages*. As children acquire their first language, these parameters and others are set, helping them to correctly make choices about word placement in sentences dozens of times every day.

Grammar provides insight into how the mind organizes language and illustrates the regularity of language systems. Beyond helping us understand one of the most fundamental aspects of the human existence, this knowledge also has practical application, for example, in the teaching of second languages. The analysis of particular syntactic structures used by students acquiring second languages is used to understand the order of acquisition of certain morphemes in the second language. This knowledge is used to create methods for helping students more easily acquire difficult structures. Syntactic rules have also made possible the programming of computers to interpret and create language. A much more complex set of the rules we have been looking at in this chapter is used to create algorithms that instruct the computer in generating language, as well as interpreting language. As linguistic research into the structures of the human mind continues, we can expect many more technological advances.

## Suggested reading

Carnie, A. (2006), *Syntax: A Generative Introduction*. Oxford: Blackwell.

Celce-Murcia, M. and Larsen-Freeman, D. (1998), *The Grammar Book*. Cambridge: Newbury House Publishers.

Huddleston, R. and Pullum, G. K. (2005), *A Student's Introduction to English Grammar*. Cambridge: Cambridge University Press.

## Questions to consider

1. What kinds of sentences can you identify that are not covered by the set of phrase structure rules from this chapter?
2. Make tree diagrams of the following sentences. Make sure you include all the information needed under the *aux*.

The children are going home.
I may have looked up in the attic before dinner.
The cheerleaders held up the bank for their pregnant captain.
She may have been leaving her husband.
Syntax is boring for the students.
The small green frog kissed the old witch.
She bought a red car for her younger brother.
The book on the table is interesting to young children.
That student goes to France in the spring for vacation.
He might have been very late on Monday.

3. Transitive or intransitive?

My car broke down.                    He threw the ball away.
Bill got off the bus at my house.     He broke down the engine.
She turned the oven off.              She was turned off by the smell.
I called off the meeting.             She passed out at the party.
He burned down the building.          The building burned down.
He left his coat.                     He left his room.

4. Prepositions or particles?

She turned down the job.              She turned down the street.
You backed down the driveway well.    You backed down from the fight.
He ran out the door.                  He ran out of beer.
He'll turn up eventually.             He'll turn up the volume.
Let's get down to business.           She bought a knockoff at Macy's.
Let's knock off at 5.                 Let's knock on the door.
She knocked over the glass.           She bought a knockoff of a
                                         designer dress.

## Notes

1   The word *determiner* refers to articles like *a, an* and *the* as well as demonstratives like *this, that, these* and *those.*
2   The simple form of the verb is the one with no markings for tense or person. Examples: *work, play, eat, talk, study* and *run.*

# 7 Semantics: Language and Meaning

## Chapter Overview

| | | |
|---|---|---|
| 7.1 | HOW IS MEANING DEVELOPED? | 133 |
| 7.2 | HOW IS MEANING ENCODED? | 134 |
| 7.3 | WORD MEANING: SENSE AND REFERENCE | 135 |
| | 7.3.1 PROPER NOUNS: THE PROBLEM OF NAMES | 136 |
| 7.4 | WHAT NATIVE SPEAKERS UNDERSTAND ABOUT MEANING | 138 |
| | 7.4.1 AMBIGUITY | 138 |
| | 7.4.2 SYNONYMY | 139 |
| | 7.4.3 ANTONYMY | 140 |
| | 7.4.4 LEVELS OF SPECIFICITY | 140 |
| | 7.4.5 MEANING INCLUSION | 141 |
| | 7.4.6 COMPOSITIONAL VERSUS NONCOMPOSITIONAL UTTERANCES | 142 |
| | 7.4.7 PHRASAL VERBS | 146 |
| | 7.4.8 FIGURES OF SPEECH | 147 |
| | 7.4.9 IRONY AND SARCASM | 148 |

In the first chapter of this book I asked, what is it that you know when you know a language? The answer turned out to be many concrete things like the sounds, words and grammar rules as well as many less tangible things like some of the more abstract rules of grammar and phonology of which most native speakers are unaware (like the word order for adjectives). These aspects of language provide us with a communication system for the transmission of meaning. However, what is the nature of what we understand about meaning?

An understanding of the concept of meaning is not quite as simple as you may think. Linguists, philosophers and others have long debated questions like: Is the meaning of an utterance what the speaker intends or the listener's interpretation of what is said? Can a 'neutral' meaning be constructed so that all people will understand a concept in exactly the same way? What is the effect of culture, social class, even gender, on the understanding or interpretation of an utterance? These are just a few of the challenges to coming up with a full understanding of meaning.

The definition of *meaning* in the dictionary is quite vague: 'the thing one intends to convey especially by language, something meant or intended, the logical connotation (or denotation) of a word or phrase'.[1] One problem with dictionaries is that they generally use words to describe words, which may leave the definition open to a wide range of interpretation because each word used has variable meanings and connotations. In the definition above of the word *meaning*, the word *logical*, used to define connotation and denotation, is certainly not unambiguous. Logical to whom, and in what sense?

This chapter and the following one will focus on two aspects of meaning: the construction of literal meaning, *semantics*, and the construction of meaning within a particular culture or social interactional context, the study of *pragmatics*.

## 7.1 How is meaning developed?

Imagine the first human speakers and the task they confronted with simply naming things. Language is not an individual phenomenon for the expression of our internal dialogues but is a group phenomenon in that people use it to share information with each other. Therefore, words and meanings must be co-constructed by a group so that meaning can be shared. If each individual maintained widely different meanings for every word, communication would be impossible.

One thought about the origin of speech is that many of the first words were iconic in some fashion. A word or sign is iconic if its sound or shape implies its meaning or some aspect of it. Modern-day examples of this are words like *meow* (the sound a cat makes) and *hiss* (air escaping from something). Printed signs can also be visually iconic in that meaning is obvious (hopefully) from the symbol provided. Restroom signs (a stick figure in a skirt) and road signs (for sharp dangerous curves) are often iconic, or partially iconic, facilitating quick understanding by native and non-native speakers alike.

Language, however, is generally not iconic because the range of human concepts is simply too extensive and abstract to create iconic words for every meaning. Therefore, the rest of the concepts that we need to express will require arbitrary phonetic strings invented by someone and agreed upon, at some level, by a community. There is no inherent reason why we use the phonetic string *dog* to refer to a domesticated canine. We could just as easily have called it a *fred*. In fact, speakers of other languages have come up with completely different phonetic strings to refer to the same animal: *perro* (Spanish), *собака* (Russian), *cane* (Italian), *mbwa* (Swahili) and *kraman* (Akan, Ghana). The ability to associate a particular meaning with an arbitrary set of sounds is what provides people with their capacity to express an infinite quantity of concepts.

## 7.2   How is meaning encoded?

In general, meaning is encoded linguistically, through spoken and written symbols; however, it may also be transmitted via gaze, gesture and other symbolic forms of communication. Most definitions of meaning imply that there is a sender, a message and a receiver. However, is it possible that meaning could exist without one of these? When people write in a diary, is there necessarily a recipient who is separate from the writer? Many people have no intention of having their diary read. You could, however, argue that when the diary writer reads it 25 years later, she or he is not the same person as the person who wrote the diary. Furthermore, people talk to themselves. Our internal dialogues are quite necessary in puzzling out information or venting frustration, but there is no receiver separate from the sender.

When we talk to our pets, we certainly encode a message, though the pet is most often quite incapable of 'understanding' the particular message that we send. You could argue that meaning exists because the relationship between the message and the signal exists, even though it is only in the mind of the sender.

It is also possible for a receiver to interpret a message when none is sent. Many people have had the embarrassing experience of thinking that someone was flirting with them from across a room at a social event. When they finally got up the courage to go across the room and chat up the flirt, they are embarrassed to find that the person had not even noticed them and was actually looking elsewhere. In this case, although a signal exists for the receiver, the person across the room has no intention of transmitting meaning.

The accidental transmission of meaning happens quite commonly with readers of literature. Readers often come up with their own interpretations of a book's message and believe that the author has created the message they have interpreted. J. R. R. Tolkien, himself a linguist, repeatedly denied that the *Lord of the Rings* trilogy was a religious allegory. Nevertheless, some people who read it endow it with this interpretation. This poses another philosophical question about meaning: is the meaning of a message what the sender intends, what the receiver interprets, or both?

There are even challenges to the message itself. A message could be encoded but in a form impossible for the receiver to interpret. I saw a wonderful example of this in a small village in the Dominican Republic. A monolingual English-speaking tourist had somehow ended up at a village grocery store where no one spoke English. The tourist was speaking very very slowly and was practically yelling the word *bread*. The unfortunate monolingual Spanish-speaking Dominican behind the counter was trying to help but did not have a clue as to what this ridiculous man wanted. If meaning is in the transmission of a message, there was no meaning here.

## 7.3 Word meaning: sense and reference

How do we define all the concepts of a language so that each word can be completely understood without ambiguity? The dictionary definition of a word is its *sense*. The sense of a word may be described using words, but as we saw earlier in the chapter, that sometimes leads to vague definitions. Some concepts can be described by a binary list of properties that eliminate the vagueness of a definition. For example, a *mare* can be described as +equine +female +mature and a *bull* could be described as +bovine −female +mature (there is no reason why either +/− male or female makes any difference for the default). These definitions are possible because you only need a limited number of binary descriptors, and you have eliminated all other possible objects. However, imagine trying to describe abstract constructs like *happiness* or *self* with binary terms. There is no list of binary terms that could be assembled that would provide an exact definition of these kinds of words. Binary descriptors will not work with gradable items like *coldness* either because there is a range of what people define as cold. The number of concepts that can be fully and singularly identified by binary terms is quite limited. Nevertheless, despite the incredible variability possible in meaning, we seem to communicate every day just fine for the most part.

It would seem to be simple to circumvent the problem of definitions solely by saying that words refer to items in the real world and using those items as referents. *Car* refers to a particular type of motorized vehicle. No need to come up with a lengthy description like: a conveyance, generally seating six or fewer people, propelled via an internal combustion engine, generally with a protective shell of some material around the passengers. *Reference* seems to be an elegant solution to the problem of definitions at first glance; however, it presents a number of problems.

First, there is the problem of function words. There is no real-world physical referent for prepositions (like *on*, *over*), articles (*a*, *an*, *the*) and conjunctions (*and*, *but*). These must be defined via sense. Not even all nouns have real-world referents. Imagine the characters from J. R. R. Tolkein's *Lord of the Rings* trilogy. If you have read the books or seen the movies, you may have a picture in your mind of an elf or an orc, but there is no referent in the real world. This is equally true for things that do exist, but are not specified. In the sentence 'The king's assassin must have died in the explosion', the assassin may be an unknown person, so there is no known referent, but the sense of the word *assassin* is still clear.

For other concepts, a referent in the real world may exist; however, the referent is distinct for almost every individual. The sense, the dictionary definition of the word *mother*, is quite clear. However, my referent for *mother* is quite distinct from yours because every mother embodies a different set of qualities. Other concepts have a disconnect between sense and reference as well. 'No *human* is native to Antarctica.' The subject of this sentence is a nonexistent being. We have no problem understanding the sense of the sentence, but there can be no logical referent.

Cultural and geographic factors, as well as other factors, may play a part in determining the sense of a word. When I taught in Tucson, Arizona, in a dry desert area, my local students disagreed vehemently with the dictionary definition of a river:

> A large natural stream of water emptying into an ocean, lake, or other body of water and usually fed along its course by converging tributaries.[2]

Rivers in the southwest of the United States may only have water in them periodically, for only a few weeks a year in total. Most local people insist that these are rivers nonetheless. They even tell a joke about a New Yorker who visited Arizona and found it too arid. So, she invited her Arizona friend to visit her in New York City. After they had taken a number of walks by the East River, she asked her Arizona friend how she liked the river. The Arizonan responded, 'I can't say. It's been covered up with water ever since I got here.'

Abstract concepts, like *happiness* or *freedom*, pose another problem for definition. The sense of abstract words like these can be quite open to interpretation, and there is no real-world referent. For some happiness is based solely on being part of a loving family that is safe and well provided for. For others, happiness is rooted in material possessions or power. Although we may have quite different interpretations of many concepts like these, in our everyday conversations we seem to be content with a general understanding of meaning and understand that any utterance is open to some variation depending on the person speaking.

## 7.3.1 Proper nouns: the problem of names

Another philosophical argument in semantics concerns the status of proper nouns (names for commercial things, places and people). One view is that proper nouns do not have semantic content (a sense), but that they are referential. From this perspective, names can only refer to a particular individual, and they have no power to denote particular qualities. The opposing view is that proper nouns are not solely referential because they may not specify a particular reference (for instance, how many John Smiths exist in the world?) and that, in fact, they may carry some semantic content, meaning that they are limited descriptions of the referent.

There are counter arguments for both views. For example, it is not very rare to hear someone say that a person does not look like a Bunny, Barbie, Billy Bob or Butch because some people have endowed some names with certain qualities. Nevertheless, for the great majority of names in English, there is no agreed general meaning that we attach to the people who are given these names. Nonetheless, names may have official meanings that may be rooted in history. My first name, *Elizabeth*, means *God is my oath* (from Greek) and *Grace* is from Latin (*gratia*) simply meaning *grace*. Unfortunately for me, grace is not one of the adjectives that anyone who knows me would use as a descriptor! Therefore, although these names have meaning, do they have sense?

Consider also cultures that have elaborate naming practices that encode meaning into the naming process. A recent Secretary General of the United Nations was Kofi Annan from the country of Ghana. In Akan naming rituals in Ghana, many names are bestowed based on the circumstances of the birth. *Kofi* is a name for a male born on Friday. *Kwadwo* is the name for a male born on Monday. Other names like *Kaakyire*, meaning *late or last born*, refer to when in the mother's life the child was born. In Akan culture, children are endowed with a number of names that provide a description of them. Therefore, do these names have sense as well as reference?

Another argument to support that names have sense is based on the feeling or idea that a string of sounds evokes. Many companies spend a lot of money on research to choose or create appropriate names for new products because they believe the name does in some fashion have semantic content or relates to some cognitive experience for consumers. There is a belief that certain sounds and words evoke certain feelings and associations.

There are dozens of companies that specialize in both creating names and all the legal work associated with them. Professional naming consultants usually follow linguistic principles about the combinations of sounds acceptable in a language as well as other principles of which native speakers are aware. Sometimes part of one invented name will take on a life of its own and become a new morpheme. A good example of this is the bound morpheme -ex, the earliest use of which I know being the facial tissue product called *Kleenex* (clean + -ex). There are many other products that have used -ex as part of their name; some of the root meanings are more obvious than others: *Pyrex* (fire + -ex), *Rolex* (roll + -ex),[3] and *Windex* (window + -ex). Medicines as well have made use of this process: *Zyrtex* and *Valtrex* are two of the more commonly advertised products with the bound morpheme *-ex*. Considering all of these names, as well as others you may know, what can the meaning of *-ex* be? This made-up bound morpheme is not productive in English beyond product naming.

Common words, and even names, are not simply referents for items in our lives, nor do they only provide one single meaning. There is a complex relationship between each word and all its possible senses and associations with other concepts. A simple definition of a word in a dictionary is rarely sufficient to get across the totality of its meaning in the real world. The mental lexicon of each individual is full of meanings that are probably much richer for each item than definitions provided by a dictionary and real-world referents are quite varied for individuals.

## 7.4 What native speakers understand about meaning

Although a definition of meaning seems to be problematic for academics, for the most part humans extract meaning from conversations, television, books and more, every day of our lives quite successfully. This is no small feat, however. There is much we must understand to comprehend the meaning of an utterance. Besides being able to deal with the fact that meaning changes as convention changes and time passes, native speakers are able to deal with the fact that almost every word has multiple meanings, and depending on context, a word may be ambiguous.

### 7.4.1 Ambiguity

As native speakers, we quite easily, and quite often, deal with ambiguity in a normal conversation. When one pronunciation can have more than one meaning, we are usually able to figure out the correct meaning from the context of an utterance. If a friend is out of money and declares she is going to the *bank*, we do not misunderstand and think she is going to the bank of a river. Because this type of ambiguity rests on the meaning of one word, it is called *lexical ambiguity*. Since thousands of words in English have more than one meaning, we are constantly selecting among possible meanings.

However, there are some instances in which the ambiguity may not be eliminated solely by context. Consider the sentence 'She cannot *bear* children'. Does this mean she physically cannot have them or intensely dislikes them? Ambiguity may also depend on how the morphemes in a word are divided. In the sentence, 'This door is unlockable', is the negative morpheme *un-* modifying *lockable* (not able to be locked) or is the suffix *-able* modifying *unlock* (that it is able to be unlocked). In the following picture, there is an unintentional humorous meaning that can be extracted depending on which meaning of 'baby' is interpreted.

Ambiguity may also be at the sentence level as well (structural ambiguity). In the sentence 'The girl heard her mother with the radio', it is not clear whether the girl was using the radio to listen to her mother who was elsewhere or whether the girl heard her mother who was singing along with the radio. In a grammatical sense, it is not clear whether the prepositional phrase 'with the radio' serves as an instrument for 'the girl' or if it accompanies 'the mother'. See if you can figure out both possible meanings of the following sentences:

> She took the pictures off the walls and washed them.
> I met a guy with a peg leg named Bill.

Although ambiguity may rest on one word, it may still be attributed to the structure of the sentence. In the sentence 'I hate boring people', the word *boring* can either be part of the main verb of the sentence or it can be an adjective modifying *people*. Structural and lexical ambiguities are often sources of humour in newspaper headlines, which because they appear out of context can easily be misinterpreted.

> Iraqi Head Seeks Arms
> Pres. Reagan Wins on Budget, But More Lies Ahead
> Miners Refuse to Work after Death

## 7.4.2 Synonymy

We also understand that a particular meaning may be expressed by different words or phrases. Expressions like 'John likes working out' and 'John likes exercising' are synonymous. Native speakers also recognize that changes in grammar do not stop utterances from being synonymous: 'Bob is standing by Jenny's sports car' and 'Bob is standing by the red sports car that belongs to Jenny' clearly have the same meaning. Synonymy in a dictionary sense, however, is not always a guarantee that words are synonymous to native speakers.

Whether words are synonymous may depend upon the culture or geographic area of speakers among other variables. In the United States, there are three words for the long stuffed piece of furniture on which people sit: *couch*, *sofa* and *davenport*, though the word *davenport* seems to be used exclusively by older speakers. Over the years, I have queried class after class about these words. For many of my students, *couch* and *sofa* are completely synonymous. For others, they are not. For those who differentiate between the two, the *sofa* is the formal one in the living room – the one you were not allowed to sit on as a child except on special occasions. The *couch* is usually in the family room. You can lie down on it, and put your feet up on it as well.

In Great Britain, the most common word for this item is *sofa*, though older speakers in the north may use the variant *settee*. The word *couch*, though commonly understood from television programmes from the USA, is generally only used in set phrases like 'crash on the couch' and is not used in general conversation about this piece of living room furniture. In Great Britain, a *davenport* is a small writing desk and not related to the American word at all. The online version of the American Heritage Dictionary[4] gives the primary meaning of *davenport* as a type of sofa that may be opened as a bed, and a secondary meaning as a desk, so at some point British and American associations of this word diverged.

## 7.4.3 Antonymy

Speakers of any language also understand that words can have opposite meanings and relational meanings to each other. Some words like *on* and *off* are absolute and have no range of meaning, but words like *cold* and *hot* are participant- and context-dependent. Words in true opposition to each other like *on* and *off* or *alive* and *dead* (ignore the zombies for now!) are called *complementary pairs* of antonyms. Other pairs of words that people often consider as opposites are not absolute; these are *gradable pairs* of antonyms because there are shades of differences between the two concepts. The word *tall* can be used to describe a 6-year-old in a group of her peers; however, the same child is not tall in a group of adults. A simple expression like 'It is hot in here' can mean quite a range of temperature depending on who is saying it.

## 7.4.4 Levels of specificity

Native speakers also recognize that words may be partially synonymous but can carry connotations and subtleties of meaning beyond the basic meaning. A basic description of an event could be 'Bob ate a sandwich'. In the USA, the same event could be related as 'Bob wolfed down the sandwich', and in Britain as 'Bob hoovered the sandwich'. Each of these utterances details 'how' the sandwich was eaten and provides a much more colourful description of the event. Consider all of the following shaded meanings of the word 'eat': *nibble, consume, gorge, gobble, munch, chomp, devour, polish off, chow down, choke down, scarf down, pick at, pig out* and *shovel in*.

## 7.4.5 Meaning inclusion

One of the most important features of word meaning is *inclusion*. As part of the meaning of any word, we understand that it includes many aspects of 'meaning' that do not need to be re-specified in a conversation. You would never say 'my male uncle' because the meaning of male is encoded in the word 'uncle'. Entailment is meaning inclusion on the sentence level. When one idea entails another it means that the truth (or falsity) of one sentence follows from the other. If you say 'Charles is divorced', the meaning of this sentence entails that at some point he was married. This is a very important aspect of language because it allows us to communicate quickly about many things since we do not have to specify everything.

How much simpler it is to say 'My mother is flying from Tennessee for a visit' than to specify 'The adult female who birthed me is coming by air-capable conveyance from Tennessee, a state of the USA in the east, to Kentucky, where we are now, to visit me'. The meaning of 'mother' includes adult and female and generally the concept of childbirth or adoption. Because I used the word 'coming', the destination does not need to be specified since it is 'here'. Furthermore, the verb 'flying' entails 'in an aircraft'. This of course is a gross example, but meaning inclusion reduces redundancy and reflects the shared meaning concepts of people from the same language and culture. Like almost everything else in language, native speaker understanding of this process and our play with it results in humour, as in bad parodies of westerns in which a character says 'I killed him dead'.

What constitutes meaning inclusion depends upon the culture or subculture. I know a number of people over 50 who react negatively to the fairly common practice of young people in the USA of referring to everyone as 'guys'. It is especially noticeable in restaurants where young people are serving older ones. Many older people do not entail 'women' as part of 'guys', as in 'What can I get you guys'? In addition, older men also interpret 'guys' as being too informal a term for a young person to use with an older person they do not know. Most young people that I have asked about this are completely oblivious to the fact that the use of 'guys' is offensive to many older people.

## 7.4.6 Compositional versus non-compositional utterances

One of the most important things that native speakers are able to do is to recognize the difference between compositional and non-compositional sentences. Compositional sentences are those whose meanings can be understood by simply adding the primary meanings of the individual words: 'I like tacos'. The subject is *I*, the verb is *like* and the object of the verb is *tacos*. However, a good deal of normal everyday talk is noncompositional: the meanings of the individual words do not simply add up but convey something other than a literal meaning. There are many kinds of noncompositional sentences. Consider the following sentences:

> What's up?
> He took down the wrestler at the end of the fight.
> She's a real pain.
> That makes my blood boil.

These are the kinds of sentences that are quite difficult for non-native speakers of a language to comprehend because their literal meaning gives little or no clue to the meaning of a particular utterance or the utterances must be understood metaphorically. I remember watching an old movie in Spanish and watching a big macho cowboy crying over his beer and saying to another cowboy 'Ella me dio calabazas' which quite literally translates 'She gave me pumpkins'. Needless to say I was confused until I learned that this expression in 1950s Mexico meant that his woman had left him. All languages are filled with thousands of these types of expressions that native speakers use without even thinking about the abstract nature of their meanings.

*Slang*

The expressions we are talking about here are the things that make learning a second language very difficult (and make geezers, geezers). One of the most significant is slang. Slang often originates in a particular group and then may spread out to parts of the general population. It tends to be transitory in nature. Many slang words and expressions last only a brief period of time (*da bomb*, 1990s, *far out*, 1960s) and others are quite enduring (*cool*, popular since at least the 1920s). Some slang words even become part and parcel of the common lexicon and may no longer be considered slang (*road rage*, which entered the American Heritage Dictionary a few years ago).

Slang expressions frequently originate from within youth culture, though others originate from workplace jargon, from technological changes, from literature and art, from foreign languages as well as elsewhere. When I was younger, I worked as a waitress. The kitchen staff used the term *86'd* to mean we were out of a menu item. Thirty years later, this term has jumped the kitchen and is used by people who have never been servers or chefs to mean 'eliminated'. I've even heard students talk about *eighty-sixing* a relationship.

Slang is cultural as well and varies from country to country in the English-speaking world. Here are a few more colourful slang expressions from different parts of the English-speaking world:

British[5]

*cabbaged*: intoxicated to a state of uselessness (vegetative state)
*garyboy*: man who drives a sporty car
*ladette*: a female equivalent of a male who might be considered *laddish*: confident, brash, loud, a drinker etc.
*panda car*: police car. taken from when police cars were black and white

Australian
*put the Billy on*: to make a cup of tea
*blue heeler*: police (from Australian cattle dog that won't let you get away)
*jackeroo*: junior hand on a cattle station; *jillaroo*: female jackeroo
*mystery bags*: sausages (don't know what is in them)

New Zealand
*bum-bag*: fanny pack
*chunder*: to vomit
*sook*: a grumpy, temperamental person
*fizzy*: soda pop

Irish
*article*: a woman, usually half in jest
*bifter*: marijuana cigarette
*black mariah*: police van
*gawk*: to throw up – especially after alcohol

Nigerian
*attachee*: someone that is only friends with you for your food or provisions
*blowing-fone*: when someone tries to speak English like Europeans to impress people
*rub your nose*: to tell a girl a bra strap is showing and to pull it into her blouse
*sparking* (also *raking*): when someone is upset with you and expresses their anger

South African
*babalaas*: bad hangover, from the Zulu word *ibhabhalazi*
*bane*: marijuana. also *number, skayf, spliff, slowboat, chellum, bottleneck, smoke*
*bark the dog*: vomit. also: *kotch, park a tiger* or *technicoloured yawn*
*naff*: wimp
*schlep*: hassle, hard work

In every variety of English, there are thousands of slang words and expressions which add colour to our language, frustrate parents and educators and provide an in-code for their users.

*Jargon*

The slang or technical expressions of a particular group, generally a skilled group, are called jargon. These may be formal or informal groups. Jargon exists for climbers, computer programmers, runners, football players (soccer, American or Australian football) even Peace Corps volunteers and Trekkies. It is the specialized vocabulary for their activities. For example, people working in hospital emergency rooms or on military bases often use technical language that may get modified or shortened because it is used so frequently. These expressions may not be understood by outsiders; however, these words and expressions may cross over into normal everyday usage because of their use in TV dramas featuring medical and military personnel and because people bring their jargon home with them and it spreads.

**Hospital jargon:**
bag: put on a respirator
circling the drain: patient who is about to die
donor cycles: motorcycles (good organ donors)
GSW: gunshot wound
preemie: premature infant (US)
SOB: shortness of breath

**Military jargon:**
beans and bullets: all types of supplies
friendly fire: accidental shooting of own personnel
bones: military doctor
jarhead: US Marine
shit on a shingle (also SOS) chipped beef on toast

*Argot*

Although quite like slang and jargon, argot is the vocabulary of criminals and, because of their association with them, police officers. Criminals create specialized vocabulary to keep their activities secret, and police work hard to learn it to be able to thwart their activities. Undercover police, especially, must be conversant with how to use this language appropriately or 'their cover will be blown' (they will be identified as police) and they could end up 'sleeping with the fishes' (be murdered).

Like all other varieties of slang, these words may be temporal, limited to particular groups of users, or may become known to the general public via television and literature (like the two examples in the previous paragraphs). The word *shiv*, to refer to a *knife*, is frequently heard in old black and white movies and television shows; a more recent term is *shank*. Police have names for criminals as well. On the television show *Law and Order*, I have heard both the terms *skel* (skeleton in the closet) and *perp* (perpetrator) to refer to suspects. Other current examples of argot are *tag* (graffitti), and *drop a dime on* or *narc* (to inform on). Some of the most interesting examples of argot are all of the words associated with marijuana. There are hundreds of these in the English-speaking world including: *pot, maryjane, grifa, weed, plant, bamma, zambi, trees, cosa, blacks, blunt, ying, doja, budda, grata, chronic, dirt, ganja* and *giggle weed,* among dozens of other words.

## Idioms

These are expressions that are not slang and are commonly used by native speakers. They are set combinations of words whose individual meanings do not add up literally to their understood meaning. Their original derivations may be lost to current users; for example, most native speakers of English know the expression 'It's raining cats and dogs', but few know that this expression comes from a very long time ago when roofs were somewhat slanted and made of plant material. Cats and dogs were often kept on the roof, and when it rained hard, the roof became slick and the animals fell off them. Other common idioms include: 'arrive in the nick of time', 'shoot the breeze', 'have second thoughts', 'get cold feet' and 'hit the books'.

## Idioms and synonyms

Besides often having colourful backgrounds, idioms behave quite distinctly from compositional phrases. For instance, in a compositional sentence, synonyms or similar meaning words can be substituted (when they exist) without greatly changing the meaning of the sentence. 'Bill argues a lot' is synonymous with 'Bill bickers a lot'. However, if you substitute a synonym within an idiom, the meaning of the new sentence is no longer idiomatic. Take the sentence 'Last night she *hit the books*' (she studied). If we substitute synonyms for the word 'hit' the resulting sentences do not have the same meaning as the idiom.

Last night she *smacked* the books.    Last night she *clobbered* the books.

Consider each of the following sentences and how the change to a synonym for part of the idiom creates a sentence that is no longer synonymous with its idiomatic counterpart:

My brother is a *sofa* potato. (couch potato)
I forgot her birthday! I'm really in *warm water*. (hot water)
She was so funny, that she had him *in a cast*. (in stitches)

*Idioms and stress rules*

The use of idioms also suspends regular stress rules for normal sentences. In a compositional sentence, different content words (nouns, verbs, adjectives) can be stressed depending on the context of the sentence. (The stressed word is italicized.)

| | |
|---|---|
| Which dress are you wearing? | I'm wearing the *green* dress. |
| Who is wearing the green dress? | *I'm* wearing the green dress. |
| Are you wearing the green suit? | I'm wearing the green *dress*. |

For idiomatic sentences, the stressed pattern is fixed. You cannot change the stress pattern to affect the meaning. The meaning is fixed.

It was her brother's *leg* that she pulled.

*Passive voice and idioms*

Idiomatic sentences can also not be put in the passive voice. Although there is no syntactic problem, native speakers think the second column of utterances is really weird.

| | |
|---|---|
| I hit the books. | The books were hit by me. |
| I shot the breeze with him. | The breeze was shot by me with him. |
| He beat around the bush. | A bush was beaten around by him. |

So, although idioms are part of the natural speech of all native speakers, they are fixed expressions that are limited in how they can be manipulated.

## 7.4.7 Phrasal verbs

Unlike many languages, English has an inordinate number of two- and three-word verbs to convey a single concept. In English, some verbs are accompanied by particles (prepositions attached to the verb) that have a distinct meaning from the verb without the particle. Other languages do this with single words, for example, in Spanish, the verb *preguntar* means 'to ask', whereas the English phrasal verb 'to ask for' is still one word, *pedir*.

There are hundreds of these combinations in English, each providing little, if any, information about the meaning of the combined words. These particles do not have meaning the same way that prepositions do. If I say, 'Phil ran down the stairs', the word 'down' tells the direction of the running. However, in the utterance 'Phil ran down his boss', the word 'down' provides no directional information. 'Run down' is a unit that means, 'hit with a car'. Learners of English must memorize hundreds of these combinations to be able to understand the normal speech of native English speakers. This is no easy task because each verb may be combined with many different particles, and in some cases, the combination may result in a noun or an adjective.

Jon *knocked off* a six-pack in less than an hour. (completed)
Harold *knocked off* his teacher for giving too much homework. (killed)
She bought a *knock-off* of a designer dress. (a copy)
Andy *knocked off* at noon. (left work)
The manager *knocked off* 10 per cent when I asked for a deal. (reduced)
The cheerleaders *knocked off* three banks. (robbed)

## 7.4.8 Figures of speech

Another problem for the literal interpretation of language are figures of speech. Like slang, the definition of this category is quite loose; it can include simile, metaphor and hyperbole. In a figure of speech, a comparison may be made with a commonly understood event or condition, or a phrase may be used to exaggerate an experience or event by creating an impression. These can be very cultural and have little translation even from one English-speaking community to another. In the United States, many of these expressions result from the culture's historical love of the games baseball and poker:

Baseball:
    *in the ballpark* (close to the expected)
      'The salary offer was in the ballpark.'
    *out in left field* (not useful)
      'As usual, John's ideas are way out in left field.'
    *way off base* (not correct)
      'The earnings for the year are way off base.'

Poker:
    *an ace in the hole* (unknown advantage, support)
      'Sandy had an ace in the hole. No one knew she could speak French.'
    *play the hand you are dealt* (deal with reality)
      'She decided to play the hand she was dealt rather than complain.'
    *know when to hold 'em, know when to fold 'em* (when to continue and when not to)
      'You've gotta know when to fold 'em in high-stakes negotiations.'

We also frame our ideas about the world metaphorically. There are abstract ideas that we relate to physical properties. Anger, for example is often expressed by heat: 'Al is hot-tempered' or 'I'm about to boil over'. We use our understanding of cold to express lack of emotion, passion or action. It is easy to see how these ideas relate; when something is frozen in ice, it can no longer move. The metaphor extends easily to many life situations.

He's a cold fish. (no emotion)
Jan is frigid. (sexually unresponsive)
The computer program is frozen. (nothing is moving)
That movie is frozen in time. (not current, locked into the past)

Hyperbole and understatement are also ways of communicating in which the literal interpretation of an utterance is incorrect at some level. Expressions like 'I'm so hungry I could eat a horse' in no way reflect the speaker's true desire. They reflect the intensity of the speaker's feeling, for example 'The fish was at least as big as the boat!' News headlines can be great examples of hyperbole. How often have we seen the expression 'the trial of the century' used by the media? Wikipedia lists no less than 16 of these including[6] the Scopes Monkey trial, the Nuremburg trials, the trials of Bruno Hauptmann, Julius and Ethel Rosenberg, Adolf Eichmann, the Chicago Seven, Charles Manson, O. J. Simpson, Bill Clinton and the police who beat Rodney King.

## 7.4.9 Irony and sarcasm

Irony can exist either within utterances or within situations or events. We are concerned here solely with ironic utterances. With irony, the literal meaning of an utterance is the opposite of the one intended by the speaker. Sometimes, an ironic statement can be sarcastic as well, but they are not the same thing. Although sarcasm also implies that the exact opposite meaning is intended, sarcasm is usually quite obvious from the tonal quality of the utterance. Irony is not accompanied by special tonal qualities.

A classic example of irony is found in Mark Twain's great American story, *Huckleberry Finn*. In one chapter, Huck is talking with a woman about a riverboat explosion:

Woman: 'Good gracious!' says the woman he's deceiving. 'Anybody hurt?'
Huck: 'No'm. Killed a nigger.'
Woman: 'Well, it's lucky; because sometimes people do get hurt.'

An understanding of irony often requires a good deal of contextual knowledge. If we read this passage from Huck Finn without knowing that Twain was an abolitionist, we may read the passage literally and miss Twain's irony. Year after year in the United States, some well-meaning parents try to have this book removed from their children's schools because they think it is racist. Twain's intent was to highlight the absurdity of racism through the use of irony.

Without context, we may miss the ironic intent of an author. Irony is cultural and locked in time as well. Imagine people 100 years from now listening to current comics, and others, who make jokes based on current perceptions of race, ethnicity and culture. How would a person from the twenty-second century understand comic Chris Rock's statement, 'You know the world is going crazy when the best rapper is a white guy, the best golfer is a black guy, the tallest guy in the NBA is Chinese, the Swiss hold the America's Cup, France is accusing the US of arrogance, Germany doesn't want to go to war, and the three most powerful men in America are named "Bush", "Dick" and "Colon".' To understand the irony behind this statement, you need to have a good deal of world knowledge going back as far as World War I and to understand popular perceptions of Americans about the French and Germans, as well as comprehending that golf had once been a sport of wealthy white men and basketball an American sport. Whether this understanding of the first names above will still be understood in 200 years is also unknown. All this makes me wonder how much of the genius of Shakespeare and other earlier English writers I have missed because I read them without the appropriate cultural context and with present-day meanings for Middle English words.

Sarcasm is much easier to identify than irony. It is usually accompanied by body language (eye rolling and shoulder-heaving), exaggerated tonal qualities of the utterance and the fact that a literal interpretation could not possibly be the correct one if common sense is applied. Sarcasm is generally accompanied by jeering and mocking and has the intent to be disrespectful. Any teenager who has said it, and any adult who has heard it, completely understands that the teenager's response 'whatever' to an adult request does not constitute agreement! Sarcasm can exist without these signals and be dependent totally on the absurdity of the statement within the context of the utterance. I once had a student ask me if he had to do the homework. I answered 'no'. As the student happily walked away, a couple of more sarcasm-savvy students informed him that my answer was clearly meant to be read as sarcasm. They were quite appalled that he did not 'get it'.

Synonymy, ambiguity, literal and non-literal meaning and the effect of context, participants, stress and intonation are only a few of the concepts we intuitively understand about meaning. As native speakers, we negotiate all of this almost instantaneously as we go about our lives creating and interpreting meaningful conversations. Although we all do this so easily, there are still a number of issues that confront the exchange of exact meaning between a speaker and a listener. One problem is that because there is rarely a one-to-one relationship between a word and a meaning, it is hard for an utterance to be completely objective. Thus, even though the word *dog* seems quite unremarkable, the mental image of a prototypical dog that each person carries is quite distinct (small, large or medium, with long or short hair). With more complex terms, variation in our understanding is even greater. For some people, *security* means living in a nice neighbourhood, for others that definition hardly constitutes security. Security may mean having a huge house with dogs and alarms for protection.

Meaning is also coloured by our experiences, culture, perceptions and conditioning. What possible association we give to a word or utterance is dependent on this as well as dry dictionary definitions. This was brought home to me when a student in a semantics class pointed out that when most people hear the word *occupation*, their first thought is of their job. However, when this student hears it, he thinks of being invaded because he is Palestinian.

Furthermore, there are generational differences in the connotations of words. In the USA, the word *sucks*, to mean 'bad', is quite commonly used in spoken language by people under 40, and is increasingly common even in more formal contexts such as network news programmes. (On CNN television news one night, I heard a middle-aged network news vice-president remark on the line-up of shows of another network by saying, 'It sucks'). For some older speakers in the USA, this word is considered quite ugly, bordering on the obscene for them; it has quite strong connotations. However, for a great deal of the under-40 crowd, it has none of these connotations at all. It is simply a synonym for *awful* or *terrible*.

These problems for meaning all have to do with the fact that meaning is constantly co-constructed by people who are members of different social networks. Our ability to connect with each other in 'meaningful' ways each and every day is even more amazing considering the fluidity of meaning and the contexts in which it unfolds.

## Suggested reading

Jeffries, L. (1998), *Meaning in English*. London: St Martin's Press.
Lakoff, G. (1990), *Women, Fire and Dangerous Things: What Categories Reveal about the Mind*. Chicago: University of Chicago Press.

# Consider the following

1. Identify ten slang words that are no longer in current use. Be sure to provide a definition of each word. Do you know how these words came into the language?

2. Identify a topic (but not poker or baseball) for which you can identify at least three figures of speech. Provide a definition of each and a sample sentence.

## Notes

1   Merriam-Webster Online: www.m-w.com/netdict.htm. Accessed 8 August 2006.
2   www.bartleby.com/61/13/R0261300.html. Accessed 18 August 2006.
3   One feature of a Rolex is that the second hand smoothly moves around the dial without stopping, unlike more inexpensive watches.
4   www.bartleby.com/61/91/D0039100.html. Accessed 22 August 2006.
5   www.peevish.co.uk/slang/ and www.lexscripta.com/desktop/dictionaries/slang.html are good sources for locating slang across the world.
6   www.en.wikipedia.org/wiki/Trial_of_the_century

# 8 Pragmatics: Language in Use

## Chapter Overview

| | | |
|---|---|---|
| 8.1 | SPEECH ACTS | 153 |
| | 8.1.1 DIRECT VERSUS INDIRECT SPEECH ACTS | 155 |
| 8.2 | SPEAKING THE UNSPEAKABLE: INDIRECTION AS A LINGUISTIC STRATEGY | 156 |
| | 8.2.1 EUPHEMISMS | 156 |
| | 8.2.2 EUPHEMISMS FOR PREGNANCY | 157 |
| | 8.2.3 PROVERBS AS INDIRECT SPEECH | 158 |
| 8.3 | LANGUAGE AND ADVERTISING | 160 |
| | 8.3.1 WEASEL WORDS | 161 |
| | 8.3.2 OPEN-ENDED COMPARISONS | 162 |
| | 8.3.3 AMBIGUOUS LANGUAGE AND MODAL AUXILIARIES | 163 |
| | 8.3.4 POLITICS AND ADVERTISING | 164 |
| 8.4 | MEANING AND HUMOUR | 167 |
| | 8.4.1 HUMOUR AND THE SOUND SYSTEM OF A LANGUAGE | 167 |
| | 8.4.2 HUMOUR AND MORPHOLOGY | 167 |
| | 8.4.3 HUMOUR AND SEMANTICS | 168 |
| | 8.4.4 HUMOUR AND SYNTAX | 169 |

Whereas semantics focuses on the interpretation of utterances in relative isolation, pragmatics looks at the contexts in which meaning develops and the purposes for which utterances are used, that is, speaker intention and hearer range of interpretation. Most of the time when we are talking, we are trying to accomplish something, whether it is something as direct as to get someone to do something or stop doing something or as abstract as to create bonds or sustain them. Each utterance that we make has a function which linguists call a *speech act*. These are all simple acts that we perform each and every day.

An utterance, taken either in isolation or within a social context, may have just one meaning. However, the function of that utterance can vary widely depending on the circumstances of the utterance. Take the sentence 'I forgot the book'. If you are in a classroom, this might be said to a teacher as an excuse for your lack of participation. However, if you say it to a friend, in a different tone, it could be an apology for forgetting her book or just providing information. The same utterance, yelled in the car on the way to school, informs your parent of your absent-mindedness and can be interpreted as a request to return to the house. In each of these scenarios, the underlying meaning of the utterance is exactly the same, but the utterance is performing a very different function.

# 8.1 Speech acts

One of the most common speech acts is a *representative*: a statement that supplies a fact (The company was founded in 1976) or a piece of information (I am tired) or a description of some physical thing or condition (The car is red). These statements simply provide information that can be evaluated as true or false.

We also make *commissives* in which the speaker has committed in some way to the truth of the statement made or has committed to some action in the future. At first, these seem very similar to representatives. In the statements 'I *assure* you that Tom has left' or 'I *know* the reports have been completed', the speaker wants you to believe something beyond the simple fact of the statement. Commissives include *promises*. A promise is activated by the words made, not by a speaker's intent or ability to keep the promise. If I say to a friend, 'I promise to pay for your university fees', I have made a promise. That promise is created by the specific words that I use. Even if I do not intend to keep my promise or am unable to keep it, I have still made one. Besides their importance in our personal lives, they have public meaning as well. Promises, in some contexts, may be viewed as *declarations* (see later section). For example, they have weight inside the courtroom. To understand the importance of their weight, you only need to watch a few episodes of *Judge Judy* or some other reality courtroom or legal show to see that they are interpreted by judges as oral contracts.

People frequently place orders, make demands or command people to do something. These speech acts are frequently *imperative* speech acts. By uttering one of these, our intent is to get someone to do something. Parents tell their children 'Do your homework now'. Employers say 'Finish the monthly report by tomorrow'. We might say to a waiter 'Bring me a drink'. Besides the imperative form, there are other ways to accomplish these same activities which we'll look at shortly.

*Interrogatives* are speech acts we use to get information that we do not know (or are pretending not to know). One student may ask another 'Is this professor fair?' An employee might ask 'What time is the meeting?' You could ask your father 'Is it cold outside?' The expectation is that the response will provide the information being requested.

Through *expressives*, speakers thank, congratulate, apologize, agree or disagree, insult, commiserate, swear, express regret or say something else that addresses the psychological state of the listener in some way: 'I'm very sorry', 'My bad', 'You're a jerk!'

Another speech act, the *directive*, is unusual in that the act of saying something officially brings about a new state of affairs. The conditions that existed before the words were uttered are now changed solely because a certain set of words were uttered. Imagine how your life could change after each of the following utterances:

You're fired!
I resign as president.
With this ring, I thee wed.
I confer upon you a Master's Degree in Humanities.

Another directive is a warning which is sometimes like a promise. Many a parent has said to a misbehaving child, 'You're cruising for a bruising, mister!' On the societal level, a leader of one country might say to another country threatening aggression, 'You are hereby warned that any attack will be met with full force'.

One special class of directives are *performative verbs*. These verbs are those which by their utterance perform an action. When a minister christens a baby, by the very act of their saying the words 'I christen this baby, Elizabeth', the baby officially becomes Elizabeth and receives the benefits of baptism. However, the same change in state does not occur if Elizabeth's 6-year-old brother Jeff says it. There are certain conditions that must be met before these words have official status; these are called *felicity conditions*. Because I am not a minister, I cannot just walk up to two students in my class and say, 'Now I pronounce you man and wife'. Well, yes, I can say it, but my words have no force. The same would be true if I declared an end to whatever war happens to be going on at the moment. I am not a governing body, queen nor president of any sort, so my words have no power to officially change the state of affairs. There are many other examples of performance verbs:

I quit this stupid job!
   (anyone with a job can say this)
I swear to uphold the constitution of the United States of America.
   (you must be a US citizen being sworn in for a federal job)
I make you, Sir Paul McCartney, a knight of the realm.
   (you must be the current king or queen of a country with knights)
I bet $500 the Jamaican bobsled team will get a gold medal in the next Olympics.
   (anyone can say this as long as there is such a team competing)
Hear ye! The court of Judge Judy is now in session.
   (the bailiff of the court must say this at the appropriate place and time)

These verbs sometimes act just like ordinary verbs. For example, when they are in the past or future tense, they are not performance verbs. 'Yesterday, I christened a baby.' The verb 'christened' is not performative in this utterance; it is solely a representative speech act. For a verb to be performative, it must also be a first person utterance. 'Now she declares you man and wife' simply does not work because the person saying it must be the one who meets the felicity conditions and performs the act him or herself. What felicity conditions must be in effect for the following utterances to be performance verbs?

I excommunicate you for heresy.
I crown you, William, successor to Elizabeth II.
I raise you $500.

I sentence you to five years in prison.
I declare today a new national holiday.

## 8.1.1 Direct versus indirect speech acts

In all of the above examples in the previous sections, the act that the speaker was performing was quite literal in that the function the speaker intended matched the sentence structure that is most appropriate to perform that function. For example, the interrogative grammatical structure was used to ask a question to solicit information. However, sometimes we use speech acts in a non-literal way to accomplish our goals. For instance, if I am having dinner at your house, and I am cold because the window is open, I could use *a direct speech act*, a question (interrogative) like 'May I close the window?' to make a request. However, much of our communication is not so direct. Sometimes we use a speech act to accomplish an act for which it was not intended.

There are other ways I can get the host to warm up the cold room. I could make a representative statement, 'It is cold in here'. This is a simple statement of fact (or opinion); however, the host is unlikely to interpret this as simply informative. It is clearly a request. I could also make an assertion, 'I think I am getting a cold' to achieve the same result.

Here is another scenario. You have invited someone over for dinner on a weeknight. It is now after midnight, and you have to be at work early in the morning. Here are some possible *indirect speech acts* that could be made to encourage your guest to go home (although the last one is certainly rude in any culture!). Notice that in all but the first and last example below the focus is on the receiver of the message and not the speaker.

(You look at your watch) Wow! It's getting very late. (representative)
I know you have to work early in the morning. (assertion)
You look so tired. (expressive)
Do you work tomorrow? (interrogative)
There's the door. (representative)

We consider the practice of using the 'wrong' speech act less direct than making a demand or a direct request. In part, this is because by our making inferences, savvy listeners are given the opportunity to address the speaker's needs, in itself a polite act. Of course, with indirect speech acts, you do run the risk of people taking them directly and not getting the 'hint' that it is time to go home, which does sometimes happen.

Imperatives are often used for purposes other than commands. In the following situations, the speaker may have no ability to command someone to do something nor have the intent to do so. In any case, a command does not make sense within the context nor do listeners interpret it as such.

Have a good time on vacation. (expressive)
Get yourself a beer from the fridge. (offer)
Swim at your own risk. (warning)

## 8.2 Speaking the unspeakable: indirection as a linguistic strategy

Indirect speech acts are part of a larger set of linguistic strategies called *indirection* which native speakers employ to accomplish the delivery of difficult content to others or to obfuscate the true meaning of an utterance. Sometimes these utterances call for the listener to interpret the context of the utterance, past history between the interlocutors and the temperament of the speakers.

### 8.2.1 Euphemisms

Euphemisms are a less direct way of expressing difficult or uncomfortable concepts. Their forms vary from culture to culture, but are often used to discuss topics like death, illness, pregnancy and war. Some are just polite ways of saying things, others are humorous responses. Sometimes, the use of a euphemism shows an intent by the speaker to make light of a difficult situation. Government officials and others create them to provide an alternative, possibly less clear, way of saying something that people do not want to hear or to provide a positive spin on a programme or policy.

One of my favourite euphemisms was uttered by Homer in *The Simpsons* when he accidentally pushed a button that caused a nuclear meltdown at the Springfield nuclear plant: 'We seem to be having an unrequested fission surplus'. An *unrequested fission surplus* certainly sounds less scary than a nuclear meltdown!

Justin Timberlake created a euphemism after the 2004 *Super Bowl* half-time show, when he 'accidentally' pulled off a part of Janet Jackson's shirt, exposing her breast. In an interview after the show Timberlake noted that 'We had a wardrobe malfunction' to describe the event in less direct words.

Aside from these comic euphemisms, which are not commonly picked up for use by the general public, euphemisms are commonly used every day by most speakers of a language. Many people of Western cultures seem to be uncomfortable speaking directly about old age and death; thus, there are hundreds of euphemisms for both. Some are simply indirect references; others are humorous expressions that 'take the sting' out of death and advancing age.

Euphemisms for age:

| | | |
|---|---|---|
| golden years | mature woman | senior citizen |
| old fart | old goat | seasoned |

Euphemisms for death:

| | | |
|---|---|---|
| pass on | go to a better place | go west |
| dearly departed | cashed in their chips | give up the ghost |
| kick the bucket | take a dirt nap | bite the big one |
| bite the dust | buy the farm | buy a pine condo |

## 8.2.2 Euphemisms for pregnancy

These are very interesting because they have recently become much less common in the USA due to changing social mores. When I was growing up in the 50s and 60s, it was not uncommon that the 'weather girl' would disappear off the news because it was considered unseemly for a pregnant woman to 'show' on TV. People often used euphemisms to refer to the state of being pregnant, like: *be in the family way, have a bun in the oven, with child, expecting* and, more humorously, *knocked up*. Because there is greater acceptance of childbearing out of wedlock, the use of these terms has diminished in the USA, directly correlated with the age of the speaker.

There are hundreds of euphemisms for unpleasant things that are used every day without much attention called to them: *adulterous* has become *extramarital, toilet paper* has become *bathroom tissue*; a *break-in* is now a *security breach*; a *brothel* is a *massage parlour* where you go to have a *happy ending*. You are no longer *addicted to drugs*, but have a *chemical dependency*. Your *juvenile delinquent* is a *problem child*. Innocent non-military casualties in a conflict situation are even given the ludicrous name of *collateral damage*.

In a print media interview, George Carlin once said that if he hadn't become a comic, he would like to have been a linguist. In fact, once you have studied semantics and pragmatics, you can see the basis for a good deal of his humour. In his album *Parental Advisory: Explicit Lyrics*, Carlin does a wonderful almost half-hour attack on euphemisms and other similar expressions. Here's a brief excerpt:

> Poor people used to live in slums. Now the economically disadvantaged occupy substandard housing in the inner cities. And they're broke! They're broke! They don't have a negative cash-flow position. They're f*** broke! Cause a lot of them were fired. You know, fired. Management wanted to curtail redundancies in the human resources area, so many people are no longer viable members of the workforce.

## 8.2.3 Proverbs as indirect speech

Another form of indirect speech is the use of proverbs. A proverb is a saying that is considered as 'common sense' or generally understood community wisdom. Their use is quite widespread across the world both as conversational elements and as formal aspects of storytelling. Anancy folk-tales of West Africa and the Caribbean, as well as Aesop's fables, make use of proverbs to sum up the wisdom of their stories. Most people can easily identify many proverbs:

> A penny saved is a penny earned.
> Familiarity breeds contempt.

Although most of the students I speak with claim not to use them, they do understand their meaning when we discuss them. Thus one aspect of proverb use in Western cultures seems to be that you must have age (and wisdom) to make use of them, though this is not always the case. Proverbs provide a neutral way to offer criticism (The apple does not fall far from the tree) or make a suggestion (Slow and steady wins the race). Because a proverb is used, the speaker is only passing on well-known information and not being directly critical of the intended receiver. Proverbs are used by political figures as well to support their contentions. In January 2003, in an interview with CNN, Senator Robert Byrd of West Virginia USA said, 'We need to pass the budget and fund programmes because *a stitch in time saves nine.*' He could have just as easily said, 'an ounce of prevention is worth a pound of cure'.

A proverb may be used to make a point indirectly because it is considered accepted community wisdom. On an American television programme called *Divorce Court*, I once heard a young rural white male say to the judge, 'Once you catch a fish you don't keep feeding it worms' to support his assertion that now that he was married, he no longer needed to buy his wife presents or take her out.

Proverb use is quite common worldwide, though in most non-European cultures their use is much more ritualistic than in European ones, even across quite varied cultures. A great deal of community wisdom seems to be shared cross-culturally. The wisdom of the following proverbs from many cultures is quite easily understood even though English proverbs for the same wisdom may be different:

> Even monkeys can fall from trees. (Korean)
> A bad wife is 100 years of bad harvest. (Japanese)
> One should choose one's bedfellow whilst it is daylight. (Swedish)
> A lie has speed, but truth has endurance. (Swahili)
> Don't speak of secret matters in a field that is full of little hills. (Israeli)
> Soft lips are able to bring a big stick down. (Ghanan)
> Eat and drink with your relatives; do business with strangers. (Greek)
> To overcome evil with good is good; to resist evil with evil is evil. (Egyptian)

Among the English-based Creole-speaking Afro-Caribbeans, the use of proverbs is quite common. They tend to be an interesting mix of translations of West African proverbs and English ones. Proverbs are used to teach children lessons either through their direct use or as endings to Anancy stories, which are tales with a proverb ending similar to Greek Aesop's fables. Adults tell Anancy stories in particular situations to indirectly insult or educate others. I was living in the Afro-Costa Rican town of Limon, Costa Rica during the impeachment hearings of US President Bill Clinton. Over and over, during discussions of Clinton's sexual misconduct, local men and women repeated the following proverb: 'The higher the monkey climbs in the tree, the more his ass you see.'

In another situation, my neighbour was commenting on the bad behaviour of a young person from the neighbourhood who had got in with a bad crowd. She simply pointed at the girl and said, 'if you lie down with dogs you get up with fleas'. No more needed to be said. The criticism was clear.

The Akan people of Ghana also use proverbs in a more ritualistic way than in most European cultures. In fact, one Akan proverb deals with proverb use itself: 'We speak to the wise man in proverbs, not plain language.' Proverbs are always perceived as coming from a third source (the community). Thus, the use of a proverb gives its user conversational immunity (meaning that because others write proverbs, the words come from them and not from you), and you may not be criticized for using one. Not only are proverbs useful for providing clarity and indirect criticism, they are accepted as evidence in tribal courts. Because proverbs come from elders and are part of traditional commonly accepted wisdom, they may be used as evidence to support a claim. They may also be used in the reading of the verdict, which may be given completely through a proverb.

The proverb below would be very useful to point out that a defendant is over-explaining or repeating some information a lot, possibly indicating that he or she is not speaking the truth.

A genuine case is argued in brief. (*Asɛm pa yɛ tia*. Original Akan)

Because their use is ritualistic, there are rules about who can use a proverb, and when, in Akan culture. For example, a commoner may not use one in the chief's court because the use asserts that the user knows more than the wise men and women of the court. A person may even be fined by the chief's court if he or she uses a proverb in the wrong situation or uses it incorrectly. Young people can use a proverb with an elder only in some very limited situations, but the utterance of the proverb must be preceded with an apology for using it. In Ghana, proverbs are such an important aspect of communication that particular patterns in cloth are visual proverbs.

There are other ritualistic or formalized contexts in which the use of indirection plays an important part in constructing a message in which the speaker or writer may be striving for a less obvious delivery of a message.

## 8.3 Language and advertising

Indirect speech is a very significant aspect of the language that advertisers make use of when promoting products or services. In the USA, advertisers are legally bound by what the language in their advertisements entails, but not what is implied (or not specifically said). In an earlier section of this chapter, I noted that a sentence can, and often does, entail certain other meanings. If I say 'John is divorced', it entails that he was once married. The sentence does not entail anything about his current emotional state: depending upon differing circumstances, John could be happily or unhappily divorced. Consider the following scenario:

> John: Am I in time for supper?
> Mary: I've cleared the table.

There are two possible ways to interpret Mary's answer to John's question. If John is on time, and he sees food cooking on the stove, the response could signify, 'I've moved my research books off the table, so we can eat'. However, if Mary looks angry, and there are pots and pans in the sink, it is likely that John is late, and she has already removed the dinner dishes from the table. Mary's answer to John's question could imply quite different meanings. Here's a familiar one for students:

Mother: Are you studying for your test?
Daughter: I'm looking at the books right now.

In the above exchange, the daughter has implied that she is studying, but she may only be looking at the books (they are between her and the TV). Sometimes an indirect answer to a question can lead the person to believe that the speaker has conveyed a certain meaning even though it has not explicitly been said. If caught, the speaker can claim that the listener did not correctly interpret the utterance and that no lie was intended. You can easily imagine how useful this escape clause is for both politicians and advertisers!

In the next section, we will see how indirection plays an important part in how advertisers get us to see their products in the best light. They achieve this by carefully manipulating language and by relying on the fact that most people choose the most positive interpretation of an utterance if it is ambiguous. Advertisers count on our goodwill not to spend too much time analysing their commercials, or we may find out that they have said nothing significant about their product at all.

## 8.3.1 Weasel words

Advertisers use a variety of words that may have a different street meaning from the dictionary meaning, or are ambiguous. For example, the adverb 'virtually' has come to be synonymous with 'almost' to many people. However, the primary meaning of 'virtually' is 'not in fact' and the secondary meaning is, 'almost, but not quite'. This makes sense when you consider the phrase 'virtual reality'. So if a cleaning product leaves your floors virtually spotless, what does that really entail?

Words used for their intentional ambiguity are called *weasel words* because of the slang expression 'weasel out' of something, meaning to wiggle out of a tough situation or the ability to not be able to be pinned down to anything. By using ambiguous language, advertisers can imply a lot about their products without fear of being held accountable for entailing something specific.

Another word that presents the same problem as 'virtually' is 'like', as in 'My friend works like a dog' which in no way means that she chases sheep or spends a lot of the day digging up bones. If a product works 'like magic' or makes your clothes 'like new', to what standard can you hold the advertiser?

'New' and 'improved', often paired together, are rarely defined within the context of the advertisement to give the consumer any real idea of how a product has improved. 'New' could simply mean that a different vegetable dye has been used and the improvements made could be minimal.

## 8.3.2 Open-ended comparisons

A very common advertising strategy is to make open-ended comparisons in which something is grammatically being compared to nothing but the consumer is left with the feeling that it has been:

> Coyote brand iced tea is better.
> Aardvark Chili has less fat.

These statements are meaningless because there is no product offered for comparison. Most consumers read these comparisons as 'with the competitor'. However, a can of Aardvark Chili could have less fat than a 20-gallon vat of fat. As absurd as this sounds, companies have made equally absurd claims. An American car company, which will remain nameless here, was fined by the FCC for making the claim that their car was 700 per cent quieter. When they were forced to support the claim, they said that the noise level inside the car was 700 per cent quieter than the noise level outside the car was when travelling down the highway – hardly a reading that any consumer would have come up with on their own.

## 8.3.3 Ambiguous language and modal auxiliaries

Advertisers often use words or phrases that are ambiguous, that can be interpreted in more than one way. Studies show that when there are two possible interpretations, people tend to interpret the stronger or more positive meaning that can be conveyed.

> The Warthog computer is designed like no other in the world.

This is of course true of all computers. Each is created differently so that it is an individual product and does not violate patents of other companies. Consumers typically read this statement as meaning that the Warthog has a better design than the others. That meaning is not entailed by the words of the sentence, it is only suggested. The only meaning that is entailed is that these computers are different (they may be worse!).

Companies also use modal auxiliaries (*can, may, could, might, should* etc.) to modify the claims that they are making about their products. Modal auxiliaries have the function of qualifying the verb in a verb phrase. In the following sentences, the modal auxiliary has a clear effect on the total meaning of the utterance:

> I *will* buy a car. (certainty)
> I *must* buy a car. (strong obligation)
> I *should* buy a car. (less strong obligation)
> I *might* buy a car. (slight possibility)
> I *can* buy a car. (option, possibility)

If a company runs an advertisement that says that 'Company X can save you up to 25 per cent on the cost of your home security system', the word *can* should be interpreted as a possibility. There is no guarantee that it will save you anything, just that it can. The claim is furthered weakened by the inclusion of the weasel words 'up to', which leave a wide latitude of interpretation concerning the possibility of savings. Consumers tend to interpret statements like this with the most positive reading – that they will get close to the 25 per cent savings. There is no objective measure here by which the consumer can judge the offer. Maybe only a small percentage of people get a discount, or the average discount may be only 5 per cent. To get the 25 per cent discount, you might have to be an employee of the company, making over $300,000 a year, with more than 20 years without a robbery claim. You just cannot tell from the advertisement as written.

Does this mean that all products that engage in these linguistic strategies have poor products? Certainly not. However, in a world where the consumer is confronted with 25 almost identical dishwashing liquids, companies are battling to get the consumer to believe that their product is better. Furthermore, these are quite often effective strategies for gaining a larger market share. Unfortunately, the same strategies employed by companies to push their products are also used by politicians to sell themselves and their policies.

## 8.3.4 Politics as advertising

> As societies grow decadent, the language grows decadent, too. Words are used to disguise, not to illuminate action: you liberate a city by destroying it. Words are to confuse, so that at election time people will solemnly vote against their own interests.
> Gore Vidal[1]

Unlike advertisers, politicians are only rarely held 'legally' responsible for what they say, except, of course, at election time, when the public has the option of voting them out. It is often argued, I think fairly, that politicians, especially those in campaign mode, must be able to create utterances that are open to the widest levels of interpretation and the most possible wiggle room, because they could not get elected otherwise. Because many people do not recognize that it is unlikely that they will ever be in agreement with any candidates on every issue, they often vote against (or later turn against) candidates for one particular view that they hold. Thus, candidates respond by giving us as little linguistic content as possible. This creates a tricky problem for both voters and candidate because the more we hold them accountable to every opinion they hold, the less likely it is that they are going to provide us with much information.

*Inference and politics*

Inference is one of the most common tools in any politician's linguistic arsenal. In the USA, the use of highly negative political advertising and political speech can lose a candidate an election because voters sometimes get fed up with directly negative advertising. Thus, candidates sometimes resort to making inferences, which are perceived by the public as being less direct, though the underlying claims are still the same. During the 2004 USA Democratic Presidential Convention, candidate John Kerry said the following in his acceptance speech:

> I will be a Commander in Chief who will never mislead us into war. I will have a Vice President who will not conduct secret meetings with polluters to rewrite our environmental laws. I will have a Secretary of Defence who will listen to the advice of our military leaders. And I will appoint an Attorney General who actually upholds the Constitution of the United States.

Clearly, his words were intended as an indictment of the Bush administration. Though he never specifically mentions anyone by name, he does make four claims about what he will not do that, presumably, was done by the Bush administration. Note that the focus, linguistically, is on Kerry, but the indictment is of the Bush administration.

Inference can be an effective weapon in another way. Sometimes, a claim is made as part of an accusation that may or may not be supported, but because of the structure of the sentence, focus is shifted elsewhere.

'The congress is completely ignoring the growing "X" crisis' (insert any crisis here). People will often assume the truth of the second part of the sentence, that there is indeed a crisis, and focus on the fact that Congress is ignoring it. There may in fact be no crisis.

You do not have to search long or hard for examples of inference in political speech in any country, and its use is not limited to any particular party or political philosophy. Columnist Molly Ivens, in one of her humorous books on Texas politics, cites this statement by Texas State House Representative, Don Rottenberg: 'There are still places where people think that the function of the media is to provide information.' Based on this inference, it is quite scary to consider what he thinks the role of the media should be in a democracy.

### Entailment and implicature in politics

Some politicians and others have also relied on entailment and the strictly literal interpretation of an utterance to obfuscate the real truth. Consider the following scenario in which a police officer has stopped a driver that she believes is drunk:

> Police: Have you been drinking?
> Driver: I've only had two bottles of beer.

In reality, the driver is telling the truth: he or she only consumed two beers. Nevertheless, the fact that the driver failed to provide the information that he or she followed each of the beers by a giant tequila chaser is assuredly a violation of the officer's expectations of the whole truth as to the sobriety of the driver.

After US President Bill Clinton's sex scandal became public, he repeated over and over again that the allegations were not true. Of course, Clinton defended himself and claimed he was not lying because the truth of his denial depended on the definition of the word 'is'. His claim was that he was asked a question about the affair in the present tense. According to footnote 1,128 of Clinton's grand jury testimony (the Starr report) 'It depends on what the meaning of the word "is" is . . . Now, if someone had asked me on that day, are you having any kind of sexual relations with Ms Lewinsky, that is, asked me a question *in the present tense*, I would have said no. And it would have been completely true.'

Needless to say, although linguistically accurate, the answer was certainly misleading. Although Clinton may assert the truth of his interpretation of the question, his response can hardly be considered to be acceptable. His answer is certainly disingenuous at best. It is interesting to note the use of modals as well (the use of *would*) in his answer to the same effect that an advertiser would use them, to mitigate the force of the verb.

*Euphemisms and analogies in politics*

Politicians and other public figures even create euphemisms to soften the impact of a particular situation or to obfuscate the meaning of some policy to which they expect the public to react negatively. The first President Bush, George Herbert Walker Bush, during his unsuccessful re-election campaign, said 'Read my lips, no new taxes', which came back to haunt him later in the campaign when he proposed 'revenue enhancers', which was a government programme in which wage earners would be forced to give the government a portion of their earnings. Hmmm . . .

Another aspect of political speech is the use of *analogies* for providing explanations or contexts for something. Their use creates a link between the sometimes foreign world of politics and something more familiar to which we can all relate. They also connect with our community process of symbol making. They may be used to create a mood or feeling as well. Speakers from both political parties made excellent use of analogies at the national presidential conventions in the USA in 2004:

> Now, again, it is time to choose. Since we're all in the *same boat*, we should choose a *captain of our ship* who is a brave good man, who knows how to *steer a vessel* through *troubled waters*, to the *calm seas* and the clear sides of our more perfect union. That is our mission.
> Bill Clinton

> Since 2001, Americans have been given *hills to climb*, and found the *strength to climb them*. Now, because we have made the *hard journey*, we can see the *valley* below.
> George Bush.

*The power of word choice*

Even the choice of word can be political and have ramifications for our worldview. The Western press and politicians have had the habit of referring to the God of Islam as *Allah*. Muslims are monotheistic and worship the God of Abraham – the same God as Christians and Jews. Many of the prophets of the Old and New Testaments of the Bible are also prophets of Islam, including Jesus, although Muslims do not view Jesus in the same way that Christians do (though neither do Jews). *Allah* is the Arabic word for *God*, like *Jehovah*, or any of the other names that are used in religious texts and speech.

What is the purpose of doing this? When the press writes about Mexicans, they do not write 'The Mexicans and their God, Dios, passed Holy Week with many celebrations'. Arabic Christians use the name *Allah*; I once asked an Iraqi Christian woman what God is called in her church, and she replied 'Allah'. Thus, we may not think of *Allah* as a synonym of *God* the same way we think of the Aramaic cognate of *Allah*, which is 'Eloi', a word heard in Christian churches. The use of the Arabic word, *Allah*, rather than the English word, *God*, is effective in promoting the mistaken belief that Muslims do not worship the same God as Protestants,

Catholics and Jews, and may contribute to the sense that Muslims are more different from Christians and Jews than they really are.

## 8.4 Meaning and humour

'Comedy lurks at secondary levels of meaning.' Eric Idle of *Monty Python's Flying Circus*[2]

I'm locating the section on humour in the chapter on language and meaning because humour is frequently found in the manipulation of meaning. However, humour also results from the ability of native speakers of a language to play with every linguistic subset of the language that we have looked at thus far.

### 8.4.1  Humour and the sound system of a language

Some humour is based on our understanding of phonetics, the rules and patterns of sound typical to our language.

> Q. Why do seagulls live by the sea?
> A. Because if they lived by the bay, they'd be bagels.
>
> Q. What do you get when you cross an elephant and a rhino?
> A. Elephino!

Some jokes reflect our knowledge of more than one linguistic principle. The following joke takes advantage of the fact that native speakers understand that a particular phonetic string of sounds can have more than one meaning and that writing often disambiguates these problems. Of course, you have to know that *borscht* is beetroot soup to get the joke.

> With all the borscht they consume, I don't understand why Russians aren't the world's greatest rock stars. I mean, everyone knows that the heart of rock and roll is the beat (beet).

### 8.4.2  Humour and morphology

Some humour is based on our understanding of the rules of how we divide up words and add prefixes and suffixes, as well as what constitutes a prefix or suffix. In one episode of *The Simpsons*, Homer is using medicinal marijuana for his eyes. At the end of the show, Homer is hanging out and getting high with Otto, the school bus driver. In his intoxicated state Otto is examining his hands and notes: 'They call them fingers, but I've never seen them fing'. This is funny because all native speakers of English understand that many verbs like *watch* and *teach* are made into nouns by adding the suffix *-er* to them.

Sometimes morphological humour picks fun at the inconsistencies of the English language. There are certain bound morphemes like *dis-*, *in-*, *un-* and others that when added to a root word are supposed to result in a new word that creates the negative of the root (*happy* becomes *unhappy*). However, the English language is perverse, and this rule does not always work. Consider the problem with the vagaries of the English language the native Spanish speaker is having in the following joke:

At a dinner party, a Latin American visitor was telling guests about himself. As he concluded, he said, 'And I have a charming and understanding wife but, alas, no children.' Listeners seemed to be waiting for him to continue, so he said, 'You see, my wife is *unbearable.*'

Puzzled glances prompted him to try to clarify the matter: 'What I mean is, my wife is *inconceivable.*' As his companions seemed amused, he floundered deeper into the intricacies of the English language, explaining triumphantly, 'That is, my wife, she is *impregnable!*'

### 8.4.3 Humour and semantics

Humour may also be based on our knowledge that words may have more than one meaning. Although this joke is partially visual, it gets the point across:

How do you know when your ass is too small?

Answer:

Semantic humour can include humour that plays with the expected meaning of utterances or violations of expected conversational practices. The following is funny because the bride does not follow convention even though she has answered the specific question asked.

> Justice of the Peace (to bride at her wedding): Do you take this man to be your lawful wedded husband in good times or in bad?
> Bride (after brief but thoughtful pause): In good times.

Humour can also result from the disjunct between the *sense* of a word (dictionary meaning) and what the word actually refers to in the real world.

> A teenage boy lost a contact lens playing basketball in his driveway. After looking for a while, he informed his parents that the lens was lost. The mother went outside and returned after some time with the lens. The teenager was quite surprised and asked her what she did to find it. 'We weren't looking for the same thing,' she replied. 'You were looking for a small piece of plastic. I was looking for $150.'

A joke may also result from the use of indirection to subtly give criticism to a group. Why might the following joke be difficult for a non-native speaker of English? What would they have to know about the culture to 'get' the joke?

> An elderly pastor, looking over his large congregation on Easter morning, startled them with this announcement: 'My friends, realizing that I will not see many of you until next Easter, may I take this opportunity to wish all of you a Merry Christmas and a Happy New Year!'

## 8.4.4 Humour and syntax

Humour may even be based on the organization of phrases in a sentence. In the following joke, the first statement may be read two ways, but the response forces one reading only.

> Knight: Your majesty, the people are revolting!
> King: Yes, very.

In the first sentence, 'the people are revolting', *are revolting* would most likely be interpreted as a helping verb followed by a verb. A synonymous sentence would be 'the people are having a revolution'. However, because of the king's response, we must read the first sentence as 'The people are disgusting', a combination of a verb (are) and an adjective (disgusting/revolting).

Grammatical humour may also result from the misplacement of prepositional phrases, which makes possible two very different readings. Groucho Marx is credited with saying in one of his movies, 'Last night I shot an elephant in my pyjamas. How he got there I'll never know!' The humour results from the mental image of an elephant wearing Groucho's pyjamas.

This type of humour is best found in the movies of the Marx Brothers, Monty Python's Flying Circus and Mel Brooks. These artists have learned the lessons of linguistics and have used that understanding to masterfully produce some of the funniest movies ever made.

## Suggested reading

Blakemore, D. (1992), *Understanding Utterances*. Oxford: Blackwell.
Yule, G. (1996). *Pragmatics*. Oxford: Oxford University Press.

## Interesting websites

Center for Advanced Research on Language Acquisition: University of Minnesota. www.carla.umn.edu/speechacts/descriptions.html
Lingua Links: Summer Institute of Linguistics: www.sil.org/linguistics/GlossaryOfLinguisticTerms/WhatIsASpeechAct.htm

## Questions to consider

1. Choose three advertisements and three jokes that are linguistically interesting (based on this chapter) and explain what linguistic strategies are employed.

2. Say whether each of the following (italicized) is a performance verb or not. If it is, describe the felicity conditions that must be in place for the sentence to have force. If it is not a performance verb, explain why not.

   a. I will *challenge* you to a debate if you win the nomination.
   b. I *dare* you to fight me.
   c. I *nominate* Arnold Schwartzenegger for President of the United States.
   d. Nixon *resigned* from the presidency.
   e. I *move* that we pass the motion as written.
   f. I *name* this bridge the John Lennon Expanse.
   g. I *swear* to tell the truth, the whole truth and nothing but the truth.

# Notes

1  'The Day the American Empire Ran Out of Gas', in *Armageddon: Essays 1983–1987*.
2  An interview on National Public Radio, *Fresh Air*, with Terry Gross, 12 May 2004.

# 9 The History of English

| 9.1 | PERIODS OF ENGLISH | 174 |
| | 9.1.1 EFFECTS OF THE NORMAN INVASION | 176 |
| | 9.1.2 THE RETURN OF ENGLISH | 177 |
| | 9.1.3 THE INFLUENCE OF GEOFFREY CHAUCER | 178 |
| | 9.1.4 THE PRINTING PRESS | 179 |
| | 9.1.5 THE INFLUENCE OF JAMES I | 181 |
| 9.2 | LEXICAL CHANGES | 182 |
| | 9.2.1 ENGLISH EXPANDS THROUGH MILITARY AND ECONOMIC EXPANSION | 184 |
| 9.3 | SOUND CHANGE | 186 |
| | 9.3.1 THE GREAT VOWEL SHIFT | 187 |
| | 9.3.2 EVIDENCE FOR SOUND CHANGE FROM OLD ENGLISH | 188 |
| 9.4 | CHANGES IN GRAMMAR | 189 |
| 9.5 | THE SPELLING 'SYSTEM' OF ENGLISH | 190 |
| | 9.5.1 FIXING THE SPELLING PROBLEM | 194 |

Chapter Overview

If you have read any Shakespeare, or suffered through translating Beowulf from the Old English in literature classes in school, you are well aware that earlier versions of English did not sound or look the same as English does now. Beowulf, written in about AD 1100, very much appears to be a foreign language full of unknown words and letters:

> Hwæt! We Gardena in geardagum,
> eodcyninga, þrym gefrunon,
> hu ða æþelingas ellen fremedon.

If you were to take a look at the full text, as foreign as it would seem, you would be able to identify words that look like English. What seems to have remained in Modern English from this older variety are the function words like the possessives (e.g. *his* or *her*) as well as many prepositions (e.g. *on* and *over*) as well as some basic nouns (e.g. *god, godfather, godson*) and verbs (e.g. *be, were, hit*) common to everyday living as we can see from the following text from the *Laws of Ine* in which we can identify Modern English words.

> Gif hwa oðres godsunu slea oððe his godfæder, sie sio mægbot 7 sio manbot gelic; weaxe sio bot be ðam were, swa ilce swa sio manbot deð þe þam hlaforde sceal. Gif hit þonne kyninges godsunu sie, bete be his were þam cyninge swa ilce swa þære mægþe.

Nevertheless, it is clear that a great deal of the system that was in place at that early time in English history has greatly changed over the hundreds of years between this writing and now. Not so foreign are the early Middle English writings of Chaucer, which are much more recognizable to speakers of Modern English. Differences in vocabulary and grammar (as well as sound) abound, but most people can get the gist of the story of *The Wife of Bath* with a little help from a glossary.

> Experience, though noon auctoritee
> Were in this world, is right ynogh for me
> To speke of wo that is in mariage;
> For, lordynges, sith I twelve yeer was of age,
> Thonked be God that is eterne on lyve,
> Housbondes at chirche dore I have had fyve, –
> If I so ofte myghte have ywedded bee, –
> And alle were worthy men in hir degree.

By the end of the Middle English period, English begins to look much more like the modern variety. Even the English we do not currently use, that was common in the time of Shakespeare, may seem familiar to us, because so much of his work is represented in movies, like Mel Gibson's *Hamlet* or Laurence Fishburne's *Othello*. Many people are also familiar with the *King James Bible* or early versions of the *Book of Common Prayer*, both of which were written in much older varieties of English. The official version of the Book of Common Prayer for the Church of England (the Episcopalian church in the USA) was written in the language of the King James Bible in 1662 and remained in use until the 1970s, when a more modern English version was developed. Though modern varieties of both do exist, many people still have a preference for the older style and they are still commonly found in many homes and churches. Even so, it is clear that the English of Shakespeare's time was quite different from modern varieties of English, and it's not just the words that make it so:

> HAMLET
> Does it not, think'st thee, stand me now upon –
> He that hath kill'd my king and whored my mother,
> Popp'd in between the election and my hopes,
> Thrown out his angle for my proper life,
> And with such cozenage – is't not perfect conscience,
> To quit him with this arm?

An analysis of Shakespeare's English reveals that the grammar and spelling are also distinct from modern varieties of English. For example, in the first line in the passage above, Middle English *think'st* is equivalent to Modern English present tense *think*. Middle English had grammatical suffixes that have long since disappeared from Modern English. It was also a common spelling convention to use the apostrophe to replace the letter 'e' in -*ed* past tense endings.

## 9.1 Periods of English

I've been talking about different periods of English as if there were distinguishable boundaries that made each form completely distinct. A better way to look at the shifting varieties of English is to think of a continuum of overlapping varieties all of which have been changing but to different degrees. The periods of Old, Middle and Modern English are arbitrary divisions bounded by important political or cultural events. The period that we call Old English covers the time period of the first Anglo-Saxon invasions of England in about 449 to the beginning of the twelfth century, after the Norman Invasion from France in 1066. We make this the end point of Old English because this invasion had a profound impact on the English language, which we'll talk about shortly. The variety of English called Middle English begins with the Norman Invasion and ends with Shakespeare and the reign of King James I of England (the 1500s). Modern English spans that time to the present. One has to wonder if from now until eternity we will be calling our variety Modern English or if at some point in the future our great, great, great grandchildren will be studying the archaic way we speak now and referring to their own variety as Post-Modern English. One thing we know for certain, all languages change and some day the way we speak now will be considered old-fashioned.

These names for different forms of English are useful to us in terms of looking at major linguistic differences; nevertheless, people didn't go to bed one night speaking Old English and wake up speaking Middle English. Changes spread slowly and were often incomplete. Imagine how long after the introduction of a new word in London in the 1500s it would have taken to reach the farthest reaches of northern Scotland. It may have been a long time, and many changes may never have arrived. Consider also that English was in competition with local languages in many areas, so local words, grammar rules and accents would have been popular with many speakers, and they may not have accepted all the changes happening, for example, in London. Variation in degree of change helps to explain the existence of so many dialects of English worldwide. A useful analogy is to imagine a new word or grammar rule being a rock you throw out in the middle of a pond. The areas closest to the rockfall are impacted first, and as the ripples travel outward, their power weakens (like the power of the linguistic change) until there are no ripples at all. For example, many new slang terms in British or Australian English never reach the US, and the converse is true as well. For now though, let's go back to the beginning.

The earliest inhabitants of what is now Britain, dating back to around 400 BC, were Celtic peoples. English is not a part of the Celtic language family; nevertheless, these people played a part in the development of English, as well as contributing significantly to modern varieties of Irish, Scots and Welsh varieties of English (which have had a major influence on the varieties of English spoken in the United States and Australia). The earliest foreign invaders were the Romans who first occupied the islands in about 55 BC. During this 500-year occupation, Latin words, especially words relating to religion, government and warfare, were borrowed into Celtic languages whose speakers later would have been intermarrying with future invaders. This Latin influence was repeated later when, in AD 597, St Augustine came to England to convert the local people to Roman Catholicism. Latin was not acquired by the local population, except for the monks, because the Romans never left a permanent occupying force in England which was at the limit of their far-flung empire. They were satisfied with receiving occasional tributes sent to Rome.

The development of English is closely associated with the history of the many invasions of England because, in fact, English is a transplanted variety of Old Germanic. The term English itself is arbitrary. What we speak could have as easily ended up being called Anglo-Saxon or Germanic. Nevertheless, for over 1,000 years, throughout a time period from around 55 BC to AD 1066, England was overrun by almost a dozen different sets of invaders. The Saxons came as early as AD 449 and were followed in 792 by the Vikings who came from present-day Norway, Sweden and Denmark. Less than 100 years later began the raids by the Danes. During this time, England was also occupied by the Angles, Jutes and Frisians, who spoke various Germanic dialects. These were not single invasions, but multiple incursions from distinct areas whose speakers would have spoken different languages, or dialects of other related languages.

As each group settled in, they intermarried and mixed with the current set of local inhabitants. The children of these unions would most likely have learned the language of their mothers, since they would be at home with them. Their father's languages would have been available to them as well though to a lesser degree. In these households, words from both languages would have been used by all the speakers in the house and spread throughout the community. Because of the mixing of all these varieties of speech, local speech forms began to emerge, and by AD 600 the still heavily Germanic speech of England was distinct enough from continental Germanic that new groups of invaders had difficulty understanding the great grandchildren of their common ancestors. However, because the invaders' languages were all related, their combined influence on the developing vocabulary of English was great. Examples of borrowed words from Norse languages of this time are: *die, leg, want, get, both, give, they* and *them*.

As settlements grew larger and as settlers became integral parts of local communities, inhabitants began to see themselves as a people. In Wessex, in the 870s, Alfred the Great became king and united these varied groups of people to defeat new invasions from the Danes, Vikings and Norwegians. After their victory, he created two kingdoms: one in the south, mostly Anglo-Saxon, which he ruled, and the northern territories which were ruled by the descendants of Scandinavian invaders. Alfred had a genius for nation-building. Besides being able to unite such disparate tribes militarily, he united them as a nation with a culture and language. He understood well the importance of language as a symbol of culture and began to make a record of this new nation, not in Latin as much of the royalty of Europe did but in English. He is responsible for the *Anglo-Saxon Chronicles*, a history kept by monks that recorded the deeds and accomplishments of the new nation. Alfred used English for all official court documents as well as for writing his own will. He gave legitimacy to what many considered a barbarian tongue, and for this and his military and political accomplishments, he was given the name 'The Great'. He is the only king of England to have ever been given this title.

For 200 years after Alfred the Great, English developed and spread across the island, becoming the language of all people of all classes. Then an event happened which could very well have heralded the death of this budding language, the invasion of William, Duke of Normandy, from France. In 1066 he defeated Harold, who was to be the last English king for almost 300 years. The Old English period ended with the Norman Invasion from France. This is as good a place as any to mark it because with this invasion came the transformation of English vocabulary and the remarkable survival of a conquered people's language.

## 9.1.1   Effects of the Norman Invasion

The major change in daily life in England was that the country became split between people of the lower classes, who spoke English, and people of the ruling class, who spoke French. Those who had to deal with both groups on a regular basis, for example merchants, priests and court officials, became bilingual. After the Norman Invasion, almost all legal documents and works of literature were written in French, and English mostly ceased to be a written language. The English monks stopped writing the *Anglo-Saxon Chronicles* because they were replaced by French-speaking monks. These French-speaking monks would have continued to perform church rituals in Latin as did their predecessors, but day-to-day activities would have been conducted in French with the nobility, and in English, as they acquired it, when they dealt with the monolingual English speakers who made up the vast majority of their parishioners.

A very limited sort of situational bilingualism sprang up as well when monolingual speakers of each group had repeated contact. For example, it is quite likely that the French nobles would have learned enough English to give orders to their field workers, who in turn would have learned some French words as well. The English peasants working in the house, who would have had more constant exposure to French, would have picked up even more French, which they most likely would have shared with their spouses and friends who worked in the fields. A good deal of unofficial language learning was certainly going on, though no official effort was made by the Normans to convert the English to the French language.

This unofficial bilingualism caused some interesting developments in English that remain with us today. The major result of contact with French is that English acquired thousands of new words from French, providing English speakers and writers with a wealth of vocabulary unparalleled by other languages. It is estimated that English has almost double the vocabulary of languages like French, German and Italian.

Because the official political, legal, cultural and religious life of England was conducted in French, and the vast majority of the people living in England were monolingual English speakers, the use of certain words from each language may have been necessary in some situations. In addition, the sole use of French words in some situations and English in others may have reflected certain cultural realities. The clash of these languages has left Modern English with some unusual sets of words from both traditions.

Imagine a typical court tribunal. It would have been likely that the peasant caught poaching deer on the king's land would have been a monolingual English speaker, yet the officials who ran the court system would have been French speakers. There certainly would have been much translating back and forth for each party to have made their case. Thus, certain words would have been paired together so frequently that they survived as a unit into Modern English, such as: *will* and *testament*, *breaking* and *entering*, *battery* and *assault* (the first in each pair are of Anglo-Saxon origin). The word *lawyer* is of Anglo-Saxon origin, whereas *attorney* and *barrister* are French.

We find a similarly interesting set of words when we look at the words for meat on the dinner table and those for the corresponding animal in the field. Again, the English-speaking workers in the field would have used English words to refer to the animals they were killing and eating, but in the castle or manor house, the Norman French would have used French words. Eventually, these words took on distinct meanings: the French-origin words are used for the food on the table and the English words for the animal in the field. Thus, we eat *poultry*, *beef*, *mutton* and *venison*, but we raise or hunt *cows*, *chickens*, *sheep* and *deer*.

Even more telling is that the same pattern exists for many of our obscene words for which the 'polite' term that we might use, for example, during a visit to the doctor, are French-derived words. The obscene counterparts are good old Anglo-Saxon words. The curious can research these words in their own time. It makes you wonder why the expression 'Pardon my French', uttered by many after swearing, shouldn't be changed to 'Pardon my Anglo-Saxon'! The point is that socio-cultural circumstances have affected what classes of terms were borrowed and which resonate more powerfully for us in different conversational contexts.

## 9.1.2 The return of English

The use of English in all aspects of society returned gradually, caused by both political and social events. In 1204, the Normans lost their lands in northern France, and thus lost their ties to French language and culture as well. Their future therrefore was tied to England. In addition, because they were vastly outnumbered by the English in the lands they ruled, they frequently married English-speaking women. Because the nobles and knights were absent from home much of the time, their children were exposed to English rather than French by the monolingual English-speaking women who cared for them as well as their English-speaking mothers. As decades passed, French was taught to these children only as a foreign language. Some interesting letters have been located from this time in which a Norman noble is petitioning the King of France for permission to educate his wife and family in the French language, so some proscription against the spread of French to English peasants seems to have been in effect. Even if the Normans had an overt passion for forcing French on the English peasantry, it is unlikely that they would have pulled their workers out of the field to teach them.

Due to all these factors, first-language acquisition of French continued to decline in England. By the 1340s, the language of instruction in most schools in England had become English, with the exception of Oxford and Cambridge where Latin continued in use. Later, in 1362, almost 200 years after the Norman Invasion, English was officially again the language of the judicial system and the language of Parliament. This was a de facto admission of reality. Spoken English had never been endangered by French, and the nobles just gave in to the reality of the English-speaking nation. Slowly, English began to re-emerge as a written language at this time.

## 9.1.3 The influence of Geoffrey Chaucer

Around 1380, Chaucer composed his *Canterbury Tales* in English, which helped English gain local prestige as a literary language. *The Canterbury Tales* were a set of stories told by a group of very diverse travellers who were making a religious pilgrimage to a faraway city. They told quite interesting and ribald stories about their lives to keep each other entertained over the long journey. Chaucer had previously written his literary works in Latin, as was the custom of many European writers of his day. Though Chaucer made a conscious decision to write in English, lending credence to its claim to be a full language, his English reflects his multilingual background. There are hundreds of words in the tales that are of French or Latin origin: words that are now part and parcel of English spoken throughout the world. Reading *The Canterbury Tales* is not that difficult for speakers of modern varieties of English. Much of the grammar is familiar to us as, well as a good deal of the vocabulary. With a good Middle English glossary his wit and humour come through the centuries quite well:

Upon an amblere esily she sat, Ywympled wel, and on hir heed an hat. As brood as is a bokeler or a targe; A foot-mantel aboute hir hipes large, And on hir feet a paire of spores sharpe.

Chaucer's writings are significant to linguists for an additional reason. In the tales, the speech of each of the pilgrims is representative of the geographical area from which they came. For example, in 'The Reeve's Tale', Oswald purposely establishes himself as a northerner via his distinct speech and use of northern slang. Chaucer was the first writer of English to make use of dialectal diversity as part of the presentation of his story.

## 9.1.4 The printing press

About 100 years after Chaucer, William Caxton brought a printing press from Germany to England in 1474. This began the long road towards the standardization of English both in spelling and in grammar. Early printers like Caxton were well aware of the effect their printing choices were to have on the language. He recognized that dialectal diversity would be reflected in the written word, not just in word choice but in grammar and spelling. Furthermore, the number of literate speakers of English would increase with much broader availability of the printed word. Caxton's musings on this very subject are available to us in the following excerpt to the preface of his 1490 printed version of Virgil's *Aeneid*:

And certaynly our langage now vsed varyeth ferre from that whiche was vsed and spoken whan I was borne and that comyn englysshe that is spoken in one shyre varyeth from a nother.

In so moche that in my dayes happened that certayn marchauntes were in a shippe in tamyse for to haue sayled ouer the see into zelande and for lacke of wynde thei taryed atte forlond, and wente to lande for to refreshe them and one of theym named sheffelde a mercer cam in to an hows and axed for mete, and specyally he axyd after eggys.

And the good wyf answerde that she coude speke no frenshe, and she vnderstode hym not / And thenne at laste a nother sayd that he wolde haue eyren / then the good wyf sayd that she vnderstod hym wel / Lo what sholde a man in thyse dayes now wryte. egges or eyren/

Translation:
And certainly our language now used varies far from that which was used and spoken when I was born and that common English that is spoken in one shire varies from another.

In so much in that in my days, certain merchants were in a ship in the Thames for to have sailed to Holland, but for lack of wind, they tarried at Forland, and went to land to refresh themselves, and one of them, named Sheffelde, a mercer, came into a house and asked for meat, specifically he asked for eggs.

> And the good wife answered that she could not speak French and she understood
> him not. And then another said that he would have eyren. Then the good wife said
> she understood him well. Lo what should a man in these days now write: eggs or
> eyren?

It turns out that in the good wife's dialect of English, the plural form of *egg* was *eyren*. This makes sense if you understand that at this time the plural ending *-en* was one of several endings that could make a noun plural. This ending remains to us solely in a few words in Modern English like *children*, *brethren* and *oxen*. In Modern English, the default form for plural is to add -s. At the end of this passage, Caxton laments (my translation) 'What should a man in these days now write: *egges* or *eyren*?' Caxton was painfully aware that the choices he and fellow printers would make would have a widespread impact on how people would write (and speak) English.

Thus English was firmly established as a literary, legal and instructional language in London by the early 1500s. Though Chaucer gave English its first push onto the English stage, it was William Shakespeare's genius (late 1500s to early 1600s) that crafted the explosion of English vocabulary that has made it such an expressive language. It is with the writings of Shakespeare, and their significant impact on the development of English, that we arbitrarily begin the period of Modern English.

A linguistic analysis of Shakespeare's works shows that his vocabulary exceeded 30,000 words. To put this in perspective, the average educated person's vocabulary is only about 15,000 words. He created thousands of words that have become part and parcel of normal everyday English. He did so not just through invention but by bringing native and borrowed words together in new combinations. Some of the more common everyday words he contributed to English are: *indistinguishable, obscene, luggage* and *zany* as well as *mountaineer, cold-blooded* and *torture*. His plays and sonnets have also left us with hundreds of everyday expressions whose users may not recognize to be Shakespearean. For example, he is the first writer to refer to *jealousy* as 'green-eyed'. Other common expressions from Shakespeare are: *fair play, cold comfort, one fell swoop, the long and the short of it* and even *wild goose chase*. There are hundreds of others as well. No other author has come even close to Shakespeare in enriching the creativity and expressive power of our language.

In the early 1600s, Elizabeth I died childless, and thus was succeeded to the throne of England by the son of her old enemy and cousin, Mary Queen of Scots. Her son, James VI of Scotland, became James I of the combined kingdoms. The choice of James had an interesting linguistic effect both on the spread of English and the variety of English that would be spread across Britain.

## 9.1.5 The influence of James I

James was a native speaker of Scots Gaelic, though reportedly a passable speaker of Scots English, which was distinct enough from the English spoken in London as to make speech between peoples of the two countries somewhat unintelligible. It was certainly plausible that once in power, James could have used his influence to promote the variety of English that he himself spoke, or even tried to force Scots Gaelic on the English. However, perhaps wisely, he did not. In fact, he declared laws that made English the national language of his united kingdoms. James is also responsible for the spread of a written variety of English across Britain. First, he decreed that English would be the language spoken in all churches and schools throughout the nation. Then, in 1611, he commissioned a new version of the Bible to be written by a committee. His intent for this Bible is reported to have been to make it a more poetic yet more readable Bible than previous versions, especially for the increasingly literate middle class. This was a particularly difficult task. At this time, Britain was fiercely divided along religious lines between Catholics and Anglicans (the church created by Henry VIII, Elizabeth's father). James' own mother was Catholic, but though he had been baptized Catholic, after his mother's imprisonment in the Tower of London, he was raised in the Scottish Anglican church. With his Bible, James was trying to find a middle road between Catholics, who wanted a flowery Bible in the Latin tradition, which would have been difficult for common people to read, and Puritans, who wanted a Bible for common people, but devoid of the passion of previous versions. It is a fair testament to James' success that this Bible is still found in many homes and churches, and sold throughout the world hundreds of years later. Once written, James ordered this Bible to be placed in all churches in all the united territories, and decreed that only this version could be read from in church. Obviously, this ruling had the effect of spreading the dialect of English in which this, the King James Version of the Bible, was written.

Of course, the decrees of James I did not immediately wipe out other languages in Scotland, Wales and Ireland, nor did the written word eliminate the divergent accents of the 'Englishes' spoken in these areas. Local preachers would have read the Bible in their own accents. Furthermore, you can imagine the reactions of many of the people to these decrees. Local varieties survive, often because of local resistance to giving up their own varieties which are a reflection of local identity. A lovely example of this is a 1983 Scots English version of the Bible in which only the devil speaks in Standard English! The resistance to linguistic change all over Britain is part of the cause of the wonderful diversity of sound heard as one travels from one area to another. In fact, there is actually more dialectal diversity across Britain than in the much larger United States because many of these varieties were established before the written word became commonplace and before the push for standardization began.

Up until now, I've focused on the historical events that contributed to the development of English as a language. The rest of this chapter will take a look at some of the changes that have taken place in English over its history, and the forces that have driven these changes. The changes have occurred in every subsystem of English, which is true of language change in general.

## 9.2  Lexical change

The most obvious types of changes to the lexicon of a language are changes to the words and their meanings. Any young person speaking with a grandparent or reading literature from even 50 years ago can note changes in word meanings and words that don't exist any more in common speech. People of my grandparents' age referred to wonderful things as *the bees' knees*, which kids in my youth would have called *groovy*. *Groovy* was happily well on its way to linguistic oblivion and would have disappeared completely from Modern English in the USA if it hadn't received a spurt of lifeblood from the Austin Powers movies.

All languages undergo changes in their lexicon, or vocabulary, every generation. Sometimes words change meaning in one dialect but remain the same in others. This is another cause of language variation within one language. In addition, new words are sometimes coined, but more often, meanings are shifted in some manner. Meanings may change completely, or they can change to become narrower or broader.

For instance, in Old English the word *docga* (Middle English *dogge*), corresponding to Modern English *dog*, referred to a specific breed of dog, not to all of the species in general as it does today. Perversely, the Old English word *hund* denoted all dogs, and now, especially in the American South, means one specific breed of dog. In German, the parent language of English, the word *hund* is still the generic word for *dog*. In this case, one term narrowed, whereas a corresponding term broadened.

The meaning of other words narrowed as well. In Old English, *girl* was used to denote children of both sexes; it didn't become gender specific until later. In King Henry VIII's time, the word for *food* in general was *meat*. They called poultry, pork or beef *flesh*.

The word *holiday* is actually derived, not surprisingly, from *holy day*. In earlier times, it referred specifically to days when work was suspended because of a religious event. The meaning has been extended in Modern English to specify any weekday that we officially have off from work. The word *butcher* has also broadened in meaning. It once specified the man whose job it was to kill goats and cut them into meat. Now it is used to refer to someone who does this for all farm animals. The many fans of J. R. R. Tolkien's *The Hobbit* will remember that he referred to the dragon Smaug as a *worm*, which is the Old and early Middle English usage of that word. Tolkien was a linguist and an Anglo-Saxon scholar; thus, his tales are peppered with words from older varieties of English.

Tracing the meaning shifts for some words can be very interesting. In Old English, the word *bead* signified *prayer*. Considering that England was predominantly Catholic until Henry VIII, it's not much of a jump to see the association between the rosary and prayer in common everyday life. Indications of this older meaning can still be found in some obscure religious words in the current language. For example, a *beadle* is a minor official at the parish in charge of keeping order at services and being an usher. Many other common English words have undergone shifts in meaning as well. Old English *lust* had no sexual connotation; it simply meant *pleasure*. This older meaning still survives in the expression *she has a lust for life* and other related expressions.

One of the more interesting transformations follows the word *silly*, which has had no less than three meanings: in Old English, it meant *happy*, by Middle English it had changed its meaning to *naive*, and it shifted meaning again by Modern English to signify *foolish* or *childish*. Another word that meant *ignorant* in Old English was *lewd*. There are thousands of these shifts in meaning over the last couple of thousands of years of English development.

Finally, some words just disappear from use altogether. Many of these words are simply slang terms, which may pass in and out of a language quite quickly and not even survive a generation of use. Others that disappear are quite common words of solid standing that die off, not from misuse, but from some other pressure in the system. The pronoun system of Old and Middle English serves as a good example of this process. Old English distinguished between *ye*, the plural form of Modern English *you*, and *thou*, the singular form. Eventually, more forms were added, and they took on an extended role. By the Middle English period, the usage for these terms started to shift. Perhaps the bilingual French-educated elite in England recognized that French offered a grammatical/social distinction that English did not: separate pronoun forms for a formal/informal distinction. Thus, *ye*, *you* and *your*, the plural forms, began to be used to denote a formal register, for example to use with someone from a different social class (usually higher), or to indicate respect for someone. What had been the singular terms, *thou*, *thee* and *thy*, became marked as the informal pronouns to be used with social subordinates, children, or those with whom one had a very friendly relationship. As some of the social class restrictions lessened and as general courtesy, in the linguistic sense, grew, the usage of the formal polite pronouns overwhelmed the informal ones, which slowly fell into disuse in normal speech. *Ye* survived somewhat longer than the others, but because both *ye* and *you* were clipped in fast speech, there was little distinction between them, and they eventually collapsed into one form. These older forms are not unknown to many of us. Those who grew up using the King James Bible and older version of the Book of Common Prayer still have at least a passing sense of some of these older forms of *you*.

For English, one of the most productive forms of language change results from the borrowing of words from other languages. English has borrowed words from practically every language with whom its speakers have come into contact. Almost half of the present-day vocabulary of English can be traced to Norman roots. The scope of the borrowing from French dwarfs borrowing from any other language. Estimates as high as 80 per cent have been bandied about concerning the number of French-derived words that are part of Modern English. Many words borrowed from French are associated with government or the law, which is not particularly surprising since these words were borrowed after the Norman Invasion when French speakers were the rulers of England. Included in this long list are the words: *parliament, baron, liberty, arrest, judge, jury* and *prison*. Other words relate to cuisine: *beef* and *poultry*. This massive influx of vocabulary, much of which added new synonyms to English for existing words, transformed English.

Up through the 1600s, Latin and Greek were the languages of science and literature across Europe. Therefore, many Latin and Greek words were borrowed into English (and other languages) at this time by bilingual authors. This list includes the names of many of our scientific disciplines including *grammar, logic, astronomy* and *geometry*, as well as the names of chemicals and scientific processes like *amalgam, alkali, arsenic, tartar, test*, and *alcohol*. Tracing the etymology (history) of words can be quite tricky because there may be more than one way a word may have come into a language. Take for instance the word *grammar*. It was originally a Greek word, *grammatikos*, which was borrowed into Latin as *grammatica*. The word is also found in Middle French as *gramaire* and in Middle English as *gramere*. We can account for influence on English from all of these sources. Latin and Greek were the languages of science and literature and were commonly understood by bilingual English writers like Chaucer and other intellectuals; thus whether the word came into English directly from Greek, or secondarily from Latin, or even more indirectly from Middle French with the Norman Invasion, may be difficult to tell. It was probably available through all of these routes.

## 9.2.1 English expands through military and economic expansion

Not only was English enriched by the nations who invaded the country, but also by the invasions, both military and economic, that England carried out abroad. For example, words were brought into English from Arabic as a result of the Crusades to the Holy Land and the 700-year occupation of Spain and Portugal by Arabs. Arabic also filtered into European languages after the Dark Ages because although manuscripts were destroyed all over Europe, many of the great works of Greece and Rome were kept safe in the Egyptian libraries at Alexandria and elsewhere. These works were maintained as bilingual documents, and later European scholars recovering their own ancient histories picked up some Arabic as well.

During their multiple invasions of the Holy Lands from the eleventh to the thirteenth centuries, the English would have encountered many new products in the markets for which they had no names. They also encountered new customs. In many cases they borrowed the Arabic names, words that are quite commonly found in today's English: *cotton*, *sugar*, *scarlet*, *mattress* and *caravan*. The peoples of this part of the world were also quite advanced in the field of mathematics; thus we borrowed from them words like *zenith*, *zero*, *almanac*, *algebra* and even *arithmetic*. However, sometimes words get borrowed with incorrect associations or definitions. During the Crusades, a secretive guerilla group of Arabs would steal into the tents of the leaders of invading European army leaders and kill them. They were often under the influence of *hashshashin* (hashish). The crusaders heard this word and misinterpreted it to mean a political murder. Thus the word *assassin* came into the English language.

Words were also brought into English as the merchant and military fleets sailed all over the world, acquired new products and had new experiences for which they borrowed words from the peoples they encountered. Many of the words borrowed from the Far East show us the importance of our trade there: words for textiles like *khaki*, a word borrowed from Urdu spoken in the area of present-day Pakistan and northern India. Other words, like *typhoon*, borrowed from Japanese, describe the terrible storms that ravaged many sailing ships. Sailors are also likely to have sampled the local alcohol in places and would have encountered *saki* in Japan as well. English borrowed another word into English from our early trade experiences in Japan: *tycoon*, which in Japanese is spelled *taikun* and spelled with the Chinese characters 人君. This word, meaning 'great leader or commander', is no longer commonly used in Japan but has survived in Modern English to refer to a very rich and powerful person.

English vocabulary continued to change and acquire new words when English was transported all over the world to English colonies. The varieties of English that developed in the colonies, and elsewhere, will be dealt with in the chapter on the worldwide spread of English.

Because many of the lexical changes have left the form of words intact over time but shifted the meanings significantly, one has to wonder how much misunderstanding goes on every day in our consumption of the literature of older varieties of English. The first time I taught this in class, it came to me that this shifting of meanings, an inevitable process, had gone unnoticed by me when I was a young student, and possibly many other students when we were assigned readings from Chaucer or Shakespeare and others. These works were difficult to understand at times because of the unfamiliar vocabulary, spelling and grammar, but I thought they were made easier by the appearance of 'common' words. I wonder how often my understanding of an event in a play or an analysis of a character's personality was completely incorrect because I gave Modern English meanings to Old and Middle English words!

## 9.3  Sound change

Another aspect of language that changes is the inventory of sounds used by speakers of languages, and how speakers may combine those sounds. Old English word structure was quite different from Modern English; for example, Old English preferred words that ended in vowel sounds and not consonants (similar to modern Japanese). Many commonly used words in Modern English used to have an unstressed vowel at the end of them in Old English. For example, the word *crab* used to be spelled *krabbe* and the word *soft* was spelled *softe*. Because these final vowels were in unstressed syllables, they were in a weak position linguistically, and many of them just disappeared over time. Some disappeared from both our pronunciation and spelling conventions, but for others, the sound was lost but the letter remained, which explains some of those seemingly extraneous *-e* letters that are not pronounced at the ends of words.

There is another type of sound loss that languages undergo: the loss of an entire sound in all environments. In modern varieties of English in Scotland, as well as in Scots Gaelic, you can still hear a sound called a velar fricative at the end of words like *loch* (as in the Loch Ness monster). Linguists represent this sound with the symbol [x]. This sound is similar to a [k] sound, but is made with the tongue raised further back in the mouth than the [k]. The sound still exists in modern German (*achtung*) and was a feature of the Saxon dialects that contributed to the development of English. English speakers may remember this word and sound from the rock and roll album by U2 called *Achtung Baby*.

Sounds may also be lost in just a single environment. This happened with the sound [h]. This sound, which represents aspiration (a puff of air), occurred at the beginning of many words in English. In Old English, this aspiration was spelled with the letter *h* and most frequently occurred before the letters *l*, *r*, *n* and *w*. Two common words with this pronunciation were *hring*, 'ring', and *half*, 'loaf'. This aspiration, though not the spelling, still exists in some varieties of Modern English in the word *which*, though it is largely disappearing in the United States. For these speakers, the words *witch* and *which* have different pronunciations. For these speakers *which* is accompanied by a significant puff of air when pronouncing *wh-*. This is called *wh-* aspiration.

Sounds may also be added to a language. The usual mechanism for this is borrowing a lot of words from another language that have the sound which gets borrowed. After the Norman Invasion, English added the sound [ʒ] to its inventory of sounds. This sound appeared in borrowed words like *azure, pleasure, measure*, and in some varieties of English it is the last sound in the word *garage* (the other pronunciation of *garage* ends in the sound [dʒ]).

## 9.3.1 The Great Vowel Shift

Perhaps the most puzzling of all the pronunciation changes that have happened to English is something linguists call *The Great Vowel Shift*. During a period of time roughly from the 1400s through the 1600s, the vowels of English underwent a systematic change. The answer to this linguistic puzzle is not completely known, but there are a number of hypotheses about what happened and why. What is certain is that all the vowels of English, except the unstressed vowels [ɪ] and [ɛ], changed in pronunciation, and that the changes are all related. It is unknown which vowel began to change first, but it was likely that it was the [i] or [u] sounds since they are the ones made with the highest tongue position in the mouth. As these vowels raised (were made with the tongue higher in the mouth than they were previously made) and became diphthongs, the other vowels shifted their position in the mouth as well. A useful analogy would be to think of a crowded elevator. People usually try to keep the optimum amount of space between themselves and others in the elevator. As people get off, those remaining often shift their positions slightly to maximize the distance between them. The vowels do the same thing. If two vowels are made too closely in the mouth, they are not different enough for people to notice the difference; so they may collapse into one vowel. Thus, as the first vowels were raised, the rest followed, preserving the distance between vowels. Another hypothesis is that one of the vowels made lowest in the mouth was raised first, forcing the rest of the vowels to be raised.

Evidence of this shift comes to us from some of the mismatched spelling and pronunciation pairs like *divine/divinity*, *serene/serenity* and *crime/criminal*, where in each set the first word reflects a post-Great Vowel Shift pronunciation and the second the vowel pronunciation from before the shift. We can also study the literature of the time and look at rhyme schemes to understand which words rhymed before the vowel shift and no longer did after it, for example the Old English word for *name* [namə] which is now pronounced [nem].

Like all other changes in a language, the spread of the effects of the Great Vowel Shift took hundreds of years to accomplish, though some words have not yet shifted and the shift only spread so far in terms of dialectal diversity. We know that before the shift the words *house, mouse* and *out* were all pronounced with the long [u] vowel, but after the shift the vowel in these words, and many like them, shifted to the diphthong [aw] in most varieties of English. However, in some Scots English varieties, we can still hear the pre-shift pronunciation of these words.

Why the people began doing this is even more of a mystery. It's hard to imagine that a bunch of people got together and intentionally set in motion a plan to raise their long vowels, and more importantly, managed to get a nation of people to follow their example. Language change is often this mysterious. Why *groovy* fell out of favour, but the slang word *cool* has remained popular for more than seven decades, is unknown. Some of these mysteries linguists are able to hypothesize about based on indications from written texts of older varieties, and others we can only make educated guesses about.

## 9.3.2 Evidence for sound change from Old English

By now, you may be curious as to how we know how older versions of English sounded since we have no tape recordings from AD 50, nor time machines to go back and actually hear the language. Although we have no direct access to the sounds of these speakers, they have left us a good deal of evidence nonetheless. One strategy that linguists employ to collect evidence of sound change is to look at letters written by common people. Normal people writing to each other are going to be less concerned with style and artifice than authors or other people who write for a living. Before an emphasis on standardization began to pressure people to write 'correctly', normal people wrote words as they thought they sounded.

Poetry, limericks[1] and other rhyme schemes are also useful in figuring out how words may have sounded and where sentence and word stress may have fallen. They may help solve the puzzle in other ways as well. In *The Canterbury Tales*, Chaucer spends a good deal of time poking fun at the accents and dialects of the people on the pilgrimage. From this teasing we get some sense of their pronunciation differences, as we saw in an earlier section of this chapter.

Linguists also look at current differences across dialects of English. Some vestiges of older English are found among speakers of all dialects, though we may learn a lot by looking at some of the more remote and isolated communities of the English-speaking world. For example, isolated religious groups have provided clues to older sounds and forms. One important note: there is a persistent myth that Shakespearean English is still spoken in some isolated place. The geographical location changes depending on the storyteller, but it is usually in some rural area in Tennessee, or North Carolina, or a northern area of Scotland. If Shakespearean English was transported intact to some remote area to where the speakers were so isolated that they had no outside contact, the language would still have changed because all languages do, if for no other reason than that teenagers, and other groups of speakers who want to separate themselves from the norm, invent new words and change the meanings of old ones, and change the language in a myriad of other ways as well.

In addition, words from languages we borrow from give us clues to pronunciation of older forms of English. Linguists look at how these words are spelled and pronounced in the original language. Because English has borrowed a lot of words, we have gained a lot of information this way. Finally, there are regular linguistic processes that help us make reasonable guesses about how sounds are likely to change. Given all this evidence, scholars can make reasonable assertions about how words are likely to have been pronounced and about sentence level stress.

## 9.4  Changes in grammar

When the grammar of a language changes, it is much easier to document than when the sound systems does because the changes are found in written texts. Why those changes occur is sometimes as much of as a mystery as with sound changes, but often we can see what causes a language to substitute one grammatical structure for another or to add a completely new set of rules.

As with changes in the sound system, changes in a language's grammar do not occur overnight, so for a time we may see two grammatical features that accomplish the same function co-existing even in a single person's speech. One such change is the loss of marking on nouns to indicate the noun's function in a sentence. Early Old English was a highly inflected language, which meant that the nouns were marked with different endings to indicate whether a noun was the subject of the sentence or some type of object. That means that the nouns in a sentence could appear in any order.

Another significant change was the change in the unmarked word order for English sentences. Languages have a normal order for what appears first, the subject, verb or object of a sentence. That does not mean that sentences in that language cannot appear in any other order, but that any deviation from the norm will be marked grammatically in some way. Currently the unmarked English sentence begins with a subject followed by a verb and possibly finishing with an object (*Jill drove the car*). However, Old English was an SOV language (Subject, Object, Verb) and shifted over time to become an SVO language (Subject, Verb, Object). In Old English, as well as early Middle English, the verb would occur after the object as in other Germanic languages. The shift in word order occurred during the period we call Middle English. By the time Shakespeare was creating his works, the shift was well under way, but we still find occasional sentences that show the older SOV pattern. Note that in each of the following two sentences from Shakespeare, the verb is in final position in the sentence.

> Neither a borrower nor a lender *be*.
> But soft, what light on yonder window *breaks*?

Other syntactic differences of Old English can be seen in a study of any Old English document. An interesting one to look at is *The Lord's Prayer* because the early Modern English version is so well known in English-speaking countries. The first two words of the opening sentence, *fæder ure* (father our), in one Old English version, reflect another word order difference: possessive adjectives followed nouns. Another example of a postposed adjective is at the end of line two (*be thy name hallowed*).

> Fæder ure þu þe eart on heofonum;
> Si þin nama gehalgod

The length of this book precludes a lengthy discussion of the thousands of changes that have occurred to English over its lifespan, but suffice it to say that English has been affected by and enriched throughout its history by an amazing series of historical events and peoples.

## 9.5  The spelling 'system' of English

At some point, most native speakers, and certainly almost every second language learner of English, have complained about the spelling system. There are certainly rules for spelling, but almost every one of them is violated frequently and many words defy any spelling conventions whatsoever. Worse yet, our spelling system provides little consistent information concerning how we should pronounce any new words that we encounter. English spelling is so bizarre that the British writer George Bernard Shaw once proclaimed that the word *fish* could be reasonably spelled, based on current spelling conventions, as *ghoti*. You take the [f] sound from the *-gh* spelling in words like *enough*, the [ɪ] sound from the -o- letter in *women,* finishing with the [ʃ] sound as found in the letters -ti- in the word *nation*. This, of course, is an extreme example, but the vast majority of other languages' speakers do not have these numerous spelling oddities. So why is English spelling such a mess?

One of the major problems with English spelling has nothing to do with its history but has everything to do with problems inherent in our alphabet, some of which were discussed in the earlier chapter on phonetics. First, there are not enough letters to make all the sounds of English. A phonetic system provides one symbol for each sound in a language, so that when words are transcribed, we know exactly how they sound. Depending on the variety of English we speak, we have approximately 40 different vowel and consonant sounds yet only 26 letters to represent those sounds. Some letters must do double duty and represent more than one sound, and we use combinations of letters to represent others. Those of you who have studied Spanish may have found great comfort in the fact that the five vowel sounds are completely predictable from the five letters used to represent them. My Mexican friends thought it was very strange that many English speakers had spelling classes and spelling tests in primary school. They didn't think you should have to be taught how to spell. Easy for them to say: their system is so much more logical. However, imagine the confusion of a native Spanish speaker trying to learn English and struggling to understand why the vowel sounds in the words *though* and *thought* differ so much when the spellings are exactly the same except for the last consonant.

Native speakers struggle too with figuring out English spelling because there are so many possible ways to make the same sound. Most English vowels can be represented with a number of different spelling combinations. Consider the following three words in which the [i] sound is represented by four different single letters or letter combinations (underlined): 1) season; 2) see; and 3) Simi Valley. Adding to the confusion is the fact that the same combination of letters may represent a different sound in other words, for example the -ea- combination in the past tense verb read which sounds like [ɛ].

| *Phonetic sound* | *Words with that sound* | | | |
|---|---|---|---|---|
| [i] | season | see | Simi Valley | review |
| [ɛ] | said | red | read | |
| [ɔ] | thought | dot | caught | |
| [o] | doe | road | rode | though |
| [e] | wait | fate | weight | |

This problem is not limited to the vowel sounds. There are consonantal letters that are used inconsistently as well. Consider the letters *c*, *k* and *s*. In the word *circus*, the letter *c* represents both the [s] sound and the [k] sound. It is interesting to consider whether we really need the *c* letter since it always represents one of these two sounds. The only exception is the digraph *ch-*, in which two letters are used to represent one sound, [tʃ]. Consider also how many nouns end in this confusing set of options: *-tion*, *-cion* and *-sion*.

Besides the spelling challenges presented by our alphabet, there are a myriad of problems associated with the peculiar development of English. The diversity and impact of the many languages that made major contributions to its development have wreaked havoc on the system as well. For instance, when we borrowed words from other languages, we often borrowed their spellings as well but only sometimes their pronunciation. From French, we borrowed words like *justice*, *charity* and *paradise*, and a few minutes with a current French dictionary makes clear that the English pronunciation of these words is quite distinct from the French. With other words like *buffet*, *ballet* and *coup d'etat*, we borrowed both the lexical item and, more or less, the pronunciation from French. There are other even more interesting borrowings. For instance, we borrowed the word *khaki* from Urdu when we began to import the material from Pakistan. This is the only word in English that begins with the letter combination *kh-* though English speakers do not pronounce this as Urdu speakers would; the *-h-* represents aspiration in this position.

There are other problems with spelling in English. For one, writing has become less phonetic over the years. In earlier times, because fewer people were formally educated, they spelled words as they thought they sounded. Since everyone did not have the same accent, this caused a lot of variation in spelling. The variation in spelling is useful though for people who study how the language may have sounded because this spelling variation provides insights into how the language may have sounded in different parts of the country.

In a more formal and intentional way, some of the strange spelling combinations of English were caused by changes made by Norman scribes, early printers and early reformers. After Caxton brought the printing press to England in the 1470s, printed materials became more widely available. With greater access to the published written word began the standardization of spelling as people copied the customs of the printers. These early printers had a great impact on English spelling, not just because they provided a model to copy, but because they introduced additional variation into the system. For example, in those times, it was the style for printers to spread their text out to reach both the right and left margins so as to form a straight line down both sides of the page. To do this they sometimes added an extra letter or two to certain words, which helps to explain why we have so many double consonants in the middle of words and extraneous silent -e letters at the ends of words. Many shopkeepers, especially of antique stores in tourist areas, still use variant spellings of the word *shop* left over from this time: *shoppe*, *shope*. In Caxton's own text provided earlier in this chapter, you can see he has spelled Modern English *eggs* in two ways: *egges* and *eggys* (as well as *eyren*, the focus of his paragraph).

After the Norman Invasion, most of the written record of English law and history were kept by Norman scribes whose primary language was French. They sometimes thought that English words of Anglo-Saxon origins were poorly spelled French or Latin words, and corrected them. Some of these were words of Anglo-Saxon origin, which had no relation to French, and others were words that may have been borrowed into both early French and Anglo-Saxon but which had distinct pronunciations in each set of languages. On such word is *language*, which in Middle English was spelled *langage*. The scribes thought it should look more like the corresponding Latin word *lingua* and so they added the letter *u* to the English version. They did the same with other English words including *debt*, which in Middle English was spelled *dette*. The Latin word was *debitum*. Other changes reflected differences in French spelling and English in the choice of digraphs chosen to represent a single sound, including the shift from Old English *sc-* in words like *scip* to the French version of English in which *sc-* became *sh-* as in *ship*. Another prolific shift was *qu-* replacing *cw-* in words like *queen*. There are dozens of these systematic changes for both vowels and consonants.

One of the more interesting changes to the spelling system of English occurred at some point after the Norman Invasion. In Old English the sound [f], represented by the letter *f*, sounded the same as it does today when the [f] was at the beginning or end of a word. However, when the letter *f* occurred in the middle of a word, then it was pronounced like Modern English [v]. The French spoken by the Normans also had this sound but they spelled it with a *v*, so their scribes and literate people wrote it the way it sounded with the letter *v*. Thus, although the Old English spelling of *knives* would have been *knifes*, the French changed it to *knives* to better reflect its pronunciation. This helps to explain all the 'odd' singular/plural pairs that exist today like: *wife/wives*, *life/lives* and *wolf/wolves*. The odd one out would be *belief/beliefs*. Because *belief* is a word often used in a religious context, it may have resisted change. As I've noted before, religious and legal terms are often preserved when spellings and grammar forms have shifted for other words.

Finally, one of the most significant reasons for the disjunct between English spelling and pronunciation has to do with *when* the standardization of spelling began to be important. Spelling was mostly set by the eighteenth century, but our pronunciation was still in great flux (for example the Great Vowel Shift was still in progress). Thus, the spelling that was made standard may have fit with that time's pronunciation but not with the pronunciation that later became standard. Lots of the words that contain silent letters, like *knife* and *knight*, reflect an earlier pronunciation that has long since disappeared in the vast majority of English dialects.

## 9.5.1   Fixing the spelling problem

Considering that the English spelling system is such a mess, why don't we use our current understanding of linguistics, accompanied by good common sense, and fix the orthography of English so that it better reflects the way we speak? The advantages are clear. Much time is spent in schools trying to teach native speakers to spell their own language, time that could be better spent in providing more instruction in maths, science and other more content-based instruction. Dictionaries could become sources for comprehension of words and usage guidelines. It would stop millions of children from having the frustrating conversations I had with my parents when asking how to spell something and being told to look it up in the dictionary. Clearly, if I couldn't spell it, I couldn't look it up quickly! Finally, second language learners of English would be thrilled. They would be able to look at a word in English and know exactly how to pronounce it and not suffer, as do the natives, with having to learn all the spelling absurdities.

As appealing as it sounds to make the system of English spelling more logical and easier to learn, the consequences of such a change are quite profound and for the most part unappealing. The first, and of course most troubling and politically difficult obstacle would be on whose variety of English would we base the system? You can imagine the hue and cry by speakers of other varieties if any particular variety other than their own was chosen. Even if we tried to make a historically based decision and chose British English since England is arguably the birthplace of the language, the original form of that language is no longer spoken anywhere, including England. Therefore, which variety of British English would we choose? The Queen's English, sometimes called BBC English, is a minority language in Britain spoken primarily by an educated elite. So do we choose another variety more commonly spoken, like Cockney or some regional dialect from an industrial area like Manchester? Or do we make the choice based on number of speakers? Some would argue that the United States is larger in size, population and influence than Britain, so the choice should be American English. But which variety? Worse yet, either of these choices would be considered linguistic imperialism in other parts of the English-speaking world. The number of first language speakers of English outside Britain and the USA is quite considerable.

Another possibility would be to have each country choose which dialect would be considered standard, and create the orthography from that variety. This would still be politically problematic in many areas for the same reasons as above. In addition, currently, we can read British, Nigerian, Indian and Canadian English among others because of our shared orthographic conventions. Not only do we share a broad cultural heritage, but our literature, science, entertainment and commercial activities can be carried out through writing. The important research presented in the British medical journal *The Lancet* is currently quite accessible, using the current orthographic system, to doctors in India, Ghana and New Zealand as well as elsewhere in the English-speaking world. This type of information exchange would become much more difficult if each group of people wrote in their own varieties.

Furthermore, if we have learned nothing else from our study of the history of languages, we've learned that despite the best efforts of those concerned about 'correctness' and 'linguistic purity', all languages change. We already know that even having standard written forms taught in schools does little to slow dialectal diversity across Britain, the USA or elsewhere. Would we have to create language committees to impose order on the unruly speakers of the English dialects?

Even if we could agree on the more political aspects, we would still confront the massive costs and time associated with transcribing all the texts written in the old orthography into the new one, as well as educating all of us who grew up with the old system. Imagine the resistance to acquiring the new system by the hundreds of millions who already know the existing system. (Consider the resistance in the USA to even acquiring the metric system that practically the entire world uses!) Finally, even if all these obstacles could be overcome, by switching systems we'd lose a great deal of knowledge about our history. The forms of words often tell us from what language they have come into English and when. They are a reflection of who we are and the road we have travelled as a people.

The history of the English language is a history of the peoples who have made us what we are and who we will become in the future. As the use of English continues to spread across the globe, English will continue to change for the very same reason: it is a living language constantly moulded by its users.

## Suggested reading

Bryson, B. (1991), *The Mother Tongue: English and How it Got that Way*. NY: William Morrow Inc.

Cook, V. (2004), *The English Writing System*. London: Oxford University Press.

Görlach, M. (1997), *The Linguistic History of English*. Macmillan, London.

McCrum, R., Cran, W. and MacNeil, R. (2002), *The Story of English*. Penguin Books, New York.

## Interesting websites

Old English Pages. Includes texts, glossary and sound files of Old English. Georgetown University. www.georgetown.edu/faculty/ballc/oe/old_english.html

A Middle English Glossary: www.librarius.com/gy.htm

## Questions to consider

Go back to the passage written in Middle English by Caxton found earlier in this chapter. How is English today different from English of his day? Look at spelling, pronunciation, grammar, morphology and pronunciation.

## Notes

1   Limericks are five-line poems that rhyme. They are usually off-colour or risqué in nature and frequently begin something like, 'There once was a lady from France'.

# 10 Language variation and change

## Chapter Overview

| 10.1 | WHY LANGUAGES CHANGE | 197 |
|---|---|---|
| | 10.1.1 LEXICAL AND SEMANTIC CHANGE | 198 |
| | 10.1.2 CHANGES IN THE SOUND SYSTEM | 199 |
| | 10.1.3 CHANGES TO GRAMMAR AND MORPHOLOGY | 201 |
| 10.2 | LANGUAGE VARIATION | 202 |
| | 10.2.1 CAUSES OF DIALECTAL DIVERSITY | 203 |
| | 10.2.2 SOCIAL ATTITUDES TO LANGUAGE VARIETIES | 206 |
| | 10.2.3 MEASURING ATTITUDES TO LANGUAGE VARIETIES | 207 |
| 10.3 | DIALECTS OF LANGUAGE CONTACT | 208 |
| | 10.3.1 CHICANO ENGLISH AND CODESWITCHING | 208 |
| | 10.3.2 CODESWITCHING | 211 |
| | 10.3.3 PIDGINS AND CREOLES | 215 |
| 10.4 | VARIETIES OF ENGLISH | 225 |
| | 10.4.1 APPALACHIAN ENGLISH | 225 |
| | 10.4.2 AFRICAN AMERICAN VERNACULAR ENGLISH | 229 |
| | 10.4.3 COCKNEY ENGLISH | 232 |
| 10.5 | LANGUAGE AND GENDER | 234 |
| | 10.5.1 USE OF TITLES | 235 |
| | 10.5.2 ASYMMETRIES IN LANGUAGE | 236 |
| | 10.5.3 GENERIC 'HE' FOR UNSPECIFIED REFERENCES | 237 |
| | 10.5.4 EFFECTS OF GENDER ON LANGUAGE | 238 |
| | 10.5.5 COMMON BELIEFS ABOUT GENDERED LANGUAGE | 239 |
| | 10.5.6 LANGUAGE AND THE WORKPLACE | 242 |
| | 10.5.7 EARLY SOCIALIZATION BY GENDER | 243 |
| 10.6 | THE FUTURE OF ENGLISH AND ITS DIALECTS | 244 |

## 10.1 Why languages change

One of the eternal truths about living languages is that they all change despite the efforts made by official institutions to halt change. Change is inevitable because speakers of every language are exposed to new concepts and ideas that require accommodation to the language. In addition to this, because there is no single form of any language the distinct varieties of each language, whether they be regional, ethnic, racial, age-based or class-based, are constantly affecting each other as their speakers live and work together. Finally, change sometimes happens for no apparent reason or explanation.

## 10.1.1 Lexical and semantic change

As we saw in the chapter on historical change, modifications happen in every language system. Language change is so slow it is almost not noticeable, except in the lexicon. New slang words are commonly acquired and lost as each generation makes its contribution to a language. Some of the changes are permanent, like the addition of the decades-old slang word *cool*, which dates back at least to the 1920s. Other words and expressions come and go quite quickly, like sayings from my youth such as *far out* and *groovy*, though *groovy* seems to have made a slight (but hopefully short!) comeback because of the Austin Powers movies.

New words and expressions don't just become part and parcel of the language overnight, nor do they disappear quickly either. It is quite common that old and new forms will co-exist for a time. When I was in graduate school, one of my professors described language change by comparing it to throwing a stone into a pond. Change, like the ripples from the stone, radiate outwards from whatever epicentre has started the change. How far the change spreads is dependent on many factors including what the source of the new expression is, what groups pick it up and whether the word is for a new concept or invention. Why certain words catch on and others do not, however, is often a mystery. There is no reason why *groovy* isn't commonly heard in hip hop music today other than the fact that it didn't survive as a slang word as the word *cool* did.

It's also true that, for a while, multiple expressions for a concept may exist as different parts of the population continue to hold on to, for example, the slang of their youth or as parents try to incorporate the slang of their children, a practice which, according to my students, is 'lame'. Use of slang often reflects membership of a culture and parents are generally not welcome to use the symbolic language of their children. A student in my semantics class was completely horrified at her father's inept use of *bling* in a conversation with her friends. He was trying too hard to be one of the gang.

Other additions to the language are of a more permanent nature; consider all of the technological words relating to computers, MP3 players, mobile phones and the World Wide Web that have been added to English over the past 30 years. These words and expressions are not replacing existing ones, but are created to describe novel inventions and concepts.

Words are not only added to English or go in and out of fashion, but they shift in their meanings and usage. A point I frequently make to my students is that obscene and profane words in American English are grossly overused. I hear words that my mother would have washed my mouth out with soap for saying, shouted quite loudly in an open area of a mall full of small children – not as obscenities, but as practically meaningless nouns, adjectives and adverbs. Is a word still obscene when it ceases to shock and offend? This weakening of a word's power is scarcely new. In Middle English, the word 'terrible' was a powerful word that meant that something truly horrific had happened, like murder or a war. It wasn't used to describe minor disappointments like missing your favourite television show.

Words also go through shifts in meaning over time. Some of these are brief slang shifts like the use of *bad* in the 1980s to mean 'cool' or the word *sick* 20 years later to mean the same thing. My nephew currently uses the word *sweet* in much the same way. These words have maintained their primary meanings for the vast majority of speakers during their faddish shift in meaning for a limited subculture of speakers. Other words make more permanent shifts in meaning. In Old English, the word *silly* had the meaning of 'blessed'. By the time of Middle English, its meaning had shifted to 'innocent'. Currently, the general definition is 'foolish'. These changes in meaning are not complete jumps; you can see how each meaning is related to the others.

As we cross the ocean from Britain to the many places to which English was exported, the same meanings are expressed by completely different words in the ex-colonies than in the mother tongue. In Britain, people snack on *crisps*, a word never heard in the USA, where teenagers gobble down bags of *potato chips*. In the USA, college students may get *trashed* or *wasted* at a party; their New Zealand counterparts get *knackered* and their Irish friends *get off me face*. At the same party, the British student could be completely *cabbaged* (so drunk he or she is practically a vegetable). Much less slangy expressions are also different from country to country. In England, farmers drive a *lorry* filled with their produce, and in the US, the farmers do the same in a *truck*. Americans walk on the *sidewalk* whereas their British friends walk on the *pavement*. Thousands of lexical differences exist between all the varieties of English spread throughout the world.

Words are the playthings not just of authors and songwriters but also of common people looking for original and possibly outrageous ways to express themselves in new and colourful ways. Sometimes these words and expressions become part and parcel of the language of an area, like *couch potato*. Just as frequently, however, they never go beyond a very small group of friends, like the adjective *pedocentric*, coined by a friend who was tired of having every conversation at adult parties eventually roll around to discussion of people's offspring.

## 10.1.2  Changes in the sound system

Although changes in the sound system may be less obvious than lexical changes as they are happening in a community, change is happening continuously. We know this happens because there is so much evidence around us: a very clear and striking example of which is how Australian, Canadian, US, Nigerian and New Zealand varieties of English, among others, differ so greatly from the varieties spoken in the United Kingdom, the birthplace of the language. Even a single variety of a language undergoes sound change, as we learned in the chapter on historical changes. For example, we know that in Old English the word *name* had two full syllables and was pronounced [namə].

The changes from Old English to Modern English happened over a great period of time before any of us were alive. However, sound change can also happen within the lifetime of a speaker. An example of this is the Northern Cities Vowel Shift. This systematic change in the vowel system has been in progress in a band of major cities of the United States across the Great Lakes areas and beyond, from upstate New York to Minnesota, since at least the 1970s. This shift in vowel pronunciation is most notable in Green Bay, Wisconsin; Detroit, Michigan; Chicago, Illinois; Cleveland, Ohio; and Buffalo, New York, though to a lesser degree it seems to be spreading to other major cities somewhat further to the south including Columbus, Ohio; Pittsburgh, Pennsylvania; and Indianapolis, Indiana. For people who have made this shift, some front vowels of English are being made with a tongue position slightly higher in the mouth, whereas the tongue position is somewhat more fronted for the low vowels. Some mid vowels are shifted to a position a little further back in the mouth.[1] It can be viewed graphically as:

The best-known aspect of this shift in pronunciation, which may also be one explanation for it, is the merger of the vowel sounds in pairs of words like *caught* and *cot* as well as *Dawn* and *Don* in much of the central Midwest and the western US where these words are pronounced the same way. In the speech of many easterners, as well as many in the upper Midwest, these have distinct pronunciations:

| | | | |
|---|---|---|---|
| caught | [kɔt] | cot | [kat] |
| Dawn | [dɔn] | Don | [dan][2] |
| hawk | [hɔk] | hock | [hak] |

However, in parts of the upper Midwest, the [ɔ] has shifted to a lower position in the mouth and thus has merged with the [a] sound in many words. In the original pronunciation of *caught* and *Dawn*, the vowel is more rounded and the jaw/tongue position slightly higher than the vowel in *Don* and *cot* in which the shape of the lips is more spread and the jaw/tongue position slightly lower.

When vowel sounds become too close in oral space or tongue position, speakers often shift the other vowel sounds near them to keep the distinctions clear. The best analogy I can come up with is the movement of people in a crowded elevator, the same analogy used on p. 187 to describe the Great Vowel Shift. When the elevator is full, everyone is pushed close together, but as people get off, the remaining passengers shuffle around so that there is optimal distance between them and the other passengers. At each stop, this accommodation happens again to maintain acceptable distance between passengers. Thus, as the jaw/tongue position for [ɔ] lowered, the pronunciation of the [a] became more fronted which in turn began a chain reaction of slight shifts in vowel pronunciation throughout one part of the system. Because the [a] is fronted in the pronunciation of these speakers, the word *block* sounds very much like the word *black*.

This is just one example of a sound change that is in progress today in one part of the English-speaking world. There is a chain shift in progress in the cities of the southern part of the United States as well which contributes to the widening gulf in pronunciation between speakers in these two regions. The sounds of English have been changing for as long as there has been an English, and as English has spread worldwide, changes have happened independently everywhere it is spoken.

## 10.1.3  Changes to grammar and morphology

Changes to grammar and morphology may be less obvious to native speakers, and may begin in the speech of one dialect group and only eventually be incorporated by speakers of standard varieties. One of the most obvious is the loss of the derivational suffix -*ly* on adverbs that are modifying other adverbs, as in 'he spoke real clear'. Although this absence of the suffix once marked a person's speech as non-standard, it is spreading across US varieties including the standard, though some people, especially older speakers, still view it as deviant.

Other changes may be limited to a subset of a population. The speech of each individual is called an *idiolect* because it is quite unique in its sound, grammar and vocabulary. No two people have exactly the same linguistic system because they have been exposed to different experiences and contexts. In my honours class one day, I was explaining how languages not only simplify but may also *complexify*. One of the students challenged my use of *complexify*, claiming that it was not an English word. So, we checked out the online dictionaries and found that it was not an 'official' American word (if we are going to allow dictionaries to dictate what is a word!), but it was a word in British English. I read British spy and mystery novels and am a fan of BBC comedy, so I evidently incorporated it into my English, as may have other Americans who are exposed to sufficient British English. It's easy to notice a distinct vocabulary item like *lorry* (if you are a speaker of American English), but the more subtle aspects of language, like morphological affixing, may get incorporated into our system without notice.

One grammatical change that is clearly underway in US and British English, is the loss of the subject/object distinction for the pronouns *who* and *whom*. Many speakers of the oldest generations still make the distinction between the two in both written and spoken language. The middle-aged speakers that I have observed and questioned over the years claim to use it consistently in writing, but only rarely think about it in spoken language. Of the under-30 crowd, I almost never see it in formal writing, and the few times I have actually heard *whom* used correctly in normal spoken language, it grabs my attention as if it were a bad word! I've asked class after class of college students about the following two sentences:

> With whom did you go to the party?
> Who did you go to the party with?

None claim to have ever said the first sentence and remark that it sounds stuck-up or snobbish. As to the British, my sources tell me that it is quite common in writing still and in formal speech, but one middle-aged British man I queried about the use of *whom* said 'speaking properly will get you stared at'. It seems that the use of *whom* is marked in speech as 'quite formal'.

There are as many distinct idiolects of English as there are speakers, yet the similarities far outweigh the differences between speakers of the same speech communities. Our language varies in the words we use, the accents we have and even in the structural aspects of the language. This is not a problem as long as the vast majority of our system is in line with the people we want to communicate with, and this is the case for the most part. Having standardized varieties does not inhibit us from being distinctive, but it does give all of us a general target to aim at which keeps us from getting so different that we can no longer communicate with each other.

## 10.2 Language variation

When linguists study language variation, they are not making value judgements about the varieties (dialects) they study. We study them to describe how they are systematically different from other varieties of the language. At the start of the book I pointed out that to linguists, all languages and all varieties of language are equal in terms of their value and complexity and that there are no living languages that should be classified as primitive or substandard. Individuals may not like certain varieties, just as they don't like certain music, but it does not make those varieties less systematic to scientists or less valuable to their speakers. Even though speakers of non-standard varieties of a language are often discriminated against for speaking them, a dialect serves as an important marker of group membership and an important aspect of personal identity for its speakers.

I remember becoming a linguist in spirit. Although I grew up in a family where my parents attempted to provide us with a model of Standard English, I lived in the foothills of the Appalachians, and my friends were mostly kids from the 'sticks'. Needless to say, like most kids, I was more interested in sounding like my peers than my parents, so I picked up much of the local variety and mixed it with my home variety.

As a teenager, my parents and my teachers attempted to correct my grammar and pronunciation, which never made sense to me because everyone I talked to understood me. One set of sentences I remember in particular: 'This car needs washed', and 'This room needs cleaned'. The missing 'to be' never bothered me, or my friends, but it sure irritated my parents. The words 'to be' are absent to this day in my spoken English passive constructions, though at this point whether it is out of defiance or custom, I can't say. This construction is not a local invention but can be traced to earlier Scottish and Irish varieties of English. Another variant form of this expression, 'needs washing', is acceptable in the north of the USA but not in the south, and British English 'wants washing', as in 'The car wants washing' is acceptable in neither the north nor the south of the USA.

It wasn't just grammar. A whole set of sounds in my speech seemed to separate me from my mother and teachers, including the tendency to stress the first syllable (instead of the second) in words like *recycle*, *descend* and *renew* and the reduction of final syllable *-ing* to *-in* (*comin* and *goin*). These particular differences are so rooted in my head that they appear even in my 'standard' speech. Although my 'teacher voice' now dominates my life, when I'm tired, angry, relaxed or with folk who don't sound like teachers, a whole set of other sounds, grammar and vocabulary make their appearance. They sound more real to me than my teacher voice, which sometimes still seems an artificial pretension.

The conflict between standard and non-standard arose again, though it was with my second language. In a graduate class on the works of author Gabriel Garcia Marquez, the native Spanish speakers criticized me for speaking like a *campesino* (villager). At the time, I thought that meant I had bad Spanish, but later I learned that I had acquired a version of Afro-Caribbean Spanish while living in a village in the Dominican Republic. Since then, I've made a vocation of studying language diversity and understanding why, in defiance of educational and social pressure, people like me persist in maintaining the voices that seem most authentic to us.

## 10.2.1 Causes of dialectal diversity

One only needs to turn on the television and listen to the many voices, both of actors in scripted programmes and real people speaking on the news, to know that people speak in quite distinct ways. It's not just a matter of accents – every language system is affected. Since we all speak basically the same language, how can there be so many different forms? The creation of different dialects is caused by a number of factors including variations in geography, time, race or ethnicity, gender and class. In fact, usually more than one of these factors contributes to the differences between varieties.


### Geographic or regional varieties

One of the primary causes of dialect diversity is the movement of groups of people. This accounts for the best-known differences in the varieties of English spoken in the dozens of countries throughout the world where English is considered a native language. The same is also true for any other language that has been exported from its original territory. Varieties of Spanish spoken in the New World differ significantly from the mother tongue in Spain. Spanish in Spain has not been stagnant since colonial times; it has undergone changes that did not affect the ex-Spanish colonies. The colonies too have been innovative. One of the most well-known differences between peninsular and New World Spanishes is the almost complete loss of the voiced interdental fricative (*th*) in New World varieties (*adios* 'goodbye' [aðios] shifted to [adios]).

Geography also plays a part in dialectal diversity within a country. Rural areas of the country often have varieties that are quite distinct from urban ones. In some urban areas, like Boston and London, locals can identify not just what part of the city a person is from, but often their race and class as well. The urban dialect of Liverpool in England, Scouse, made famous by the Beatles, is quite distinct from the speech of other urban areas of Britain. One local described it as 'one-third Irish, one-third Welsh and one-third catarrh'![3] The nasalized congested sound of the variety was often blamed on the horribly contaminated air of this once-industrial city. The air in Liverpool has been greatly cleaned up over the past decades and some say that the congested sound of the accent is disappearing as well.

Immigration within a country can account for the spread of certain features as well. One can trace the migrations of the Scots and Irish through the Midwest, South and West by looking at who today uses the expression *(a) fixin to*, as in *I'm (a) fixin to go* (I'm getting ready to go). It is quite commonly heard as *a fixin* in the northern Appalachian territory, but moving further south through Kentucky, the 'a' is mostly lost but *fixin*, as an expression meaning 'about to', is still commonly heard. The use of *fixin* itself finally died out in west Texas where colonial settlements were sparse, and early settlers began to intermarry and blend their speech varieties.

Although native speakers usually understand whether concepts are synonymous or not, there is one particular set of words (*this* and *next*) that can cause serious misunderstanding, and yet many native speakers are unaware of it. Imagine that today is Monday 1 May. Your teacher tells you that a homework assignment is due next Friday. For about 75 per cent of speakers in the United States, that means the homework is due on 12 May; for the remainder, the homework is due on 5 May. For these speakers, the meaning of 'next' in this utterance refers to the very next one. For the majority of speakers though, it means the one in the following week. What makes this even more confusing is that it depends on where in the week an utterance like this is made. In my dialect (the majority one), if it is Saturday and you say next Sunday, I think of the one in eight days even though the next actual Sunday is in the following week. Interestingly, the same problem exists for speakers of Mexican Spanish with expressions like 'viernes proxima' (next Friday).

*Social class varieties*

In the United States, social classes are less obvious and less structured than in Britain. One particular speech form for the elite across the country does not exist. One accent in English that could be viewed this way is the Boston Brahmin dialect (best known through the voice of television character Frasier Crane). One very notable feature of this dialect is the loss of [r] at the end of syllables typified by the expression: 'Park your car in Harvard Yard', which speakers from outside the region say teasingly to imitate the locals. This dialect, unfortunately, is slowly disappearing, and there is no concentrated effort by the elite in other parts of the USA to acquire this form of English, so it will not be spreading to new elite groups.

In Britain, however, there is an official variety of English that is associated with the educated elite of the country, which is a marker of the speaker's social class, called Received Pronunciation (RP), The Queen's English or BBC English. What is interesting about RP is that, unlike Boston Brahmin, it says nothing about the place one comes from, only the class. One obvious feature of this variety, to non-speakers in Britain, is the pronunciation of [h] at the beginning of words like *hotel*, which often goes missing in other commonly spoken dialects of Britain.

*Ethnic and race-based varieties*

Some varieties of language differ by the background of people who speak them rather then their social class or location, though both may also play a role. In the southwest of the United States, there are varieties of English called Latino, Hispanic or Chicano English that are spoken primarily by people of Latin American descent. The families of these speakers may have been in the USA for many generations and may no longer speak Spanish; however, their English is richly coloured by their Spanish language heritage including differences in pronunciation and the inclusion of Spanish vocabulary in their English. Unfortunately, other English speakers have often considered these varieties to be incomplete attempts of these speakers to learn English, and think that they are not systematic languages. Nevertheless, because these speakers are a sizeable group in the southwest, some of the features of their language have been acquired by other groups as well. When I lived in Tucson, Arizona, it was not uncommon to hear people with non-Spanish backgrounds freely using Spanish words that had become part and parcel of the local variety of English.

African American varieties of English, sometimes called Ebonics, are varieties that are spoken, obviously, primarily by African Americans. These varieties of English have long been a subject of debate in terms of their origin and value. People ignorant of linguistics who do not completely understand speakers of these varieties have claimed that they are broken English. Many have negatively judged speakers based on this false understanding of the systems of African American Englishes, and have ignored the rich heritage that they illustrate. Even more than for Chicano English, there is a long history of contributions to American language from African American English, especially in the arts and music. The history, social context and structures of both of these varieties will be elaborated on later in this chapter.

## 10.2.2 Social attitudes to language varieties

That people have attitudes to differing varieties of language has been true since the beginning of language. These attitudes generally have more to do with people's perceptions of particular groups of people than with any real lack of systematicity on the part of the variety. Thus, it is often the varieties of minority groups that receive the most negative evaluations. There are a number of incorrect and negative stereotypes that Wolfram and Christian[4] have identified with speakers of non-standard varieties including: 1) speakers of these varieties are not able to acquire the standard completely or correctly, 2) the speech that these speakers do produce is unsystematic, 3) these speakers are slow to learn a language because they are not as able as standard speakers and, finally, 4) using non-standard varieties prevents speakers from being able to think clearly or deeply.

Linguistic prejudice can do the same damage that racial, ethnic or class prejudice can. Imagine the reaction of small children in primary school who are told by their teacher that they sound ignorant because of the way they speak. Most children internalize this commentary as meaning that they are ignorant, which can have a disastrous effect on the rest of their school career. The importance of the standard language in the community is clear. If you do not acquire it, then you may well suffer occupational, educational and social discrimination. Many teachers see dialectal speech as an evil that they must stamp out, rather than a system that has its place in other parts of a child's life. The approach should be additive. Add the standard variety to the tools that a speaker may draw upon in the appropriate contexts. I say 'appropriate contexts' because the use of the standard can alienate a person from their social group, or be distancing. I know that when I am in a casual social situation, my teacher voice is generally put away (maybe in the same place as the suit I wear for job interviews and then never wear to work!).

## 10.2.3 Measuring attitudes to language varieties

Linguists have tested people's sense of what is acceptable in their native language as well as their attitudes to different speech varieties. These tests often tease out the fact that although 'proper grammar' is taught in school, the reality of people's normal language usage differs. They also identify the relative acceptability of structures that may be in different varieties of a language, and they measure people's attitudes to certain varieties and constructions.

In graduate school, another student and I created and tested an attitude survey of people's attitudes towards Appalachian English. We each read a short story, once in our standard voice and once in our local voices. We then created tapes in which both a standard and a non-standard reading of the story were presented. Each tape had one version of my voice and one version of hers so that the subjects would not hear two voices of the same person. We played these tapes for more than 100 students who were not linguistics majors. We asked them to rate the speakers based on a series of polar qualities like: urban/rural, college educated/high school, wealthy/poor, white collar/blue collar, clever/not clever, lazy/industrious, tall/short as well as others. The results were sadly predictable. In my teacher voice, I am smart, educated, white-collar, urban and tall (I'm 5'2" in reality, but tall in Western culture patterns as a positive trait). In my local voice, I scored the opposite on all these traits. I'm short, uneducated and lazy. Imagine being able to make all of those decisions based solely on a speech sample. What makes this test even more interesting is that a large number of the people in the classes we tested grew up in areas where Appalachian English is spoken and may even be speakers of it, or some closely related dialect, but they reported negative responses to that voice.

When we meet people, the first things we are able to base our judgements about them on are the way they look and the way they sound. These judgements may prevent us from going beyond the superficial and really learning the truth about people. People who have distinct accents and dialects have learned to mitigate these negative reactions by losing or 'softening' the aspects of their speech that mark them as distinct. Accent reduction and speech therapy are huge industries, not just for second language speakers who are trying to make their English more clear, but for native speakers as well who have suffered the consequences of linguistic prejudice.

## 10.3 Dialects of language contact

Some language varieties develop due to the intensity of language contact. In these cases, completely different languages have a major influence on the direction of language change of a variety, or can play a major role in the development of a completely new variety. In the first case, the borrowing of words and accent features, and less frequently structures of another language, create a distinct variety that may have important cultural meaning for its speakers. An example of this is Chicano English, which will be described below. Pidgin and creole languages, however, are created in quite unique situations in which source material from a number of languages is used in the creation of a new language. Unlike the vast majority of languages which are handed down from parent to child, these languages are created abruptly. Many creole languages were created only in the past 500 years and have provided linguists with a unique opportunity to understand language creation and development.

### 10.3.1 Chicano English and codeswitching

Chicano English (CE) is an ethnic variety of English spoken primarily by people with Mexican-American heritage. CE is a linguistic name that may not be acceptable to all speakers of this variety. The word *Chicano* itself is not accepted by all members of the community. It is sometimes seen as a political designation rather than a cultural one, and not everyone in the community holds the same political views. Like other varieties of English, most speakers will just call their local variety *English*.

Speakers of Chicano English are speakers of English. Many speak little or no Spanish at all or only speak it non-natively. Like other non-standard varieties, CE is a group of varieties systematically different from other Englishes. CE speakers differ in their usage and application of rules from other English varieties. They are also able to range across their varieties as the situation requires: for example, some speakers might use a variety of CE that is less influenced by Spanish in the presence of English monolinguals, and use more marked features in groups where everyone is Chicano.

Carmen Fought (see reference at end of chapter), describes Chicano English by challenging the myths concerning CE. So many misconceptions about CE exist because most people are ignorant of its history and structure. The perpetuation of these myths encourages discrimination against this variety of English and its speakers. One of the most persistent myths is that CE is the result of Spanish speakers' inability to fully acquire English. Speakers of CE may speak Spanish, but many of its speakers do not speak Spanish at all. They grow up in homes where English is spoken. They are speakers of a variety of English that reflects its historical contact with Spanish, as African American varieties of English reflect West African traditions and Appalachian English its Irish roots.

Perpetuation of this myth has ramification for school classrooms because teachers may incorrectly assume that children with this variety are not native speakers of English when they are. Like children who enter school with other non-standard varieties, speakers of CE should be taught to honour their home varieties while still acquiring Standard English, which is so necessary for success at school and work.

A second myth about CE concerns its linguistic structure. Some believe that CE is just a mix of Spanish and English, a hybrid of sorts, a form that is neither good Spanish nor good English. There is a type of language production that we'll talk about later in this chapter for when fluent bilinguals, who are competent in two or more languages, actively choose to mix their languages a process called codeswitching.

One of the most damaging myths is that CE is the language of urban gang members. Unfortunately, television programmes have helped to promote this myth. In an attempt to be more 'authentic', actors playing gang members often use Chicano-like speech. Sadly, the use of this variety by less objectionable members of the community on television is rare. Nevertheless, many educated middle- and upper-class people in the real-life Chicano community make use of the differing varieties of Chicano English for their communication with other Chicanos. Linguists have contributed to this myth in a different way because we tend to focus our study on the varieties that are most distinct because we find them the most interesting. Some speakers of Chicano English are not so distant from the speech of other groups.

The same accusation that is levelled against other non-standard varieties of English is also levelled against CE – that it is just incorrect grammar. Like other non-standard varieties of English, CE is systematically different from SAE. It is a patterned variation on the standard. Some of the differences can be attributed to contact with Spanish whereas other differences from SAE cannot.

*Chicano English sound system*

Like other non-standard varieties of English, CE varies in all its linguistic systems: sound, grammar, vocabulary and usage. Nevertheless, the differences are most notable in the sound system. Some of these differences can be traced to Spanish (contact with older relatives who are monolingual or bilingual Spanish speakers). CE certainly has a subset of features from Spanish – but not all the sounds of Spanish. Other features can be traced to the dialects CE speakers are in contact with: for example, African American varieties of English like putting the stress on the first syllable of words like *police* and *Detroit* where SAE speakers put stress on the second syllable.

Another feature of the CE sound system is the lack of reduction of vowels in unstressed syllables. In SAE, there is the tendency to change the vowels in unstressed syllables. Speakers shorten the sounds and make them lax. CE speakers use the long form of the vowels:

|  | SAE | CE |
|---|---|---|
| together | [I]-[tɪgɛðr] | [u]-[tugɛðr] |
| because | [I]-[ bɪkʌz] | [i]-[bikʌz] |

One of the most marked features of Chicano English is the lack of a distinction between the high front vowels, a linguistic process called neutralization. These speakers do not distinguish between the sounds [i] and [ɪ], thus words like *sister* and *mister* are rendered [sistr] and [mistr] rather than [sɪstr] and [mɪstr]. This merger of the two sounds can be traced to influence from Spanish, which does not make this distinction because it does not have two high front vowels.

Another feature of CE that can be traced to Spanish is the replacement of -*th*- sounds with [t] or [d]. Thus the word *something* would be pronounced [sʌmtiŋ]. Consonant cluster deletion is also common in word-final position. When two or three consonants come together the final consonant may be lost, for example, the word *least* would lose the final [t] sound and the word *state* may be rendered as [ɛstet], the added vowel at the beginning serving to break up the string of consonants. Although these features may be attributed to Spanish, consonant clusters are disfavoured in many of the world's languages and are also disfavoured in some African American varieties of English whose speakers are commonly in contact with Chicanos in urban Los Angeles.

### Chicano English syntactic system

The grammar of Chicano English differs as well from other varieties of English in some interesting ways. For example, speakers may eliminate some of the irregular forms of other varieties, in other words get rid of all the pesky exceptions to the rules. One such case is the reduction of the *was/were* distinction. Another is the loss of the *don't/doesn't* difference. CE speakers generally use only *was* and *don't* for both plural and singular subjects and objects (later we'll see that speakers of other dialects do this as well). This cannot be attributed to influence from Spanish.

> We knew the Dallas Cowboys was gonna win.
> She don't know nutin.

CE also shares with other dialects we'll look at later the use of double negatives and the use of *ain't*, both of which are present in the following sentence: 'I ain't got none'.

The lexicon of Chicano English has been enriched by its historical contact with Spanish. Speakers of other varieties of English sometimes borrow these words as well. Examples: *barrio* (neighbourhood) and *fiesta* (party). It is the lexicon of these speakers that is most likely to be picked up by speakers of mainstream varieties of English as contact with this variety increases.

Speakers of this variety of English are often discriminated against because of their use of CE, so why do they continue to use it when they also acquire more standard varieties in school that are modelled on television and elsewhere? As we'll see with African American Vernacular English (AAVE), Appalachian English (AE), Cockney English (CE) and other non-standard varieties, its use by its speakers is an act of identity, a cultural marker. Speakers of CE show no more signs of abandoning it than speakers of any other non-standard variety.

## 10.3.2  Codeswitching

Most of the world's people live in bi- and multilingual communities, a result of which is that many people have communicative competence in at least two languages. Sometimes in these communities, the two languages co-exist. However, the use of each language is relegated to particular functions or social settings where only one of the languages would be used at a time. For many speakers of Spanish, Hindi or Navajo (as well as other languages), they use English in contexts in which English speakers are present: i.e. work and school. However, the heritage language is used in the home, for community cultural events and even in some elementary schools. There are many speakers in these communities who incorporate aspects of one language into the speech of another language. This practice is called codeswitching because fluent bilinguals choose to mix the languages available to them for some reason.

> One beautiful día one mariposita was flying en el garden when, de repente, she azotó. 'Ay jijos,' she said. 'I forgot my alitos.'[5]

This is a common practice in large urban centres, the best examples of which for English speakers may be London and New York City. In New York City, English is shared with dozens of languages, but there are huge ethnic enclaves where particular language mixes are found. For example, in Queens, you hear the mix of Dominican and Puerto Rican Spanish with English. In other neighbourhoods the mix may be with Chinese, Italian or Yiddish. In London, the same thing goes on in neighbourhoods with Urdu and Hindi as well as other languages. In other cities of the USA, the sheer number of languages may be smaller, but we still get codeswitching where there are large bilingual populations: Arabic in Detroit and St Louis, Polish in Cleveland, Haitian Creole and Cuban Spanish in Miami, Spanish, Chinese and Croatian among others in Los Angeles; and of course Spanish all across the southwest, in places where Spanish speakers settled long before English speakers did.

If you travel to the border of the United States and Mexico, especially along the Río Bravo area, you'll find an intense mix of English and Spanish which the locals call *Spanglish* or *Pocho*. Outsiders believe these people are not competent in English or Spanish, but that is not accurate. These speakers are competent in both languages, though the variety of English or Spanish they speak may be non-standard. Here the fluid mixing of Spanish and English characterizes communication between bilinguals. When I lived in northern Mexico, I used to go to the border town of McAllen, Texas every few months. The mechanic I used there was a study in codeswitching. I'd sit in the waiting room in his small shop for hours waiting to get my car repaired, listening to the mix of conversations going on around me. When monolingual Spanish speakers would come in, he would address them in Spanish. When the clients were monolingual English speakers, he'd speak to them in English. When his friends, family, or local suppliers would come in, the banter would all of a sudden change to a fluid mix of the two languages, moving so quickly from one language to another, sometimes within the same sentence, that it was clear that this was not a planned affectation. It was just the way two people who are bilingual and bicultural made use of the codes available to both of them. No confusion at all. A customer would come in and the mechanic would effortlessly slip back into monolingual mode in the language necessary for the customer. It was a riot to listen to.

Here's a conversation I was able to note down between two middle-aged waitresses in a restaurant in McAllen, Texas. Note how they switch languages in the middle of the sentence:

> A: Por limpiarse es mas facíl take everything out, me entiendes?
> B: Eso es un good idea.

> Translation:
> A: In order to clean it it's easier to take everything out, do you understand me?
> B: This is a good idea.

So, why do people codeswitch? The simple answer is because they can! Having more than one language gives you double the resources in which to express yourself. For some speakers, certain topics may be conducted in a particular language because it is more comfortable. I remember going to a linguistics conference and hearing a paper about young girls from the Catalan area of Spain who would switch from Catalan to Spanish to talk about boyfriends because to them Catalan represented a more conservative culture in which boyfriends were frowned upon at an early age, a proscription that they didn't associate with the use of Spanish.

The use of two languages is also a signal of a bilingual and bicultural identity. Just as a speaker of a southern variety of US English may stress their variety in a part of the south to which they are new to indicate they are not 'damn Yankees', bilinguals will make use of both their varieties to indicate their complex identity expressed through their language use. Their usage of both has been characterized as an 'act of identity'.[6]

This switching is fluid and effortless. It is not done because speakers lack the vocabulary necessary to communicate in one language or the other. Bilingualism is a necessary condition for codeswitching. Codeswitching behaviour is a matter of personal style. Some speakers switch only at sentence boundaries, and others will engage in intense intrasentential switching. Codeswitches can be distributed into three categories. One is called tag switching, which is the insertion of a word or phrase from one language, when the rest of the sentence is in another. These are often expressions that sit on the edges of sentences (words like *so*, *truthfully*, etc.) that may be a commentary on the sentence. This is one of the most frequent types of switch as typified by the English expression, *just kidding*, in the first example and the use of Spanish *entonces* in the second.

> *Felicidades por la 4x4, también tienes barba, barriga cerveza?* Just kidding!
> 'Congratulations on (buying) the 4 x 4 (truck), have you got a beer belly and a beard now? Just kidding.'

> *Entonces*, drink and go to heaven.
> 'So, drink and go to heaven.'

Other speakers will keep entire sentences in one language and only shift to another at a sentence boundary.

> *Esta idiota es loca!* And she makes me crazy!
> 'This idiot is crazy.'

The most interesting switches, however, are those that occur in the middle of sentences. This intra-sentential switching is syntactically the most difficult because it occurs within a clause or sentence boundary and the two sets of grammar rules from both languages come into play.

> Hay room *aquí* for us. I plan to get drunk.
>         (here)
> Tell the *psicopata* to email me something.
>         (psychopath)
> That son of a *perra* screwed up all of my plans!
>         (female dog)[7]

In all of these examples, the switches are quite easy because the switch is simply one noun for another. More complex combinations, however, are quite possible, as seen in these examples from Quebeçois (Canadian French).

> Je pouvais *choose between* rester à Nova Scotia . . .[8]
> 'I could choose between staying in Nova Scotia . . .'
>
> . . . ont *settle* à Lafayette. Mais Cajun c'est *short* pour Acadien.
> . . . 'settled in Lafayette. But Cajun is short for Arcadian.'
>
> Ça me *gross out.*
> 'That grosses me out.'

The fact that this variability in codeswitching style exists suggests that switching is motivated by choice and open to the creative whim of the individual. That the use of codeswitching can be part of our creative play with language is quite obvious in the following rendition of the classic tale of the night before Christmas. A Spanish dictionary will provide enough information to get the gist of the story. If you know some Spanish, read it aloud to feel the rhythm of the story or ask a Spanish-speaking friend to read it to you.

Twas the night before Christmas and all through the casa,
not a creature was stirring. Caramba! Que pasa?
Los ninos were tucked away in their camas,
some in long underwear, some in pijamas.
While hanging the stockings with mucho cuidado,
in hopes that old Santa would feel obligado,
to bring all children, both buenos and malos,
a nice batch of dulces and other regalos.
Outside in the yard there arose un gran grito,
I jumped to my bed like a frightened cabrito.
I ran to the window and looked out afuera,
and who in the world do you think that it era?

Saint Nick in a sleigh and a big red sombrero,
came dashing along like a loco bombero.
And pulling his sleigh instead of venados,
were eight little burros approaching volados.
I watched as they came and this quaint little hombre,
was shouting and whistling and calling by nombre:
'Ay Pancho, ay Pepe, ay Cuco, ay Beto, ay Chato, ay Chopo, Maruco, y Nieto!'

Standing erect with his hands on his pecho,
he flew to the top of our very own techo.
With his round little belly like a bowl of jalea,
he struggled to squeeze down our old chiminea.
Then huffing and puffing at last in our sala,
with soot smeared all over his red suit de gala.
He filled all the stockings with lively regalos.
None for the ninos that had been very malos.
Then chuckling aloud, seeming very contento,
he turned like a flash and was gone como el viento,
And I heard him exclaim, y esto es verdad! Merry Christmas to all y Feliz Navidad!

## 10.3.3 Pidgins and creoles

When the European merchants set out in their sailing ships to begin trade with Africa and the Far East hundreds of years ago, they could hardly have imagined the amazing number of peoples with distinct languages that they would encounter and with whom they would want to trade. Clearly they would not have available to them bilingual translators to handle their negotiations for them at every port. They did, however, already have on hand a kind of trade language that had been used by sailors for trade throughout the Mediterranean Sea that had served them well.

The Portuguese were the dominant merchant fleet for some time and their vessels travelled extensively. Sailors from many countries manned their ships, and so on-board communication between peoples of different languages was quite rudimentary using many words from Portuguese, and words from other languages as well. Through these communications, sailors cobbled together enough common language to be able to give and understand orders and make trade in the many ports at which they stopped. There was never any emphasis on creating a grammar, just on communicating the needs of the sailors. This incomplete form of communication is called a *pidgin*.

As they went port to port in many countries, they not only collected new words for the things they found and experienced, but they left pieces of their languages as well with the people with whom they traded. The people in the ports found it useful to remember the phrases the sailors used to further their business with them. In addition, the sailors didn't just land in port, conduct their business and leave; they also ate and drank with the local people, and often had relationships with local women and even left behind children. Depending on the winds, a group might stay in an area several weeks. As sailors moved from port to port and from ship to ship, they took with them their linguistic skill with the pidgin, which they shared with other sailors and the locals at the ports at which these ships stopped.

The longer this went on, the more established certain phrases and words became both with the sailors and with the people in the ports they visited over and over. When the English, the French and the Spanish began to trade in these same ports, they found the Portuguese pidgin well entrenched and used it as well. They also added bits and pieces of their own languages. However, Portuguese remained dominant. So much so that we have found pieces of Portuguese throughout the areas where the pidgin was spoken including slave plantations where English was the dominant language. On plantations in the American south, a slave child was called a *pikanini*, a word that is derived from Portuguese *pequeño*, meaning 'little one'. Another derivation of this word is still used in both Limonese Creole (spoken in Costa Rica) and Jamaican Creole: *pikni*. Another Portuguese word, *saber*, which means 'to know,' is also found throughout the peoples of the old European trade routes as *sabe* and *savve*.

Linguistically, a pidgin is a lingua franca or trade language. Because a pidgin is a communication system born of temporary necessity, it generally does not develop into a full language. No one needs it to. Everyone who uses a pidgin has his or her own native language, therefore, there is no need for the pidgin to handle the full complexity of a culture's communication needs. Pidgins have a simplified grammar that may not reflect the rules of any one particular language. There will be little to no morphology for making nouns possessive or plural or verbs past or future. The forms used from person-to-person and situation-to-situation vary greatly. This is true because there is no standard form with native speakers for new speakers to pattern themselves after. The vocabulary will be drawn from the languages of all the contributors, though in the case of Nautical Pidgin, more words come from Portuguese than any other single language.

Their extent is quite widespread. They are found on every continent except Antarctica. Some are the result of massive immigration like the Turkish-German pidgins spoken in Germany. Others reflect ongoing language contact like the Basque pidgin of the region between Spain and

France. However, most of the better-known pidgins in the world are found along old colonial shipping routes in Africa and Asia.

Sometimes the pidgins disappeared as the need for communication was eliminated or as bilingualism increased. Many of the so-called pidgin languages have become quite stable and are the native language of many peoples. One pidgin that has expanded only within the last couple of generations is Tok Pisin (Talk Pidgin) which is the co-national language of Papua New Guinea. Although the name used by its speakers still has the word *pidgin* as a part of it, linguistically it no longer is one because it has become a full language with native speakers. Tok Pisin is used on the radio, in newspapers and in schools. Right now there are families whose children are learning Tok Pisin as their first language because the parents communicate in Tok Pisin.

Why did Papua New Guinea end up with a pidgin? Papua New Guinea has over 700 local languages. Previous to colonization, there was not a need for a language to unite all of the country's ethnic groups. Because Papua New Guinea was colonized by the English, an English-based pidgin developed. It began as a trade language used throughout the country. Over the last few generations, it has continued to spread and has become more complex and is used for all communication needs. Rarely have linguists had the chance to study creolization, the process of a pidgin becoming a creole, in action. In this modern age of tape recordings and written language, Tok Pisin affords us a wonderful opportunity to observe language creation in progress and to learn much about the workings of the human mind.

*Creole languages*

The expansion of Tok Pisin into a full language with native speakers is a process that has happened in many parts of the world over at least the past five centuries. It is part of a collection of languages that are of a unique type in terms of their original development. Languages are usually handed down from parent to child in an unbroken transmission of structures from generation to generation. The children acquire the language of their caretakers and in turn pass it down to their offspring. Changes in every system of the language may happen during the lifetime of the speakers, but the majority of the basic structures remain the same. As we saw in the history chapter, languages do undergo major changes, but they generally happen over a long period of time. However, when a pidgin becomes a full language, it often does so quite abruptly, within a generation of speakers. When a language is created thus, linguists call it a creole.

In the most important ways, creole languages do not differ in significant ways from non-creole languages. They are systematic varieties that are capable of handling all of the complex communication needs of their speakers. What makes creole languages unique is the sociolinguistic situations from which they develop and their unique and abrupt development into full languages.

Most creole languages, like the pidgins that spawned them, are located near the old European nautical trade routes, though there are some notable exceptions. Many are associated with the advent of slavery and the forced and violent relocation of Africans from many ethnic groups to the plantations of the New World. But the story, and often the languages, begin in Africa.

We'll mostly focus here on the slave trade carried out by the British because we will focus on the development of African American English in a later section of this chapter. The slave trade dates to the early 1500s; in fact less than 20 years after Columbus first landed on the island of Hispañola (Haiti/Dominican Republic). Ships left England bearing goods for trade to the West Coast of Africa where these goods would be traded for other goods or slaves.

During the slave trade, the European slave traders collected slaves from a swaths of the west coast of Africa, roughly from about present-day Senegal stretching south to Angola. The sailors of the slave ships generally did not land at some port and just go ashore and round up whoever was convenient and ship out for the New World. Slaves were often captured and brought to centralized areas and kept hostage for as much as a year before a ship came to take them away. One place they were collected was the island of Cormantin located off the coast of present-day Ghana. While there, they were 'cared for' by local Africans who worked for the English who controlled the port. Many of these workers were part of the local Twi or Asante ethnic group whose descendants currently populate Ghana. These workers were often little more than slaves themselves and many ended up on the ships as slaves. Slaves were brought to this fort from many of the surrounding ethnic groups, thus, they spoke many different languages. Because the captured Africans had little contact with the English slave traders who controlled the fort, they had little need for acquiring English. They did, however, find it useful to learn as much Twi as possible, since the Twi were their direct caretakers. Since many of the languages spoken by the slaves, including Twi, were Niger-Congo languages (which are similar in the same sense that Romance languages are), picking up some Twi may not have been too difficult. Combine this with the fact that bi- and multilingualism were and are quite common in Africa, so it was not unusual for people to pick up other languages. Because of the mix of Twi, English and other peoples, a pidgin developed and was used for communication between the slave traders and their workers, and between the workers and the captured slaves. Through the pidgin, Twi words as well as English (and some of the Portuguese Nautical pidgin) would have been acquired and transported to the New World with both the slaves and the slave traders. Even today, we find features of Twi language, and other Niger-Congo languages, in African American varieties of English, Limonese Creole, Jamaican Creole, Cuban and Dominican Spanish and Southern White Vernacular English among many others.[9]

Examples of African retentions in the New World:

*bayɛre* (a type of yam) from Akan is maintained in Limonese Creole as *yeri yam*
*bobo* in both Akan and Limonese Creole means a fool or an idiot
*Cho*! An exclamation of surprise in both Yoruba and Limonese Creole

During the Middle Passage, the many-months-long journey across the Atlantic, the pidgin would have continued to be used for shipwide communication. Furthering the need for the pidgin was the general practice of separating slaves from the same ethnic groups who shared a common tongue. The thought was that a slave revolt would be less likely if communication was made difficult and slaves from rival groups were placed together. The general demographics of a plantation meant that the African population far outnumbered the owners and overseers, thus any advantage the slave owners could orchestrate, they did.

There were as many as 1,200 slaves on some of the bigger plantations. The contact between the slave owners, the overseers and their families, maybe a dozen or so people, with the field slaves would have been quite limited. This entailed that, for the vast majority of slaves, access to English was quite limited as well. House slaves and the slaves of small homesteads would have had much more access to English because they would have had more hours of exposure to native speakers every day, giving them a better shot at acquiring the language. House slaves would pass on aspects of the language they were learning to the other slaves.

An interesting question is, what English were they acquiring? Many of the white overseers and skilled plantation workers were either immigrants from Ireland or indentured servants. Their varieties of English would have been greatly different from the English of the plantation owners. Even the speech of the plantation owners may not have been a prestige variety of English. As we'll see again in the section on Appalachian English, the same Irish who fled the famines, unemployment and continuing persecution by the English, ended up on slave plantations in Barbados, Jamaica, Georgia and Louisiana as well as in the coal mines of Appalachia. Fragments of the sound system, grammar and vocabulary of these immigrants resonate in the speech of people in all these areas and in many varieties of both Black and White English in the Americas.

Thus, on each plantation, you had a large multilingual population trying to pick up whatever bits and pieces of language were possible from the group in power to best facilitate their survival. Meanwhile, the slaves were communicating among themselves using the pieces of pidgin they'd acquired, and the grammar they had in common from both African and European languages. Still, they had their first languages in their heads and sometimes they were fortunate enough to have other speakers of their language near to them. It's highly likely that on the larger plantations, despite efforts by the slave owners to separate them, speakers of the same languages would end up together. Thus, African languages would not have immediately died out in the New World. Words and features from these languages would have continued to be incorporated into the developing language on the plantation.

Then the slaves did what all humans do – they began to fall in love and have children. Many of these children were born to parents who had no native language in common and communicated solely through the pidgin. The children born into this environment picked up bits and pieces of the parents' native languages, as well as the pidgin, and other languages in their environment. Since children were usually cared for in large groups by the oldest slaves, they were also exposed to their languages as well. In the chapter on language acquisition, we learned that all children need is the input of their parents or other caretakers to acquire their native language. For these children though, there wasn't a community language available to them to use as a target. The African languages would not have been consistently available to most of these children, nor was the language of the slave owners, thus the language they were most exposed to would have been the pidgin. Unfortunately for these children, pidgins are not full languages capable of the complexity necessary for a human life.

The language acquisition device helped structure the quite varied input to which the children were exposed. The African languages spoken by the children's caretakers also contributed in significant ways to the expansion of the creole, especially in the areas of the language's structure and sound system. The language of the slave owners and overseers contributed much of the vocabulary. This is not unexpected since the words of a language carry primary aspects of meaning, and being able to understand and respond to their owners and bosses would have been critical to survival.

### What happens to creole languages after creolization?

How a creole develops after its initial expansion and stabilization, a process called creolization, is dependent on a number of sociolinguistic factors, most especially the relationship of creole speakers to speakers of other languages. The direction of language change is dependent on the amount and type of contact with different groups or the loss of contact with these groups. One of the most significant is the relationship with speakers of the superstrate language, the language spoken by the dominant group, in other words, the language of the plantation owners in the case of the English creoles of the New World.

### Close contact with the superstrate language

If there is a continuing relationship between a creole community and a community in which the superstrate is the primary language, then the superstrate language will continue to be influential, and it is likely that creole speakers will acquire aspects of the superstrate. A good example of this relationship is the relationship between Jamaican Creole and British English. Britain maintained direct political control over Jamaica until 1962 and since then has remained an important political and linguistic influence. In Jamaica, English is the language of tourism, so there is an economic motivation for people to have an internationally understood variety available to them. Standard Jamaican English is used in the schools, the media, government and with tourists. Jamaicans have access to international varieties of English through TV; both BBC and CNN are available as well as local Jamaican programming. The internet certainly provides an outlet for the use of International English as well.

In Jamaica, a rich collection of language varieties exist, and many people have the ability to shift to varieties of English that could be labelled Standard Jamaican English and reflect close contact with Britain. In other contexts, especially social and cultural ones, Jamaicans make use of the many voices available to them to express themselves. There is a *continuum* of varieties that range between Standard Jamaican English and cultural and creole varieties: including, but not limited to, Maroon Spirit Language, Rasta Talk and Jamaican Creole. Because of the contact with international varieties of English, *some* of the varieties of language spoken in Jamaica have continued to become more like Standard Jamaican English. Depending on people's social and business contacts, they may be able to vary their speech greatly depending on the context. For example, a union organizer must be able to communicate well with workers in the cane fields as well as to make contractual agreements with the management of major companies. To do this well, he or she must be able to speak naturally with both groups. Not all of these varieties are easily understood by outsiders, like the tourists who visit. The street sales people understand this well, and when they approach tourists they shift their variety to the most standard variety they speak.

Jamaican Creole plays an important part in the culture of Jamaica, not simply as a speech variety used in social contexts. Creole is widely used throughout the country in a variety of artistic genres including dub poetry and reggae. It also is used on television and more frequently in wider and wider social circles as it gains acceptance. Among the Jamaicans there has been a growing movement to recognize the value of the cultural varieties of English like Jamaican Creole. Nevertheless, not all Jamaicans value all the varieties, an attitude found in other countries as well where the use of standard and non-standard varieties are battlegrounds for cultural identity.

*Greatly diminished relationship with the superstrate language*
In other creole-speaking countries, like Haiti, speakers of the superstrate are no longer in constant contact with creole speakers in significant ways. When this happens, it is likely the creole will begin to diverge from the superstrate rather than converge with it as in Jamaica. Haiti gained its independence in 1804, during the time when Napoleon was losing power and control over French territories. The French had controlled Haiti for almost 300 years and during this time the creole, called Kreyol by its speakers, was developing. However, since the French mostly left as the Haitians were gaining their freedom, there was no continual French

presence in Haiti that spread the use of French, rather than Kreyol. Because the French turned their attention away from Haiti, Haitian Creole (HC) was under no pressure to become more like French.[10] Therefore, as HC developed and changed, as all languages do, it became more distinct from French. In addition, unlike Jamaican Creole, HC has maintained a greater number of non-French (African) features in all aspects of its systems.

When I did research in Haiti in the late 1980s, approximately 7 per cent of Haitians spoke a variety of French that would be understood by speakers in France, and these speakers were generally part of the elite classes. Haitian Creole is taught in the elementary schools and is used in almost all domains of use except high levels of government, tourism and business. To go to a government high school you must pass a French exam, but since French is not taught in earlier grades access is generally restricted to the children of the elite and children fortunate enough to get into the limited number of free religious schools. Because of high unemployment, many Haitians leave the country for jobs, often to the Dominican Republic or the United States. Thus many are fluent speakers of Spanish or English as well as HC. Because there is little French influence in the area, both Spanish and English have become more useful second languages than French for local trade and tourism.

### Loss of the creole

Creole languages may die off for the same reasons as other languages do. Many of the creoles developed in the USA on plantations have either disappeared or have shifted into modern versions of African American English. Others remain, but the number of their speakers is quickly dwindling, for example, the use of *Gullah* is now limited to the Sea Islands off the coast of Georgia and some limited mainland areas. Other varieties disappear because they merge with the superstrate language and only minor differences remain that signal the language was once a creole. Some worry that Bahamian Creole is getting more and more like Standard Caribbean English with each generation and may eventually be lost.

### Shift in direction of language change

Lastly, on rare occasions, creoles end up in significant and sustained contact with a language that is not the original superstrate language. Limonese Creole (LC) is an English-based Creole spoken in Costa Rica which has recently begun to incorporate Spanish lexicon and grammar into its systems. LC is a daughter language of Jamaican Creole which was transplanted to Spanish-speaking Costa Rica in the late 1800s when thousands of creole-speaking Jamaicans went there to live and work. Although most never intended to immigrate there permanently, they created communities in which to live where the English-based creole was dominant. Since few Spanish-speakers lived in the area, these communities were self-sufficient and grew in size and economic prosperity. Few of the Limonese ever bothered to learn Spanish because it was unnecessary to a successful life in the province of Limon.

In the 1950s, the migration of thousands of Spanish-speaking Costa Ricans caused a shift in demographics that eventually resulted in the Afro-Costa Ricans becoming a linguistic and cultural minority in the province they once controlled. At this point, the government began to require that the community's children attend Spanish-language schools. Within a couple of generations, the majority of community members became bilingual in Limonese Creole and Spanish.

At first, due to their bilingualism, LC speakers began to codeswitch with Spanish because both systems were readily available to them. Later, it became clear that Spanish was having a more permanent effect on LC: even monolingual creole speakers were using Spanish words and structures in their creole speech, a sign that the creole system was being permanently affected rather than soley reflecting a bilingual's ability to shift back and forth between two systems. In addition, there were some creole words and phrases that were being permanently supplanted by Spanish ones, another sign of a system change.

Here are some examples of how LC is mixing with Spanish (Spanish words are underlined and glossed below the word). In the first two examples a single word is borrowed into each, a noun in the first case and a verb in the second. The word *parada* has almost completely displaced *bus stop* in the community. Note the form of the Spanish verb. When verbs are borrowed they are always borrowed in the infinitive form (the 'to' form of the verb in English, e.g. 'to run').

> Yu gwain siem *parada* as Puerto Viejo.
> 'You are going to the same *bus stop* as Puerto Viejo.'

> Mi a fi *recolectar* mi buk dem.
> 'I have *to collect* my books.'

Sometimes, a Spanish meaning will be borrowed, but the creole word will remain. This is the case with the word *taym* (time), the creole use of which corresponds to the Spanish word *tiempo* which is used to refer both to the hour or the weather.

> Di *taym* chieng up.          Di *taym* luk layk it a rein.
> 'The weather is changing.'    'The weather looks like rain.'

There is evidence that the verbs being borrowed are not just simple lexical switches because they have acquired inflectional morphology, in the case of the example below the *-ing* suffix, which in LC, as in Appalachian English, sounds like [in].

> Luk laik im *kedarin*. (from Spanish *quedar*)
>               staying

> Tamara wii spen da huol die *paesearin*. (Spanish, *pasear*)
>                              running around

Yu jus *basilarin*. (Spanish, *basilar*)
(fooling around)

The grammar is affected in other ways as well. Whenever a Spanish adjective or noun is borrowed into a creole sentence with both, the word order rules change. In English, adjectives come before nouns (*the red car*), but in Spanish, they follow the noun (*el carro rojo*). But in LC, Spanish word order is beginning to dominate, sometimes even in sentences in which there are no borrowed Spanish words as we see in the third example below:

Jus di English *corriente,* what we would speak  (*corriente* = street or common)
　　　adjective  noun

So, shi studi der an shi gradjiet az sekritari *bilingüe*. (*bilingüe* = bilingual)
　　　　　　　　　　　　　　　　noun  adjective

Well, if I see a black . . . somebody, a person black, I feel good . . .
　　　　　　　　　　　　　　noun adjective

This linguistic situation is quite rare and the opportunity to study the effect is as well. I have been documenting changes in the community for almost a decade and the influence of Spanish is quite remarkable. Because we are able to observe and document these changes at first hand, we may gain new insights into how languages in contact affect each other and what are the mechanisms of language change.

## 10.4 Varieties of English

There are hundreds, if not thousands of varieties of English spoken natively worldwide. The actual count depends on how you slice up the pie. How different does one variety have to be from another before it warrants its own designation? As we've seen with languages like Swedish, Danish and Norwegian, which are remarkably similar in form and sound, native speakers may decide that their variety is distinct enough to be called something else. With varieties of a language, or dialects, we find almost the opposite situation. Most speakers of non-standard varieties of a language would not give their a variety a distinct name. If you asked someone walking down the street in Chauncey, Ohio (a rural area where Appalachian English is commonly spoken) what language they were speaking, they'd consider it a ridiculous question, but most would probably answer 'English'. I got the same response when I asked speakers of Limonese Creole what they were speaking. They simply said 'English'. The more specific names are a convenience for linguists, though they may get picked up by locals, especially if for some reason they decide to promote local culture and language.

Part of the reason that this answer is so common and so logical is that speakers of most non-standard varieties are also able to use speech forms that are standard. These speakers are able to vary their speech depending on the context in which they find themselves. If speakers in a conversation are all in-group members, the variety used will most likely be more non-standard (real) because it is an important symbol of group membership. The formality of the situation affects choice of variety. People understand that they are judged by their speech, and thus manipulate their speech to get what they want. People who are bi-dialectal have more varieties at hand to manipulate and to use to express their uniqueness. Thus many speakers of non-standard varieties are able to shift their usage depending on the situation. In a job interview, people may speak their most formal variety, which may almost sound like writing. At a party with friends, people will use the variety that is most accepted by the group they are with. They can choose to use the variety of language that serves them best, depending on the context. The continuum of varieties a person masters can be viewed graphically as:

| very distant from standard | less distant | very close to standard |
|---|---|---|

In the following sections, we'll take a brief look at two regional dialects, one urban (Cockney English) and one rural (Appalachian English) as well as African American Vernacular English, a variety based on ethnicity. We'll finish up with a variety that most people don't look at as a dialect, gendered English.

## 10.4.1 Appalachian English

The language varieties labelled as Appalachian English are a regional variety of American English spoken primarily in the Appalachian Mountains and the surrounding areas, stretching from the most southern and eastern parts of Ohio through parts of West Virginia, eastern Kentucky, Tennessee and the Carolinas, and south through southern Missouri and northern Arkansas. The speech throughout this broad area is not completely uniform, but speakers share features that make their speech distinct from that of surrounding areas. The geography of this part of the country is harsh and hilly, and so the communities tended to be, and some still are, somewhat isolated from each other and from the rest of the country. Small communities that were settled high up in the 'hollers' had virtually no communication with the outside world. As time went by, the communities became more and more insular and so less likely to be exposed to or to adopt linguistic changes from other speech communities.

Major immigration to this area came from Ireland and Scotland, where English was spoken as a second or an adopted language. Both Irish and Scots English varieties were and still are quite distinct from those spoken in England, a fact which was exacerbated by the 'troubles' between the English and the Irish. The English never made a serious attempt to change the type of English spoken by the Irish, thus their varieties were quite distinct from those of the English. When these immigrants came to the new world, they brought their dialects along with them. After 1640, a large immigration of the Irish and the Scots began. The heritage they brought is still evident in the area's language and music.

Speakers of these dialects have been stereotyped as ignorant, poor and uneducated by outsiders. The saddest part of this situation is that many native speakers of these dialects also claim that their own language is 'bad English'. Whether we like it or not, the prestige dialect is the one determined by or spoken by those in power. Varieties like Appalachian English are looked down upon because they are used by people who are from socially stigmatized groups not because of any real structural deficit of the language.

*Features of Appalachian English*

The grammar of AE differs in a number of ways from Standard American English (SAE), for example in the use of double modals by its speakers. Modals are helping verbs like *should, could* and *would*. The rules of SAE do not permit the use of two of these in succession; however, AE speakers do this: 'I *might could* go'. For the same meaning, speakers of SAE would say 'I *might be able* to go'. Another double modal that occurs in this area is *shoulda oughta* which is really a combination of 'should have' and 'ought to', which in a sentence is rendered as 'He shoulda oughta come to work today'. In this case the function of the double modal is intensification. The use of double modals is a very marked feature of AE that is quite noticeable by speakers of other varieties.

As mentioned in the introduction to this section, speakers of AE also commonly delete the 'to be' in some passive constructions, as in 'This car needs (to be) washed' or 'Your room needs (to be) cleaned'. In that same section, I also talked about the use of 'a fixin' or 'fixin' plus the infinitive form of the verb as in 'He's a fixin to run away'. The use of '(a) fixin' is limited to events that are imminent. You can say 'I'm a fixin to go to town this afternoon' but cannot say 'I'm fixin to retire in 30 years'.

One of the most marked grammatical features of AE is the use of double negatives, which of course are quite common in many other non-native varieties of English across the English-speaking world as well as in the writings of Shakespeare.

> He can't get nothin' done with her a hollerin.
> I ain't gonna do nothin'.

The other features of AE that is quite noticeable to outsiders are the differences in the sound system and intonation. The sound system of AE has a number of features that are quite distinct from SAE, including the shift from [ŋ] in final unstressed syllables to [n] as in *comin'* and *goin'*. This shift to the alveolar nasal only happens in unstressed syllables, so words like *sing* [sɪŋ] do not become [sɪn]. Another patterned change is the tensing of high lax vowels, both front and back. The vowel [ɪ] is pronounced [i] in words like *fish* and *dish*, and the [U] vowel sound in some SAE words is pronounced as [u] in words like *push* and *bush*. The mid vowel [ɛ] may also be tensed, for example the first vowel in the word *special* is pronounced as an [e]. Another notable feature of many of the dialect's speakers is a tendency to draw out the vowels in single-syllable words so that they become, in essence, two-syllable words. In college, my boss used to call me by my childhood nickname *Beth*, which in her pronunciation was rendered as [bɛ·ɛθ]. Previously in this text, I also remarked on the practice of shifting the word stress to the first syllable of words like *Detroit*, *recycle* and *rewind*.

The lexicon of AE also differs from SAE. In some ways it is more conservative than SAE, preserving some older English forms that are not in common use in SAE, like *vexed* for 'angry'. Other differences in the lexicon can be accounted for by regionalisms distinct to the area, like *wood pussy* or *polecat* for the smelly animal that SAE speakers call a *skunk*. AE speakers are also comfortable with the contraction *ain't* as well as another contracted form, *y'all*, which in my home community was also sometimes pronounced *y'ins* or *y'uns* by some speakers. The pluralization of *you* is a particularly interesting phenomena. English used to distinguish between *you* singular and *you* plural (*thou* singular and *ye* plural), but that distinction has been lost. I've asked foreign students from many countries if their languages make this distinction, and almost all report that they do. One German student told me that German only has one form, but later came back to tell me that non-standard varieties of German do have separate forms for *you* singular and plural. In the USA, other non-standard dialects have a form for this as well. In New Jersey you get 'youse guys', and in southern Indiana 'youins' (from 'you ones'). My father told me of an older female friend in southeastern Ohio who used to ask, 'Are youins goin to the doins?' ('Are you all going to the party/festival?' etc.).

Despite the fact that Appalachian children are schooled in standard varieties of English, often by teachers who have little appreciation for their local variety, and despite the fact that adult speakers may be discriminated against for its use, Appalachian English is alive and well throughout this area. Many speakers have made accommodations towards standard English and may use their distinct varieties as it best suits them. Other speakers' lives are happily bound to local communities where their speech is the norm and outsiders' speech is what attracts attention.

## 10.4.2 African American Vernacular English

> That mainstream English is essential to our self preservation is indisputable but it is not necessary to abandon Spoken Soul to Master Standard English, any more than it is necessary to abandon English to French or to depreciate jazz to appreciate classical music.
>
> (John R. Rickford and Russell J. Rickford, 2000).

Ebonics? Black English? Black Vernacular English? African American English? African American Vernacular English? These popular and linguistic names, old and new, refer to a group of systematic language varieties spoken by many black Americans, and others, throughout the United States. Just as with SAE, African American English is an abstract concept. Not all African Americans speak it or any of its variations, and not all of its speakers are African Americans. Just as with any other dialect, its speakers apply its rules in varying degrees, and just like other dialects, it rules are applied systematically.

The history of these varieties is part of the history of slavery and the development of pidgins and creoles, which we discussed at length in an earlier section of this chapter, so that history will not be repeated here. Suffice it to say that African American varieties of English have features that can be traced to Niger-Congo (NC) languages of West Africa, and other features which can be traced to varieties of settler English including Irish varieties of English, now Appalachian English (AE) and Southern White Vernacular English as well. This history is significant, among other reasons, because the linguistic status, especially of the most radical form, African American Vernacular English (AAVE, also called Ebonics), is still hotly debated in some circles. Is AAVE a Niger-Congo language of West Africa or is it a variety of colonial American English? As we look at the distinctive features of this language, we'll see that arguments can be made for both positions.

*Features of African American Vernacular English*

Some of the most recognizable differences in the speech of AAVE speakers are the differences in the sound system. Many people even claim to be able to tell the race of a person over the telephone. Due to a discrimination case involving fair housing, a study was conducted that shows that this is true to some extent. This unfortunately meant, in the case of this study, that some landlords were discriminating against African Americans based solely on features of their language.

One of the most noticed differences is the shift away from the voiceless interdental consonant [θ], the *-th-* sound. There is a pattern to the pronunciation differences. In word-final environments (at the end of words), the interdental fricative [θ] is labialized; it is realized as [f] in words like *mouth* [mawθ]. When the voiced *th-* sound is word-initial, then it is realized as [d], thus the words *this* and *that* are pronounced [dɪs] and [dæt]. Other word final consonants, specifically [t] and [d], are simply lost, as in 'last beer' [læst bir] becoming [læs bir]. This final consonant deletion has been attributed to the fact that Niger-Congo languages show a preference for no consonant clusters.

A frequently misunderstood feature of AAVE concerns the pronunciation of the past tense morpheme. Uninformed speakers of other dialects have claimed that speakers of AAVE don't use the past tense grammar. Actually, this is a sound system issue. As we saw, final consonant deletion is common as well as the loss of consonant clusters.

> He walked to school yesterday.
> SAE [wakt]     AAVE [wak]

We know that speakers of AAVE have a past tense morpheme because the full form is heard in root words that end in [t] or [d] like *elected* and *voted*.

Another widespread sound feature is the shift from [ŋ] to [n] in word-final unstressed syllables in words like *comin'* and *goin'*, a feature also found in Appalachian English, Jamaican Creole and Limonese Creole. Did this feature originate in one of the substratum languages of West Africa? (Substratum in this case means a language contributing to the English pidgin.) Or was this feature present in the speech of Irish indentured servants who ended up on slave plantations in the American South and throughout the Caribbean? Or both?

Like speakers of Appalachian English, AAVE speakers have a broader range in pitch than speakers of SAE, a feature which is also common to present-day varieties of Niger-Congo languages. In addition, the shift to first-syllable stress in words like *Detroit*, *hotel* and *police* occurs in both AE and AAVE.

Evidence suggests that the metathesis (switching) of consonants in the word 'ask' to 'aks' may be a residual from an earlier form of English. It certainly was an acceptable alternative pronunciation in Old and Middle English as can be seen from this excerpt from William Caxton, the full text of which is found in the History chapter. Although the spelling is variable, it is pronounced the same.

> A mercer cam in to an hows and axed for mete, and specyally he axyd after eggys.

AAVE has made, and continues to make, the largest contributions to SAE from its vocabulary, often through the medium of music, especially jazz, and culture. African words like *banjo, bandana, tote* and *banana* are now part and parcel of SAE. Other words came into English later via pop culture. Many were words relating to music: *hep* (from Cab Calloway's Hep Cats), *boogie, gig* and *jazz*. Other words describe day-to-day life events and situations: *ashy, crib, funky, phat, bling.* As with all dialects, these words come and go in popularity. Some of these are slang words that will disappear with time, but others will cross over into mainstream English.

The grammar of AAVE is unique as well. Again, as with other varieties of English, the differences in grammar can sometimes be attributed to a systematically different application of the rules. One example of this is in the absence of helping verbs (auxiliary verbs or modals) in some constructions. Standard English speakers can contract the verb phrase in the sentence 'He is a good boy' to 'He's a good boy', or 'I have got it' to 'I've got it'. In AAVE the rule is systematically different and can be represented as 'where SAE speakers can contract, AAVE speakers can delete': 'He a good boy' and 'I got it'. Other examples I've heard: 'He jammin'' and 'Dey runnin''. Niger-Congo languages don't have helping verbs like these, so that may be the source of this rule, but this sometimes happens in AE as well, where it is not uncommon, to hear 'He got it'.

Another feature of AE, not unexpectedly present in AAVE, is the acceptability of double negatives:

> I didn't have no lunch.
> Can't say nutin to nobody.

However, double negatives are not uncommon in Niger-Congo languages either. Speakers of AAVE and AE both also use double modals (*might could* and *shoulda oughta*) as well as quasi modals, akin to *liketa* (meaning 'almost'), for example in the utterance 'I liketa died!' They also share the use of the expression *ain't but* meaning 'only', as in 'She ain't but five feet tall!'

One of the most remarked-upon features of AAVE by speakers of other varieties is the systematic difference in usage of the 'be' verb, the most common of which is the use of 'be' as a habitual marker to grammatically mark that an event or state is customary, as in 'That child be bad'. SAE has no grammatical way to mark a verb as habitual. Its speakers do so through the use of adverbs like *usually*.

One African American linguist I used to work with told me that she grew up in a rural, mostly white community and lived there until she was about 15, when she moved to an urban black neighborhood. When she got to school, she realized that her language was quite different from her peers and in an effort to fit in, she started dropping the *be* verb in all over the place. Very quickly she was informed that she wasn't using it correctly. Even the teenagers, the people we think are ignorant of grammar rules in every culture, understood that there is a systematic usage of this form.

The tense system of AAVE is somewhat more complex than that of SAE:[11]

He runnin. (He is running)
He be runnin. (He is usually running)
He be steady runnin. (He is usually running in an intensive, sustained manner)
He bin runnin. (He has been running)
He *bin* runnin. (He has been running for a long time and still is).

In addition to the influence of African languages and varieties of English that certainly contributed to the unique development of AAVE, we must add the effects of creolization. The English spoken by most of the slaves was a creolized variety that reflected not just influence from superstratum and substratum languages, but the effects of universal language acquisition processes by the first native speakers of the creoles.

At the beginning of this section, I pointed out that the lineage of AAVE is a matter of debate. Some see the present-day speech of African Americans to be so similar to current varieties of English that it is a dialect of English. Certainly, SAE and AAVE are more alike now than ever before. This is not particularly surprising. Many speakers of AAVE are also speakers of some version of SAE, and SAE has been enriched throughout its history by the appropriation of features of AAVE into SAE. In addition, we have been living, loving and working together for long enough now that most dialects of English have become more commonly heard and less unfamiliar to our ears.

For people who prefer to go back to the beginning of things, it is the root of this variety, spoken by Africans who began with African languages and forged the creoles that became AAVE, that is the most significant aspect in determining how to categorize AAVE.

So the answer is not simply that AAVE is a variety of English or a Niger-Congo language, or a descendant of a creole language. It seems simplistic just to call it English, given its exceptional history. The reality is that language is a messy business, and trying to adopt a simple explanation won't give you the true picture of this unique speech form.

## 10.4.3 Cockney English

Cockney is a working-class variety of British originally spoken in London, within hearing distance of the Bow Bell, which rang in a church, St Mary le Bow, long since destroyed. Cockney has spread beyond its original habitat including by some reports to as far away as Liverpool in younger groups of speakers. American readers may be most familiar with the dialect by way of the BBC soap opera *Eastenders* or through the voice of Eliza Doolittle and her father in the movie *My Fair Lady*. Fans of Monty Python may remember Eric Idle's cockney accent in the song 'Always look on the bright side of life' from Monty Python's movie, *The Life of Brian*.

Originally the term Cockney simply referred to the working-class inhabitants of London. No negative association was linked with the term until, because of the rising middle class in the eighteenth century, grammar books for 'proper English' began to proliferate. Needless to say, a variety spoken by the working class was not viewed as 'proper'.

## Features of Cockney English

Although it is a non-standard variety of English and greatly stigmatized by speakers of more standard varieties of British English, many speakers take covert pride in its forms and usage, especially in Cockney Rhyming Slang which is a playful pairing of related words to come up with, at least to outsiders, a totally unrelated meaning, but a similar pronunciation to the second item in the pair. Although some of these creations have been around for quite some time, and are known to people outside of the community, some are created on the spot and may never be repeated again. Here are some of the more common examples in each the pair of words has the same meaning as the word after the equals sign:

| | |
|---|---|
| trouble and strife = wife | bees and honey = money |
| apples and pears = stairs | plates of meat = feet |

The distinct vocabulary of Cockney reflected through the rhyming slang has also been enriched by borrowings from other languages, borrowings that did not come through other varieties of British English. For example, Cockney has acquired a considerable number of Yiddish words including: *schlemiel* (a fool), *nosh* (food), *spiel* (an exceedingly long or pointless talk), and *mazel tov* (good luck), all commonly used by Cockney speakers. Cockney soldiers also brought home French words from the two world wars including *ally toot sweet* ('quickly' from *allez tout de suite*) and a *parleyvoo* ('a chat', from *parlez-vous*) as in 'Let's 'av a parleyvoo'. If your grandparents are old enough, they may remember a song from after World War I called called 'Hinky Dinky Parley Voo'. Here's one verse:

Mademoiselle from gay Paree 'Parley voo'
Mademoiselle from gay Paree 'Parley voo'
Mademoiselle from gay Paree
You certainly did play heck with me
Hinky dinky 'Parley voo.'

Other expressions typical of Cockney are *hang about* ('wait a minute') and *straight up* ('honestly'). Some Cockney expressions came to America with Cockney immigrants and caught on, like the expressions *out of order* (out of line) and *taking liberties* (getting fresh).

The sound system of Cockney is the other feature that is quite distinct from other varieties of British English. One of the most remarked-upon feature by outsiders is the absence of word initial [h] in words like *'umble*, *'ospital* and *'ouse*. Cockney speakers, like many speakers in the rural south of the United States, insert an [r] in word-final position in unstressed syllables, as in *tomater* and *potater*. Another feature found in both southern varieties of American English and Cockney is the replacement of word final [ŋ] with [n], a feature that is also found in Limonese Creole, as in *livin'* and *drinkin'*.

Cockney speakers commonly substitute a glottal stop [ʔ] for the [t] preceding unstressed syllables in words like *bottle* and *water*. For speakers of American varieties of English, the glottal stop is the sound in the expression *uh-oh*, which is made at the glottis.

The -th- consonants are replaced in Cockney by the voiced and voiceless labiodentals [f] and [v], the result of which is one of the most well-known Cockney words, *bruvver* (brother). Substitution of -th- sounds is common in non-standard varieties of English.

Grammar differences from other non-standard varieties of English don't seem to be very prevalent, However, as for seemingly every other non-standard dialect of English, the use of double negatives is quite common in Cockney:

> That ain't got nothing to do with it.

Cockney grammar shares another feature with many varieties of US English, the absence of -*ly* on many adverbs or the use of an adjective in place of the adverb:

> The mates are playing normal.
> The girls done good.

Cockney speakers simplify the *was/were* set to *was*, as do speakers of a number of non-Standard US dialects:

> They was dressed good.

Cockney not only came to America, but also became the speech of many of the immigrants, both voluntary and involuntary, who settled Australia and provided the base for what was to become Australian English. If you are interested in more examples of Cockney, visit Cockney Online at www.cockney.co.uk.

## 10.5 Language and gender

'We need to talk.' These words strike terror into the heart of many males when uttered by their girlfriend or spouse. Much of this fear stems from the fact that men often see women's utterances as code for something much more than they say. Frankly, women are equally baffled by some of the communication breakdowns and misunderstandings they have with men. Although men and women seem to use the same words and grammar, at times we seem to be reading from different playbooks.

So, if there is a different code, why don't our parents just let us in on the dirty little secrets and save us all a whole lot of trouble? It doesn't happen because we seem to believe that we are speaking the same language. Most people are unaware that there are subtle, and sometimes not so subtle, differences both in the structure and meaning of our gendered varieties as well as how we choose to use them.

There are two aspects to language and gender. First, we need to look at how a particular language may be gendered that reflects current or past social values. Language is a social construction and reflects our attitudes (or someone else's) about the world around us – or reflects the way previous generations saw the world. Features of language may persist a lot longer than attitudes. Second, are there gender dialects? Do men and women use language in such distinct ways that they can be considered separate varieties of a language?

## 10.5.1 Use of titles

Is English a gendered language? Not in the sense of French, Spanish or Italian, for which nouns are assigned arbitrary genders which have specific grammatical requirements. If we look closely at English though, we can see that there are asymmetries in sets of words that reflect gender. For example, look at all the titles that have been used before women's last names. For men, there is only one title: *Mr*. This title reflects nothing about a man's age or marital status. For women, there are several (*Miss*, *Ms* and *Mrs*), though in the US, the use of *Miss* is rapidly disappearing. When I was growing up in the early 1960s, *Miss* seemed to be used for all unmarried females regardless of age. By the 1970s, especially with the rise in popularity of the term *Ms*,[12] the use of *Miss* began to diminish. Of course in the United States, this decline in the use of *Miss* coincides with a general drop in the use of formal titles for both males and females in many environments, both public and private. It's important to remember that the idiolect of any speaker may reflect a number of different varieties, based on age, gender, geographic location, social class and ethnicity. Dialects do not exist in a vacuum.

I've surveyed many women with a variety of backgrounds, marital status and ages about their use of titles. The great majority of them reported that they generally didn't use a title at all. They introduced themselves to strangers in formal situations by using both their first and last names. None reported using *Miss* self-referentially, though some reported that older relatives used it with them when they were small (and *Master* with their brothers). Only one maiden aunt of my husband, well over 75 years of age, used *Miss* to refer to herself.

The use of *Mrs* is much more interesting because there is so much variation in usage. One very old speaker uses *Mrs* plus her husband's first name (he has long since died). The only other usage of *Mrs* plus a husband's name came from a particularly class-conscious respondent who does not work outside the home, who is married to a medical doctor. A number of the respondents use *Ms* in professional circles and *Mrs*, plus their own first name, in purely social ones when a title is required. For the women who kept their own name after marriage, the overwhelming majority use *Ms*, though there was some suggestion that you couldn't be a *Mrs* plus your own last name because *Mrs* is supposed to go with a man's name, which none of them took. Clearly in the US there is a wide variety of naming options available to women.

The distribution of these terms is cultural. My understanding after querying a number of British women is that although the term *Ms* is not unheard of, it is not commonly used, although titles are much more frequently used than in the more egalitarian US culture. One respondent said that the title *Ms* actually carried a negative connotation for many British people.

The whole point of having a single term is to match the single male term which makes no reference to matrimonial status. Some people clearly don't understand why one term for women of both marital conditions is appropriate: 'If you use *Ms* for a female, please indicate in parentheses after the *Ms* whether it is *Miss* or *Mrs*.' 'Instructions given to Pennsylvania public information officers.'[13]

I had one funny incident with the word *Ms* in the late 1980s. I was a substitute teacher in the inner city of Los Angeles. One day in a class of third or fourth graders, I foolishly corrected a child who called me Mrs Winkler, and said that my name was Ms Winkler. When the child asked his neighbour what *Ms* meant, he patiently explained that Ms was the word women used when they didn't want you to know they weren't married!

## 10.5.2 Asymmetries in language

Asymmetries exist in other parts of the system as well. Consider the difference in connotation, at least in American English, between the words *bachelor* and *spinster*. When I pressed students in my classes to describe a *bachelor*, the comments were all positive; a *spinster* however elicited negative comments. A *bachelor pad* is a party place with lots of beer, a big-screen TV, and a lot of mess. There didn't seem to be a corresponding term like 'spinster pad', but when I suggested it, the description was a place with a lot of cats and knick-knacks.

Of course the use of these terms varies by culture. In October 2003, I saw an announcement on the TV show *Entertainment Tonight* about the marriage of Prince Andrew many years before. Here's what they reported was in the official court record:

> Announcement of a Marriage Licence:
> Andrew Duke of York, Bachelor (age 24)
> Sarah Ferguson, Spinster (age 26)

Frankly the word *spinster* is disappearing among the younger generations in the USA. Again, this can be attributed to age as much as to a change in gender consciousness. For the most part, Americans no longer consider women (or men) who are not married at 30 to be out of the ordinary, so the label is less useful than previously. The same is true for *bachelor*. We are marrying later in life than we did a generation ago.

Asymmetries also extend to words that have acquired asexual connotation. The words *master* and *mistress* were both once used as titles and terms of respect; while *master* has almost completely disappeared as a title (except for young boys in the south of the USA), *mistress* has taken on the meaning of 'the woman with whom a husband cheats on his wife'. The same happens with *mister* (*Mr*) and *Madam*. *Madam* is very rarely used in the USA, only in very formal business correspondence and even rarely there. The word *madam* is now more commonly used to refer to the woman who is in charge of a house of prostitution.

Such asymmetries do not always disfavour women. Consider the difference between the seemingly parallel expressions *mothering* and *fathering* in normal usage. While *mothering* entails a set of positive nurturing characteristics, *fathering* only refers to the actual donation of genetic material to create a child, reflecting what I personally think is our culture's ongoing devaluation of the importance of fathers in the emotional life of families.

Defaults in meaning may also be looked at as asymmetries. Many professions are still dominated by one gender or the other, and without labelling the person or saying a name, many people assume a particular gender. Consider the following statement:

> The model was very attractive.

For most people, this sentence stimulates a mental image of a woman and not a man. We use the expression 'male model' when the default gender is not the one we are referring to. Here are similar expressions I have heard over the past few years:

| | | |
|---|---|---|
| a lady doctor | a lady lawyer | a girl professor |
| a male nurse | a male prostitute | a male stripper |
| a male slut | | |

There is an episode of *The Simpsons* in which Marge can't get hired because she is a 'lady carpenter', and all the male characters who answer the door explain that she can't be a carpenter because she is a woman.

## 10.5.3 Generic 'he' for unspecified reference

The use of *he* as the generic pronoun is slowly disappearing in the USA (e.g.: A student works hard. He deserves a break). Its use as the generic pronoun is no longer as an appropriate style for academic writing by the American Psychological Association (APA) and other groups who issue style sheets for college and academic writing. Generic *he* isn't even historical. In 1850, an Act of Parliament was passed in Britain which made *he* the only legal form for third person singular generic. The use of generic 'he' is exclusionary, and it does have a subtle impact on the culture. In the 1990s, some studies showed that elementary schoolgirls did better on reading comprehension tests, when the texts they read were gender-neutral rather than filled with male pronouns used for generic references.

In US English, in informal speech and sometimes even in writing, the use of *they* is becoming more common as a replacement for generic *he*. This usage sends writing teachers over the edge, but there really is no reason why *they* cannot become the default pronoun, both singular and plural anymore than it was incorrect to change *thou* (singular) and *ye* (plural) to *you*. Native speakers of a language quite happily ignore the proscriptions handed down to them by 'protectors of the faith', oops, I mean language purists. Time marches on, and so does the language. Only time will tell if *they* catches on and becomes part of Standard English.

## 10.5.4  Effects of gender on language

Language is not only gendered, but the genders use language differently. The differences go well beyond commonly heard statements like 'When women talk, they are more polite' and 'Men swear more than women'. The differences are in every aspect of the linguistic system, only one of which can be explained by our genetics: the differing range of pitch available to men and women. Some of the differences we'll look at are more obvious than others. Some are just humorous, but other differences may cause us problems in communication and in how our lives turn out. Many of the differences are subtle enough that we are unaware of them, and our lack of awareness may mean that we miscommunicate with each other in important relationships both at home and at work.

This is not about either men or women using language properly. There are differences in our language use and forms, but neither form is correct; they are just reality. It's also true that we are gendered people, but we are not locked into roles that lack variation. You may identify features of the other gender that are in your own system. Perfectly normal. These roles and the use of language also vary across cultures. What is true for one culture may not necessarily be true for another. As I've said before, dialects are affected by many factors.

Studies over the years have looked at many aspects of gender. The more recent studies are in general better than some of the earlier ones because of the approach that many researchers took. Women's language was studied as deviant from the norm, which of course was the use of language by males, and for the most part, white middle-class males. This bias did a disservice not only to women, in labelling their speech thus, but also to men, because many interesting aspects of male usage have been left unstudied, as though men's speech was 'normal' and there wasn't anything of import to learn from studying it.

## 10.5.5 Common beliefs about gendered language

There are many stereotypes about how men and women use language, some of which reflect reality or at least part of it. Other stereotypes are really just too simplistic, and the reality of our usage is much more complex. One of the stereotypes that is credible is the use of more standard varieties of language by women.

Women are more likely to use prestige forms rather than non-standard varieties of language, when they are available to them. There are a couple of reasons for this. Women are more often, or at least feel that they are, judged by their appearance rather than their ability. More important though, I think, is the role of women in raising children. Women are still the primary caregivers in the home. Because they often equate standard language with power, they want their children to acquire the standard. Men use non-standard varieties as a way of bonding (talking like one of the boys) or establishing rapport or arousing fear in others, especially other males. The social repercussions for using non-standard varieties differ by gender. Women may be penalized at work for sounding, or trying to sound, too much like one of the boys.

One critique of women's language use is that it is somehow less direct and less authoritative than male use of language. Much of this has to do with how women use questions. Women often make assertions (statements) in the form of questions, which many men read as hesitance and lack of competence because it seems that women are looking for affirmation of their statement. Women see questions as being more polite than direct assertions. Thus, a woman giving her boss a set of accounts might not choose to say: 'The facts are accurate', but might rather say, 'The facts are accurate, aren't they?'

Some women also use questions in place of statements when they are offering criticism, as in the oft-heard question on television programmes, 'You know where you're going, don't you?' From personal experience with my husband, I know these questions not only irritate him but can cause other problems as well. We were driving in the desert one day, way out in the country, and were moving at a good speed down the road. I saw a stop sign coming up and we were not slowing down, so I said, 'Is that a stop sign?' For my husband, a typical guy, a question is a request for information, so he first answered and then realized what I meant and slammed on the brakes. As all the stuff in the back seat came flying into the front, it occurred to me that perhaps a question was much less useful than simply yelling 'Stop sign!'.

Women use a particular type of question, the tag question, in a markedly different way from men. Yes/no questions can be in two forms. 'Are you coming?' is a simple request for information. Nothing else can be read into it. A tag question is constructed in a grammatically different way, and provides some additional information to the listener.

Consider the difference between the following two questions:

> You are coming, aren't you? (indicates speaker hopes/believes that you are)
> You aren't coming, are you? (speaker hopes/believes that you are not)

The use of tag questions, however, goes far beyond this simple usage. Studies show that men tend to use tags almost solely to confirm information they think they know. They prefer this style of question, which indicates that they already know the answer, rather than a simple request for information question ('When is the meeting?') because that puts them in a position of looking as if they don't know something.

> The meeting is at 8, isn't it?
> You completed the study, didn't you?

Like men, women also use tags to confirm what they already know. However, studies have shown that US women, at least, have a whole range of other reasons for using them as well. For example, at dinner one night, a woman looks at her companion and says:

> We've been dating for six months, haven't we?

What's the function of this utterance? She knows this information, and so does he, so it isn't likely to be a simple request for information. She wants him to talk, maybe about their relationship, or is just trying to make conversation, to get him to talk. It would be very weird for her just to say, 'Let's have a conversation'. Women perform the supportive work in conversation to encourage and facilitate the participation of others, both male and female.

Men do not interpret these utterances in the same way. They often see them as a trap. You can imagine a cartoon with this scenario, and the bubble above the poor guy's head is full of questions like: Does she think this is an important anniversary? Does she want a present? Is she looking to go to the next level? Which way can I run?

Tag questions may also be used to co-opt a negative response, which may actually be useful to guys because it signals that this is something you'd better agree with me about.

> My meatloaf is good, isn't it?
> You'll enjoy going to my mother's with me this weekend, won't you?

Of course the best-known and most dangerous tag question, 'This dress makes me look fat, doesn't it?' only has one safe answer, guys, just memorize it and you'll be fine: 'I can't imagine anything that you could put on that could make you look fat.' In some ways this is an unnatural, albeit a safe response. This particular tag question is a problem, not solely from the aspect of content, but because of the form. Usually when a tag question is asked in which the tag (the last part) is in the negative, the speaker is signalling to you that they are looking for agreement: 'You like football, don't you?' The speaker expects you to answer yes, though you may not. But 'yes' is a totally inappropriate response to 'This dress makes me look fat, doesn't it?'

According to another stereotype, women are supposed to interrupt men frequently. This is a case where a simple answer is really not sufficient. It turns out that you have to not just measure interruptions, but look at the context in which interruptions occur. It turns out that women do interrupt men more often in the context of personal discussions in the home and at casual social gatherings. Men, however, interrupt women more often than they interrupt other men and more often than women interrupt men, in the context of the classroom and in business contexts.

Another aspect of interruptions is 'choral discourse' or overlapping talk. This is a conversation style more commonly associated with women, though across cultures both genders may do it. For many women, a conversation is considered to be a collaborative effort of all the participants, especially in the construction of group narratives. If you think about opera, several voices may be heard at the same time, but the audience is still able to follow the story.

Another linguistic feature that is handled differently by gender is 'back channel support', both verbal and physical. Back channel support is providing ongoing feedback though verbal commentary (*uh-huh*, *yeah, you don't say?*, *sure, wow*) or physical reaction (shaking the head) in response to a speaker's narrative. Women perceive that feedback encourages the speaker to continue and that silence indicates boredom or lack of understanding. Men neither provide nor expect back channel support, which is probably the source of women sometimes asking their male partners 'Are you listening?' It's quite likely that these questions either confuse or irritate men who, in fact, are listening. They just don't provide the back channel support that women expect.

This same approach to conversation is also reflected in the fact that men generally do not feel the need to respond to a simple assertion or statement of fact (unless they disagree with it). Unlike many women, they do not necessarily interpret an assertion as a question.

A friend of mine related the following conversation she had with her husband. One evening, they were taking a walk in the desert. They had been walking in silence and enjoying the view and the exercise. The following exchange occurred:

> Heidi: It's a really beautiful sky.
> Husband: (silence)
> (15 seconds go by)
> Heidi: Isn't it? (she's irritated)

She explained to me that he clearly didn't 'get it'. She considered her comment to be the opening volley in a conversation. However, because he happened to agree with her, he did not see a reason to respond. She didn't ask his opinion; she just made a statement. If she had asked him a direct question, he would have responded.

## 10.5.6 Language and the workplace

Our differing approaches to language by gender have an impact on our work lives as well as our personal lives. Women have had to accommodate to male communication styles in the workplace, where men have dominated for a very long time. If women are unaware of the differences in language use, it can have a profound impact on their success in the environment. If men don't understand the differing language use by women, they may be unable to have fully successful business relationships as well.

Here is some of what we've learned. Men are four times more likely than women to negotiate for higher pay at their first professional job interview, which can mean a lifetime difference in pay of up $500,000 for women who don't negotiate.[14] Why don't women negotiate? Women report that they are less comfortable with both the process of negotiation and the act of self-promotion often necessary to get rises and promotions. From childhood, women are socialized to be modest and not act in a conceited way. Girls are much more likely to be admonished by their parents and teachers for bragging: 'it's not ladylike'. Bragging is, however, an expected part of a boy's behaviour. Thus, men are less uncomfortable with the acts of self-promotion necessary to get ahead and understand that this is just part of the process. Even knowing this, I was extremely uncomfortable writing the cover letter for my current professorship, in which I listed my educational and professional accomplishments.

Once they get a job, women are sometimes easier for bosses to deal with in terms of rises and promotions. For example, women have been known to apologize for asking for more money and benefits, possibly giving the impression that they don't really deserve it, which of course makes it easier for employers to turn them down. Men will often not immediately take 'no' for an answer, and will respond to their boss with a counter offer and negotiate for getting something. They don't hear the 'no' as the end of the conversation.

So, why does speech differ by gender? A lot of it has to do with early socialization patterns, both in terms of how we are taught to act (or what we see modelled for us by adults) and the types of play that boys and girls engage in. These play patterns have an impact on how we behave as adults.

## 10.5.7 Early socialization by gender

Young girls frequently play in very small groups, and generally have one very close best friend. Their groups are quite private and other girls don't just join in, but must be invited into the group. The girls in the groups are generally the same age and the groups are characterized by a lot of cooperative play. If a girl is excluded from a group, she may often be shunned.

For young boys, their play groups are quite different. Almost any boy can just walk up to a group and join the fun, no matter what their age or status. In fact, the older boys in the group make use of younger or weaker boys as objects of victimization. Unlike the girls, boys don't usually shun; they like keeping their victims around, and as boys age, the victims sometimes become the victimizers, so roles change as well. The organization of boys' groups is completely hierarchical, which teaches boys how to get what they want by either controlling or manipulating members of the group. Often one boy will take over the group and get the group to do what he wants.

These play groups teach us very different sets of rules about how we go about getting what we want out of life and work. Boys learn to capture the floor and be the centre of everyone's attention, and to push themselves forward when another boy has taken over. Girls, on the other hand, look at their peers as a group and focus on things that benefit the group as a whole. Of course not all children fit into these patterns. Most of us are a mixed bag of gender patterns, especially if we were solitary children or tomboys.

So what do these gender differences say about us? Does all this mean that men are insensitive bores? Does it signify that women don't use language in direct ways? Of course not. Neither gender is evil; we're just speaking different dialects of the same language. What makes this one tough is that we usually don't recognize that we are speaking different dialects. Imagine you are from the USA and are talking with an English speaker from Britain. If the British person says something strange like 'It's in the boot' (in response to 'Where is my suitcase?'), the American will most likely ask what the word 'boot' means in this sentence. We don't expect there to be such significant differences in the use of language between two people who are from the same social class, who grew up in the same region. We don't expect them to misunderstand each other.

## 10.6 The future of English and its dialects

Numerous predictions have been made about what could happen to English because of its status as a continually growing global language. One accusation is that it could become 'the killer language', wiping out scores of lesser-used languages. Another prediction, from a historical perspective, is that although English could be utilized worldwide, because it mixes with local languages, many Englishes will be formed that will eventually become so distinct that they might as well be classified as different languages. English could break up, like Latin did, and form many new languages. A third possibility is that English will continue to spread worldwide in the form of an international language, with local varieties of English as well. However, bilingualism will be maintained with English and local languages will continue to flourish. This street sign was photographed in North Carolina, where the Cherokee language is promoted alongside English.

An important argument against International English wiping out the world's languages is that, for most of the people in the world, bilingualism, and even multilingualism, is commonplace. Thus it is possible for lesser-used languages to remain vibrant and useful, and some of the larger ones (Arabic, Spanish and Swahili for example) will remain important regional lingua francas. This also makes any global or regional language less of a threat to local identities. In addition, because English is fast becoming a local language in so many parts of the world, it can become a neutral lingua franca without imperialistic connotations. People can have more than one variety of English – just as many of us do now!

It is unlikely that English will go the way of Latin. Even though regional varieties of English are quite distinct from each other, especially those spoken in other countries, most people can shift along the continuum of their varieties to a variety that is less local. This 'international' variety of English is already available as merchants travel from country to country doing business and people from every walk of life communicate directly via the Internet, which has made global communication instantaneous, inexpensive and easy. The understanding of diverse varieties of English is also spread via the media. People in Ghana watch CNN News; Americans can watch news and comedy programmes from Britain and Canada. Our diverse voices are spread across the globe in ways that speakers of the dialects of Latin never had available to them.

## Suggested reading

Fought, C. (2003), *Chicano English in Context*. New York: Palgrave Macmillan Inc.

Lakoff, R. T. (2004), in *Language and Woman's Place: Text and Commentaries* (ed. M. Bucholtz). Oxford: Oxford University Press.

MacNeil, R. (2005), *Do You Speak American?* Films for the Humanities and Sciences. www.films.com

McWhorter, J. (2005), *Defining Creole*. Oxford: Oxford University Press.

Rickford, J. R. and Rickford, R. J. (2000), *Spoken Soul: The Story of Black English*. New York: John Wiley and Sons Inc.

Wolfram, W. and Schilling-Estes, N. (1998), *American English*. Oxford: Blackwell.

## Interesting websites

The Dictionary of American Regional English: www.polyglot.lss.wisc.edu/dare/dare.html

African American Vernacular English, California Center for Applied Linguistics: www.cal.org/topics/dialects/aae.html

University College London, Estuary English: www.phon.ucl.ac.uk/home/estuary/

Atlas of North American English, TELSUR Project, at the University of Pennsylvania: www.ling.upenn.edu/phono_atlas/home.html

Rethinking Politeness, Impoliteness and Gender Identity, by Sara Mills: www.linguisticpoliteness.eclipse.co.uk/Gender%20and%20Politeness.htm

'Sex, lies and conversation. Why is it so hard for men and women to talk to each other?' Deborah Tannen, The Washington Post, June 24, 1990. www.georgetown.edu/faculty/tannend/sexlies.htm

## Consider the following questions

1. Ask several of your friends or family the following questions about the varieties of English that they are familiar with:

a) What is the geographical area whose people, in your opinion, speak the least attractive or least pleasant type of English? You may base your answer on accent, slang, or any other criteria you can think of.

b) Next, what is the geographical area whose people speak the most attractive or most pleasant type of English?

c) Finally, what are the typical characteristics that you associate with the people who speak those varieties of English?

After you describe their answers, explain in the homework what the information tells you about normal people's (people who haven't studied linguistics!) attitudes to language varieties.

2. If you are an international student with family in an English-speaking country or you live with other non-native speakers of English, or you are a foreign resident whose family speaks another language at home, do any of them (and you) mix English and another language together in the same sentence, or between sentences? Do people switch from English to another language depending on the topic of discussion or some other factor? Or does the mixing seem to be random? Are there people you know who have attitudes, either negative or positive, about mixing two languages together in the same sentence or conversation? Also, which is the most common language used in your home situation? Why do you think this is so?

3) If you or members of your family are part of a minority group that speaks in a different way explain, in linguistic terms, how you are different. Also ask people in your family (or your in-group friends) how they feel about their variety. However, don't first lecture your family on the systematicity of AAVE or Cockney English and then ask them if it is a legitimate variety. This will slant their answer. Just ask family/friends from the same group how they feel about their own way of speaking. You may be surprised at some of the answers you get.

# Notes

1 According to Wolfram and Shilling-Estes, 'the low long vowels are moving forward and upward, and the short vowels are moving downward and backward', p. 138.

2 Another example is Pauley/Polly.

3 'Easy on the Adenoids. Clean Air, Social Mobility Cleans Up Old Liverpudlian Accent'. Leela Jacinto. 23 February 2001.

4 Wolfram, Walt and Christian, Donna, 1976. 'Appalachian Speech'. Washington DC. Center for Applied Linguistics, p. 131.

5 [One beautiful day, a butterfly was flying in the garden when, accidentally, she fell down. 'Oh damn,' she said. 'I forgot my wings.'] Mexican children's chant.

6 From *Acts of Identity: Creole-based Approaches to Language and Ethnicity*. Robert B. Le Page and Andree Tabouret-Keller, 1985. Cambridge University Press.

7 All of the examples in the previous two sections come from bilingual speakers in Monterrey, Mexico.

8 These Quebecois examples are courtesy of Dan Golembeski, Grand Valley State University.

9 What many forget, or never learned, are the ways in which African languages influenced Southern English. On the typical plantation, the primary caretakers of the owners' children were African slaves. Transmission of their language to these children, and to the adults on the plantation as well, was the vehicle for Africanisms to enter their language.

10 The French do maintain some cultural and economic ties but they are dwarfed by the importance of the ties with Spanish and English-speaking countries.

11 Example from Rickford, John, 1999: *African American Vernacular English*. Blackwell Publishing, p. 293.

12 Contrary to popular belief, the title *Ms* is not a product of the 1970s women's movement. The term actually predates it by at least 20 years. It was created by a business looking for a neutral word for its female employees.

13 From *Language, Gender and Professional Writing* (1989), Frank and Treichler (eds.).

14 Laschever, Sara and Babcock, Linda, 2003. *Women Don't Ask: Negotiation and the Gender Divide*. Princeton University Press.

# References

Adams, M. (2001), 'Infixing and Interposing in English: A New Direction'. *American Speech*, 76.3, 327–31.

Baptista, L. (2000), 'What the White-Crowned Sparrow's Song Can Teach Us About Human Language'. *Chronicle of Higher Education*, 46 (44), B8.

Baugh, A. and Cable, T. (1993), *A History of the English Language*. 4th Edition. New York: Simon and Schuster.

Bickerton, D. (1990), *Language and Species*. Chicago: University of Chicago Press.

Blakemore, D. (1992), *Understanding Utterances*. Oxford: Blackwell.

Bright, W. (ed.) (1998), *International Encyclopedia of Linguistics*. Oxford: Oxford University Press.

Bryson, B. (1991), *The Mother Tongue: English and How it Got that Way*. New York: William Morrow Inc.

Cameron, D. (1992), 'Not gender difference but the difference gender makes' – explanation in research on sex and language. *International Journal of the Sociology of Language*, 94 13–26.

Carnie, A. (2006), *Syntax: A Generative Introduction*. Oxford: Blackwell.

Celce-Murcia, M. and Larsen-Freeman, D. (1998), *The Grammar Book*. Cambridge: Newbury House Publishers.

Coates, J. (2004), *Women, Men and Language*. Harlow: Pearson Longman Inc.

Cook, V. (2004), *The English Writing System*. London: Oxford University Press.

Crystal, D. (1997), *English as a Global Language*. Cambridge: Cambridge University Press.

—— (2003), *The Cambridge Encyclopedia of the English Language*. NY: Cambridge University Press.

Culpeper, J. (1997), *History of English*. NY: Routledge.

Curtiss, S. (1977), *Genie: A Psychological Study of a Modern-day "Wild Child"*. NY: Academic Press.

Doughty, C. J. and Long, M. (2003), *The Handbook of Second Language Acquisition*. Oxford: Blackwell.

Fasold, R. (1987), *The Sociolinguistics of Society*. Oxford: Blackwell.

—— (1990), *The Sociolinguistics of Language*. Oxford: Blackwell.

Fought, C. (2003), *Chicano English in Context*. New Tork: Palgrave Macmillan, Inc.

Fromkin, V., Rodman, R. and Hyams, N. (2006), *An Introduction to Language*. 8th Edition. Boston: Thompson / Heinle.

Görlach, M. (1997), *The Linguistic History of English*. London: MacMillan Publishers.

Harley, H. (2006), *English Words: A Linguistic Introduction*. Oxford: Blackwell.

Herzfeld, A. (1991) (ed.), 'The pragmatics of proverb performance in Limonese Creole'. Mid American Linguistics Conference Papers. Lawrence, KA.

Helmuth, L. (2003), 'Birds can put two and two together'. *Science Now*, 5649:1323.

Holm, J. (1989), *Pidgins and Creoles*. Cambridge: Cambridge University Press.

Huddleston, R. and Pullum, G. K. (2005), *A Student's Introduction to English Grammar*. Cambridge: Cambridge University Press.

Jarvis, E. (2005), 'Opinion: avian brains and a new understanding of vertebrate brain evolution'. *Nature Reviews Neuroscience*, 6(2), 151–9.

Jeffries, L. (1998), *Meaning in English*. London: St Martin's Press.

Lakoff, G. (1990), *Women, Fire and Dangerous Things: What Categories Reveal about the Mind*. Chicago: University of Chicago Press.

Lakoff, R. T. (2004), in *Language and Woman's Place: Text and Commentaries*, ed. by Bucholtz, M.. Oxford: Oxford University Press.

Le Page, R. and Tabouret-Keller, A. (1985), *Acts of Identity: Creole-based Approaches to Language and Ethnicity*. Cambridge: Cambridge University Press.

Lightbown, P. and Spada, N. (2006), *How Languages are Learned*. Oxford: Oxford University Press.

MacNeil, R. (2005), *Do You Speak American?* Films for the Humanities and Sciences. www.films.com

McCowan, B. and Reiss, D. (December 2001), 'The fallacy of "signature whistles" in bottle-nosed dolphins: a comparative perspective'. *Behaviour*, 62, 6.

McCrum, R., Cran, W. and MacNeil, R. (2002), *The Story of English*. New York: Penguin Books.

McWhorter, J. (1997), 'It happened at Cormantin: locating the origin of the Atlantic English-based creoles'. *Journal of Pidgin and Creole Languages*, 12:1, 59–102.

—— (2003), *The Power of Babble*. NY: Perennial.

—— (2005), *Defining Creole*. Oxford: Oxford University Press.

Michel, A. (1980), *The Story of Nim: The Chimp who Learned Language*. New York: Knopf: distributed by Random House.

Milroy, L. and Muysken, P. (1995), *One Speaker, Two Languages: Cross-Disciplinary Perspectives on Code-Switching*. Cambridge: Cambridge University Press.

Montgomery, M. (1989), 'Exploring the roots of Appalachian English'. *English Worldwide*, 10:2, 227–78.

Myers-Scotton, C. (1993), *Social Motivations for Codeswitching: Evidence from Africa*. Oxford: Oxford University Press.

Obeng, S. G. and Winkler, E. G. (2002), 'A comparison of reduplication in Limonese Creole and Akan'. In S. Kouwenberg (ed.), *Twice as Meaningful:*

*Morphological Reduplication in Pidgins and Creoles*. London: Battlebridge Press.

Obeng, S. G. (1994), 'Verbal indirection in Akan informal discourse', *Journal of Pragmatics*, 21:37–65

Pepperberg, I. M. (1999), *The Alex Studies: Cognitive and Communicative Abilities of Grey Parrots*. Cambridge, MA: Harvard University Press.

Premack, A. J. (October 1972), 'Teaching Language to an Ape'. *Scientific American*, 92–9.

Rickford, J. R. and Rickford, R. J. (2000), *Spoken Soul: The Story of Black English*. New York: John Wiley and Sons Inc.

Rickford, J. (1985), 'Ethnicity as a sociolinguistic boundary'. *American Speech*, 60:2, 99–125.

Riley, K. and Parker, F. (1998), *English Grammar: Prescriptive, Descriptive, Generative, Performance*. NY: Allyn and Bacon.

Romaine, S. (1995), *Bilingualism*. Oxford: Blackwell.

—— (2000), *Language in Society: an Introduction to Sociolinguistics*. Oxford: Oxford University Press.

Ryan, E. B. (1979), 'Why do low-prestige language varieties persist?' In H. Giles and R. St Claire, *Language and Social Psychology*, 145–57. Oxford: Blackwell.

Slobodchikoff, C. N. and Ackers, S. H. (1999), 'Communication of stimulus size and shape in alarm calls of Gunnison's prairie dogs, *cynomys gunnisoni*'. *Ethology* (105) 149–62.

Thomason, S. G. and Kaufman, T. (1988), *Language Contact, Creolization, and Genetic Linguistics*. Berkeley, CA: University of California Press.

Tserdanelis, G. and Wong, W. Y. P. (eds) (2004), *The Language Files*. Ohio State University Linguistics Dept. 9th Edition. Columbus: Ohio State University Press.

Valdman, A. (1988), *Ann Pale Kreyol. An Introductory Course in Haitian Creole*. Bloomington, IN: Creole Institute.

Valdman, A. (ed.) (1977), *Pidgin and Creole Linguistics*. Bloomington: Indiana University Press.

von Frisch, K. (August 1962), 'Dialects in the language of bees' *Scientific American*, 207, 2, 78–89.

Winford, D. (2003), *An Introduction to Contact Linguistics*. Oxford: Blackwell.

Winkler, E. G. (1998), 'Limonese Creole: a case of contact-induced language change'. Unpublished PhD dissertation: Indiana University, Bloomington.

—— (2001), 'Cambio de códigos en el criollo limonense'. *Revista de Filología y Lingüística de la Universidad de Costa Rica*. 26(1), 189–96.

Winkler, E. G. (2003), 'Limonese Creole: a rose by any name'. *Southern Journal of Linguistics* 25, 16-27.

Winkler, E. G. and Obeng, S. G. (2000), 'West Africanisms in Limonese Creole English'. *World Englishes* 19(2), 155–71.

Wolfram, W. and Schilling-Estes, N. (1998), *American English*. Oxford: Blackwell.

Yule, G. (1996), *Pragmatics*. Oxford: Oxford University Press.

Zentella. A. C. (1997), *Growing Up Bilingual*. Oxford: Blackwell.

# Index

acronomy   96, 98
adjectives   7–9, 18, 48, 52, 68, 79, 84–8, 92, 106, 108–9, 116, 119–20, 125, 128, 132, 137, 139, 146–7, 190, 200, 224, 234
adverbs   11, 16, 18, 54, 84, 88, 92, 108, 115–6, 119–22, 125, 128, 201, 231, 234
advertising   99, 160–5
affixes   85, 87, 92, 201
affricates   71–3
African American Vernacular English   87, 206, 209–11, 218, 222, 225, 229–32, 246
African Grey Parrots   32–5
Alfred the Great   175–6
alveolar ridge   65–6, 68, 71, 89
ambiguity   5–6, 135, 138–9, 150, 161, 163
   lexical   5–6, 138,
   syntactic or structural   139
antonymy   140
apes   30–2
Appalachian English   18, 203–4, 207, 209, 211, 219, 223, 225–30, 247n
argot   144–5
article (see also determiner)   4, 8–9, 43, 53, 85, 88, 108, 110, 135,
articulator   64–6, 70, 73, 81n
aspect   121–6
aspiration   3, 67, 72, 79
attitudes   56, 206–7, 221, 235
auxiliary verbs   122–6, 129, 163, 231

babbling   46–7, 49
BBC English (see also Queen's English)   13, 194, 201, 205
bee communication   24–6, 28, 34
Behaviorism   37–40, 50–4
Berko-Gleason, Jean   42
bird calls and songs   23, 26–9, 32–4
Bloomfield, Leonard   37
borrowing   3, 15–16, 71–2, 175–7, 180, 183–8, 191–2, 208, 210, 223–4, 233
Broca's area   43–4

Chaucer, Geoffrey   173, 178–80, 184–5, 188

Chicano English   205–6, 208–11, 246
chimpanzees   30–2
Chomsky, Noam   38–40, 58, 113, 127, 129
clipping   93–4, 98
Cockney English   67, 194, 232–4
codeswitching   208–9, 211–14
coinage   94, 98
commissives   153
compounding   93–4, 98
conjunctions   85, 88, 110, 113, 118, 135, 
consonants   3, 47, 63–73, 78, 80, 81n, 89–90
content words   84–5, 88, 146
contrastive analysis   52
Creole languages   8, 12, 159, 208, 215–26, 229–30, 232
   Gullah   222
   Haitian Creole   8, 130, 212, 221–2
   Limonese Creole   217–19, 222–6, 230, 234, 246
   Jamaican Creole   217–18, 220–2, 230
   Tok Pisin   217
Critical Age Hypothesis
   first language   45
   second language   57

deep structure   129
derivation   86–9, 91–4, 98, 145
determiner (see also article)   115–16, 127–8, 130
dialect (see also language variety)   2, 4, 11–20, 23, 26, 34, 74, 76–7, 94, 103, 107, 174–5, 179–82, 186, 188, 194–5, 201–11, 225–46
Dichotic Listening Test   44
dictionary (see also lexicon)   4–5, 77, 86, 100–2, 132, 135–6, 138, 140, 142, 150, 169, 246
diphthongs   74
directives   153–4
dolphin communication systems   28, 34
double negatives   1, 9, 16, 18, 210, 227, 231, 234

English as a global language   244–5
entailment   141
error   40–2, 49, 51–5, 107,
Estuary English   246
euphemisms   86, 156–7, 166
expressives   153, 155–6

felicity conditions   154–5
figure of speech   147
first language interference   52
fricatives   70–1, 73
function words   49, 84–5, 88, 135, 172

gender   97, 182, 234–44
generification   95, 98
glides   72–3
glottal stop   67, 70, 234
glottis   65, 71
grammatical gender   19
Great Vowel Shift   187–8, 194
Gunnison's Prairie Dogs   23, 29

Hemispherectomy 44
humour   5–6, 20, 141, 167–70

iconicity   133–4
idioms   5, 83, 145–6
imitation   31–2,  37, 40–2, 50, 54
imperatives   113, 153, 155
implicature   160–1 165
indirection   156–61, 169
infixes   85–6, 89, 103
inflection   86–90, 92, 121, 223
Innateness Hypothesis   38–9, 43–4
International Phonetic Alphabet   73–4, 80
interrogatives   129, 153, 155
intonation   47, 79, 150, 227
intransitive verbs   86, 127–8
irony   148–9

James I   173–4, 180–3
jargon   142, 144

language acquisition   36–49, 55–7, 170,
      220, 232
   first language   36–49
   individual difference in language
         learning   55–7
   language acquisition device   38–9, 43, 45
   second language   50–60
language contact   82, 99, 176, 184, 188,
      208–34

lexicon   4, 58, 98, 138, 142, 182, 198,
      210–11, 222, 227–8
lingua franca   216, 245
liquids   72–3

manner of articulation   64, 66, 70–2
meaning inclusion   141
minimal pairs   65–6, 71
modal auxiliaries   11, 18, 122, 163, 165,
      226, 231
morphological misanalysis   96–8
morphemes   82–104, 230
      bound morphemes (see also prefixes
         and suffixes)   85–93, 96–7, 102,
         137–8, 168
      free morphemes   85–6, 88–9, 92, 96,
         98, 102
motherese, caretaker talk   41

names (see also proper nouns) 95, 136–8,
      166, 235–6
nasal sounds   69–73
native speaker intuition 8, 37, 106, 112–13
Niger-Congo languages   20, 109, 218,
      229–30
Norman Invasion   14, 174, 176–8, 184,
      186, 192–3
Northern Cities Vowel Shift   200
noun (and noun phrases, see also pronouns
      and proper nouns)   7–9, 18–19, 40,
      42, 49, 52, 68, 79, 84, 87–8, 92, 108–9,
      111–17, 168, 172, 180, 189–90, 216,
      223–4

onomatopoeia   95, 98

palate   66, 71–3
particles   119, 146–7
passive voice   49, 54, 129, 146, 203, 226
Pepperberg, Irene   33–4
performative verbs   154
phonetics   62–78, 80,
phrasal verbs (2-word verbs)   118, 146
Phrase Structure Grammar   111, 113–17,
      119, 126, 128–9
Pidgin Languages   37, 208, 215–20,
      229–30
place of articulation   64–6, 70–2
plosives (see also stops)   66
plurality   7, 18, 42, 86–90, 109, 180, 183,
      193, 210, 228, 238
politics and language   161, 163–6

possessives   40, 86–7, 109, 172, 190,
prefixes   7, 82–3, 85–7, 89, 109, 127, 167
prepositions   1, 4, 15–6, 43, 85, 88, 105–6,
    108, 112, 114–22, 135, 169, 173
prescriptive grammar   105
principles and parameters   129–30
printing press   179–80, 192
pronouns   41, 98, 112, 115–16, 128, 130,
    183, 201, 237–8
proper nouns   79, 95, 136–7
proverbs   158–60

Queen's English   13, 194, 205

recursion   117
reduplication   95, 98
reference   135–7
reinforcement   37–40, 50
representatives   153

Sapir, Edward   37
sarcasm   148–9
sense   135–8, 140
Shakespeare   16, 87, 94, 149, 172–4, 180,
    185, 188–9, 227
Skinner, B. F.   37, 39
slang   5, 15, 84, 86, 91, 96, 100, 102–3,
    142–5, 149, 161, 174, 183, 187, 198–9,
    231,   233
sound system (see phonetics)
Southern White Vernacular English   218,
    229
speech acts   153–6
spelling   63, 71–2, 76–7, 79, 89–91, 101,
    173, 179, 185–7, 190–5, 230
Standard English   12, 15–16, 18, 77, 107,
    179–80, 192, 194–5, 201–3, 206–9,
    211–12, 216, 226, 228–9, 231, 239

stops   66–71, 73
stress   2, 78–9
Structuralism   37–8
suffixes   7, 68, 82–3, 85–9, 109, 127,
    167–8, 173, 201, 223
suprasegmentals   78
synonymy   54, 118, 139–40, 145, 150,
    161, 166, 169, 184, 204
syntax   8, 32, 105–31, 169–70

tag questions   240–1
tense   11, 19, 42–3, 54, 59, 68, 73, 86–7,
    89–90, 121–5, 154, 173, 191, 230–1
Transformational Grammar   129
transitive verbs   86, 127–8,
tree diagrams   111, 114–21, 124–6

Universal Grammar   113, 129

velum   65–6, 69–70, 73, 81n
verbs   10–11, 16, 18, 40, 49, 68, 84–8, 92,
    108–9, 112–13, 118–23, 125, 127–30,
    146–7, 154, 169, 173, 189, 191, 216,
    223, 227, 231
vervets   29–30
vocabulary (See also lexicon)   4, 7, 13,
    49, 55, 82, 91–102, 142–7, 173–8,
    180, 182, 184–5, 201, 203, 205, 216,
    219–20, 230, 233
voicing   64–8, 70–2, 74
vowels   3, 20, 47, 62, 64–5, 68, 73–5,
    77, 80, 186–8, 190–1, 193–4, 200–1,
    209–10, 227

weasel words   161, 163
Wenicke's Area   43
whale songs 23, 28
word order   10, 32, 110–11, 189, 224